FAITH IN THE FIGHT

D0937785

FAITH
IN THE FIGHT

Civil War Chaplains

Edited by

John W. Brinsfield

William C. Davis

Benedict Maryniak

James I. Robertson, Jr.

STACKPOLE
BOOKS

Published by
STACKPOLE BOOKS
5067 Ritter Road
Mechanicsburg, PA 17055
www.stackpolebooks.com

Printed in the United States of America

10 9 8 7 6 5 4 3 2 1

A Virginia Center for Civil War Studies Book

FIRST EDITION

Library of Congress Cataloging-in-Publication Data

Faith in the fight : Civil war chaplains / by John W. Brinsfield ...
[et al.].
  p. cm.
  Includes bibliographical references and index.
  ISBN 0-8117-0017-8
  1. United States—History—Civil War, 1861–1865—Chaplains.
2. United States. Army—Chaplains—History—19th century.
3. Confederate States of America. Army—Chaplains—History.
4. Chaplains, Military—United States—Biography. 5. Chaplains,
Military—Confederate States of America—Biography. 6. United
States—History—Civil War, 1861–1865—Religious aspects.
7. United States—History—Civil War, 1861–1865—Registers.
I. Brinsfield, John Wesley.
E635.F35 2003
973.7'78'0922—dc21

2002011181

Contents

Introduction

Late in July 1864 two mighty armies were locked in combat for control of Atlanta, Georgia. Near twilight one day, Chap. James H. McNeilly of the 49th Tennessee came up to the front to conduct a religious service. McNeilly later wrote:

> I take my place midway of the line, a few feet back of the trenches, so that those who remain there can hear and those who gather around me, from five hundred to a thousand, can spring back to their places at a moment's notice. We can't make a light, for it would attract the fire of the enemy. I have a great many earnest Christians, officers and men, to help me. The colonel is a Presbyterian elder, the lieutenant colonel a shouting Methodist.
>
> There is a gigantic fellow with a voice corresponding to his size beside me. . . . While he is singing the gathering song and the men are coming out of the trenches, the picket stops for a moment on the way to the front.
>
> As they stand by me, one of those stray bullets comes through the embrasure, strikes one in the temple, passes through his brain, and lodges in the breast of the man next to him. There is confusion for a few minutes. The dead man's body is cared for by his comrades. The wounded man is taken to the infirmary.
>
> Quiet is restored and the song starts again, and I preach the sermon with a vivid illustration of the nearness of that mysterious, unseen world that lies so near us and claims some of us every day. I finish the sermon and ask those who wish to take Jesus Christ as a Saviour to rise up. Maybe two hundred rise.[1]

For the overwhelming number of Union and Confederate soldiers, religion was the greatest sustainer of morale in the Civil War. Faith was a refuge in great time of need. Troops faced battle by forgetting earthly pleasures and looking heavenward. Only a minority of the men of blue and gray belonged to any formal denomination, yet large numbers read their Bibles conscientiously and prayed regularly. Religion was always present and highly personal. In mid-August 1864 James Parrott of the 16th Tennessee confessed to his wife: "I have ben in several hard fites I can say thank god that I have never bin harmed when I go into a fite I say God be my helper and when I come out I say thank God I feel like he has bin with mee."[2]

Guarding and guiding the spiritual well-being of the soldiers was the primary responsibility of army chaplains. Neither side ever had a sufficient number. Regulations for chaplains were so vague and varying that most of them had an identity problem in the army chain of command. Many chaplains themselves were unsure of precisely what their duties were.

Frederic Denison was an energetic minister who served as chaplain to two different regiments. He was surprised on entering the army to learn that a chaplain had "no appointment or recognized place . . . on a march, in a bivouac, or in a line of battle; he was a supernumerary, a kind of fifth wheel to a coach, being in place nowhere and out of place everywhere."[3]

In time, however, the chaplains learned. The process was often painful. While the first wave of clerics to enter the armies left something to be desired in ability, the ministers who served in the field for any extended period were capable, devoted, and hardworking.

Soldiers' opinions of chaplains naturally varied. In January 1862 a New York sergeant referred to his chaplain as "the Old Woman, for he ain't fit to be called a Chaplain." Sunday prayers "would sicken anyone." The sergeant felt that his chaplain "should be tarred and feathered and drummed out of the service."[4]

Pennsylvania captain Francis Donaldson initially thought his chaplain "loud, ranting, boisterous, and roaring." Three months later, Donaldson's feelings had melted somewhat. "This being Sunday our chaplain went for us, his text being the last verse of XXV Proverbs—'He that hath no rule over his own spirit is like a city that is broken down, and without walls.' He attacked us in front, all along the line, worked around our flanks and got well into our rear, and as he let loose his reserves and routed us completely he hurled his Anathema Marantha upon the evil doers until we couldn't rest. A man of powerful lungs is the Chaplain."[5]

Many chaplains were not averse to participating in a battle for the good of the cause. In an official report of the fighting at Prairie Grove, Arkansas, the colonel of the 94th Illinois stated: "Chaplain R. E. Guthrie proved himself to be a soldier in every sense of the word. . . . He was on the field throughout the whole engagement, encouraging the men on in their good work, calling on them to trust in God, do their duty, and fire low."[6]

Lucius Barber of the 15th Illinois had an entirely different view of his chaplain. It was one most often found in soldiers' writings. "Although not a gifted man or an eloquent speaker," Barber stated, "yet I will venture to say that there was not a harder working chaplain in the whole army or one that did more good. With a good education, he combined goodness of heart with an indomitable energy and perseverance. . . . Our chaplain could not rest unless doing something for the good of the men."[7]

Several small studies of chaplains have appeared in the past century. Regrettably, most of them present only a superficial analysis of the men who carried religion into the field. This is evident from the small rosters of 200 to 300 chaplains that normally appear as an appendix.

Identified here for the first time are 3,694 ministers who were duly commissioned as chaplains in the Union or Confederate armies. This descriptive roster is the amalgamation of research done over a long span of years by three men working independently and, for a time, ignorant of the labors of the others. Benedict Maryniak of Lancaster, New York, devoted over a decade amassing Union chaplains' names and units. In a similar vein, U.S. Army chaplain John W. Brinsfield of Atlanta, Georgia, had been doing the same for clergy in Southern armies. James I. Robertson, Jr., at Virginia Tech, meanwhile had been compiling a Civil War chaplains' roster of his own.

The work of the three men eventually became known to one another. Under the auspices of the Virginia Center for Civil War Studies at Virginia Tech, an organizational meeting occurred with a view of combining the three rosters and getting them published.

The compilers agreed on the principles to be followed. An overriding concern was to include not merely a chaplain's surname and initials, but full name, life-dates, denomination, and unit(s) in which he served. Broadening the base resulted in two more years of research in obscure church records.

To make the completed roster more meaningful, two essays and samples of chaplains' unpublished writings have been added. They are intended to enrich rather than to distract from the roster, which is the core of this volume. It is hoped that the book will henceforth be the starting point for any research into the neglected area of Civil War chaplains.

This is the first book-length study published through the Virginia Center for Civil War Studies. Grateful acknowledgment is made to the Lilly Endowment of Indianapolis, Indiana, for a grant that greatly facilitated research and production. Deep appreciation is also extended to The Society of the Order of the Southern Cross for its financial support of this project. Special thanks for help generously given go to Dr. Gaston de la Bretonne, Beth R. Brown, A. J. Chiesa, Ron Coddington, Dr. Timothy J. Demy, John Gorto, C. Peter Jergensen, Stephen D. Lutz, Sara Mummert, and Bob Willett.

Leigh Ann Berry of Stackpole Books displayed her usual skill in being the connecting link between editors and publisher. To everyone else who sent a tidbit for the roster, or suggestions for the book, go sincere feelings of appreciation.

"Holy Joes" of the 1860s were dedicated servants who, in the main, strove mightily to bring a sense of caring to a war environment of callousness. In the midst of hate, they taught love. In the midst of greed and destructiveness, they taught unselfishness. In the midst of death, they pointed men to eternal life. The overwhelming number of chaplains in the Civil War did the best they could, and better than anyone had a right to expect.

Stanton Allen of the 1st Massachusetts Cavalry never forgot the eve of the May 1864 Wilderness campaign. The regimental chaplain conducted a brief service. He read from the Bible about buckling on the whole armor of God, and he extolled the soldiers to be "prepared to stand an inspection before the King of Kings." High-spirited troopers listened in silence, Allen noted, and many of them wept openly.[8]

Few monuments exist today to Civil War chaplains. This poetic testimonial would be a fitting tribute:

> Press on—press on, nor doubt nor fear
> From age to age, this thought shall cheer
> Whate'er may die and be forgot
> Work done for God, it dieth not.[9]

INTRODUCTION NOTES

1. *Confederate Veteran*, 26 (1918): 398–99.
2. Bob Womack, *Call Forth the Mighty Men* (Bessemer, Ala., 1987), 409–10.
3. Frederic Denison, "A Chaplain's Experience in the Union Army," in Soldiers and Sailors Historical Society of Rhode Island, *Personal Narratives*, 2 (1891–1893): 17.
4. Paul J. Engel, ed., "A Letter from the Front," *New York History*, 34 (1953): 206.
5. Francis A. Donaldson, *Inside the Army of the Potomac* (Mechanicsburg, Pa., 1998), 223, 321.
6. U.S. War Department, *War of the Rebellion: A Compilation of the Official Records of the Union and Confederate Armies* (Washington, D.C. 1880–1901), ser. 1, vol. 22, pt. 1, 134.
7. Lucius W. Barber, *Army Memoirs of Lucius W. Barber* (Chicago, 1894), 103.
8. Stanton P. Allen, *Down in Dixie: Life in a Cavalry Regiment in the War Days* (Boston, 1888), 176.
9. Edmund D. Patterson, *Yankee Rebel: The Civil War Journal of Edmund DeWitt Patterson* (Chapel Hill, 1966), 139.

Essays

Union Military Chaplains

Benedict Maryniak

The heavy hand of August pressed down on Missouri. For General Rose-
crans and his Army of the Mississippi, it was one more oven of an afternoon during which the scenery shimmered from the heat. Members of the
36th Illinois Infantry had already begun yet another daylong search for
patches of shade. Part of the "Pea Ridge Brigade," the 36th were notorious
for having gunned down Confederate generals Ben McCulloch and James
McIntosh at the very outset of that battle down in Arkansas.[1] But after
these exhilarating moments of combat came five excruciating months of
unvarying repetition that was camp life. Though nearly everyone had volunteered in an impetuous moment, imagining himself prepared to come face to
face with death, no one had expected this grueling, grinding sameness. It
was a momentous age for America, a time of heroic figures and mighty
deeds, but none of that excitement, change, and growth was evident in
southwest Missouri.

Clattering in the road suddenly drew all eyes to a wagon that usually
brought their rations of poor coffee, rusty bacon, and hard bread, all of it
inaccurately termed "subsistence" by the army. With a stream of abuse that
singed the air, the teamster finally cursed his intractable mules to a halt. The
kicked-up dust settled to reveal grimy, sunburned faces that surrounded him
in anticipation of grub. Some of these men voiced their hopes about the
hostler's cargo, calling out "butter" or "sugar," while others pulled at the tar-
paulin to get a look inside.

The rowdy soldiers suddenly froze, however, poleaxed by the sight of a
black suit, far too immaculate, crawling out of the wagon's bonnet. Baptist
minister William M. Haigh sheepishly climbed down under the collective

glower of his new flock. Fresh from the greener pastures of his ten-year ministry along the Fox River just north of Chicago, Haigh had come not only to follow the drum, but also to watch over hometown boys who marched off with the 36th Volunteers to personally see that they had a good hope in Christ. "I am Brother Haigh, here to take Chaplain [George G.] Lyon's place," he announced. A sergeant snorted with derision, eyes slitted. It was at this moment that a corporal finally got his head inside the wagon and promptly reported it was "Empty! She's empty!"

Annoyed disgust on the hairy faces in front of him made the Baptist minister wish he was Elijah, swept away by a whirlwind to anywhere but this awkward situation. Reverend Haigh had spent a long time rehearsing for this moment when he would meet the regiment, but he concealed his disillusionment under a thick layer of false heartiness, only confiding his upset to his journal that night. "I first arrived to join the unit in a wagon the men thought to be loaded with rations, and they were disappointed to find me inside." He went on to do admirably by his boys for the next twenty-seven months, and even received a commendation from his regimental commander that cited his "active religious effort" and "great service in providing reading matter and ministering to the wants of sick and wounded" during the Atlanta campaign.[2]

William Haigh's unfortunate introduction to his unit was not all that unusual for an army chaplain because smoothly operating conventionalities of government, of the military, and even those of religious denominations fell to pieces as North and South rushed to prepare for a war after the opening shots had been fired. Organizational chaos reigned while both sides scrambled to raise and maintain military forces larger than either had anticipated. While Columbia prepared to part the Red Sea of slavery, the chaplains of her armies were abandoned to red tape.

Before 1861, except for the years of war with Mexico, the U.S. Army had no units larger than a regiment. In order to meet the modest needs of detachments that were scattered from Atlantic to Pacific, an equally modest staff system evolved. It was this rudimentary administrative framework, suffused with thousands of volunteers, that ballooned into the Northern military machine that fought the Civil War. The Medical Department of 1860, for example, consisted of the surgeon general, thirty surgeons with the rank of major, and eighty-four assistant surgeons with ranks of either captain or first lieutenant. In its amplified form during the war, the department counted just more than 12,000 surgeons and assistant surgeons. Though it had its share of shortcomings, the U.S. Medical Department exerted contin-

Chaplains of the 9th Corps, Petersburg, Virginia. LIBRARY OF CONGRESS

uing influence upon the Federal government to improve military medicine and advocate for its army surgeons.[3]

Back at his Missouri camp in 1862, Chaplain Haigh had no recourse to a special advocate for chaplains in Washington when he needed help with snarled red tape or sustained incivility from particular sectors of the army. Except for the possibility of now and then convening a commiseration of chaplains who served in the same brigade or division, Brother Bill would continue through the war on his own because the army chaplaincy had no organization higher than regimental level until the first chief of chaplains was appointed in 1920.[4]

Worse still, the book of army regulations barely mentioned the place and duties of a chaplain. Colonel Thomas W. Higginson, a Congregational minister who led the 33rd U.S. Colored Troops (the first regiment in national service entirely composed of former slaves) came up with the best description for this sorry state. "In a little world of the most accurate order, where every man's duties and position are absolutely prescribed, the chaplain alone has no definite position and no prescribed duties. In a sphere where everything is concentrated on one sole end, he alone finds himself

Sunday morning mass in camp of 69th New York State Militia. LIBRARY OF CONGRESS

of no direct use towards that end and apparently superfluous. He cannot succeed without both moral energy and tact."[5]

A procession of earnest, sturdy, and buoyant churchmen nevertheless
entered into national service as chaplains of volunteer regiments. That each
one made a great bounding leap of faith is unmistakable. Despite unfavor-
able portents, each knew in an instant that his place was with the army, and
they mustered in at an average rate of sixty per month from May through
December 1861. "The very spirit of the revolution of 1776 is aroused, and
the most striking sign of it is the attitude of the clergy," proclaimed a
Methodist newspaper in Boston on May 23. "Pastors, so many that they
cannot here be enumerated, offer their services as chaplains. . . . [W]hole
companies are formed from single churches and go forth with the solemn
approbation of their spiritual fathers." The article concluded that "the most
sacred of sanctions is that of religion and with that sanction the people gird
themselves to this quarrel."[6]

It was this sacred sanction that the first volunteer chaplains believed to
be their most valuable contribution to the army. Any initial hostility that
they met would surely fade as the hour of combat drew near and compelled

thoughts of mortality and eternity. In his study of Civil War soldiers, Bell Wiley accurately observed that "religious sanction was demanded by the righteous—always a powerful minority, approved of by the lukewarm, and accepted by the wicked. All felt better to have the church's blessing." Only the government and the church could legitimately ask Northern men to selflessly risk everything in pursuit of a common good. Americans would, in fact, quickly embrace the concept of military duty as a divine imperative because, to some degree, all felt that Heaven had favored their country. Their Union was "the city on the hill," meant to be viewed by the rest of the world as God's model for the Millennium—the thousand years of ideal society described in the Book of Revelation.[7]

During early June 1861, an editor of the *New York Tribune* described his visits to various "camps of the Volunteers" and was struck by the chaplain's part in rallying a regiment's good men. "The Christian men do not know one another, but those of a certain moral and earnest cast will naturally seek to know the chaplain; to gather as a Christian community and speedily draw in others. Thus a high moral tone can be commenced in many bodies of our army. The North are fighting this battle as one of law, liberty, and righteousness, and they must fight it as their Puritan forefathers, with Bible and Psalm book in hand."

There is no better example of the potential power in a chaplain's words than a perfect message delivered at a perfect moment in the public square of Elmira, New York, on a morning in mid-September by Chap. Thomas K. Beecher, 141st New York Volunteers.[8]

Reverend Beecher first came to Elmira in June 1854, as a high-school principal, but soon assumed a pastor's role at the Congregational Park Church. A contemporary described Beecher as "free of vanity, forthright, with a grim humor and a not too hopeful view of human nature, but stubbornly devoted to helping his fellow man." Beecher had to have been the most unorthodox of Lyman Beecher's seven sons but likely the truest Christian. He used a Sunday service as the occasion to announce his appointment as chaplain of the 141st New York Volunteers, and gave the following reasons to his congregation:

Of the nine hearty men in Elmira called ministers at least three ought to be doing duty and I am one of those three.

There are no enterprises of great importance which I could serve by staying.

The 141st regiment is gathered from companies in which I am known. No other minister could enter the regiment and be recognized so quickly.

The determination of the colonel to have me.

I can serve the regiment in various arts and handicrafts.

Every man in the regiment knows it is no gain for me—but a great loss—to go with them and this will give me sincerity and authority.

It will be easy to see if I succeed and easy to resign if I don't.

After he had pulled himself onto a heap of baggage, Chaplain Beecher straightened to his full six feet and addressed the regiment as they waited to board a train bound for the "seat of war." It must have looked to him as though every living soul in Chemung County had come to town. A throng of relatives embraced and clenched each other's shoulders; women cried and men pummeled the arms of departing sons. These were last good-byes, and some galvanizing words were in order. Pointing at a National banner overhead, Beecher recounted the familiar, consoling description of a war fought for God's purposes. "For whom the Lord loveth, He chasteneth," went the quote from Hebrews, and the chaplain spoke of war's regenerative chastisement as necessary preparation before the nation could proceed to fulfill its destiny as appointed by Providence. He closed with a brilliant version of the "sacred sanction" recently used by his older half brother, Henry Ward Beecher, in sending off the 67th New York Infantry from Long Island.

You go on a sacred mission. The prayers and sympathies of Christendom are with you. You go to open again the shut-up fountains of liberty and to restore our disgraced banner to its honor. You go to serve your country in the cause of liberty. And if God brings you into conflict with those misguided men of the South—when you see their miserable, new-vamped banner—remember what that flag means: Treason! Slavery! Despotism! Then look up and see the bright stars and glorious stripes over your own head, and read in them Liberty! Liberty! Liberty! And if you fall in the struggle, I will wrap you in the flag of your country. You will die with its sacred touch upon you. Your hometown and kin will not forget you. You will return from the conquests of liberty with a reputation and a character established—forever—to your children and your children's children. And that shall be an honor. And that shall be a legend. And that shall be historic truth. And your posterity will be able to say, "Our fathers stood up in the day of peril and laid again the foundations of liberty that were shaken; and in their hands the banner of our country streamed forth like the morning star upon the night."

As Washington frantically geared up to fight a war, seven notes went from the desk of Abraham Lincoln to clergymen in the city. Initially stunned at the sight of President Lincoln's signature, each recipient must have been completely nonplussed by the statement that he would soon be needed as a military hospital chaplain. All of these clerics probably knew that the largest army hospital in Washington at that time held forty beds. The president, however, had recently reviewed plans of organization and architectural drawings for several extensive facilities that were soon to be in operation. The president hoped they could begin immediately, working as volunteers until Congress arranged for their rank and remuneration. Though there was a great deal left unsaid in Lincoln's note, all seven ministers—William Y. Brown, John G. Butler, George G. Goss, Henry H. Hopkins, and John C. Smith, along with Catholic priests Matthew F. McGrath and Francis E. Boyle—promptly complied with Lincoln's wishes. It was sixteen months before Congress named them as "hospital chaplains of U.S. Volunteers."

Prior to this, their lack of official status caused them constant embarrassment and annoyance at the hands of surgeons who presided over the hospitals.[9] The president of the United States had to ask these men to work without pay and rank because in 1861 he did not have the lawful wherewithal to appoint them. After eighty-five years of underwriting men and matériel for the army and navy, Congress had only "customs" regarding military chaplains. The Constitution, after all, could not be clearer that "Congress shall make no law respecting an establishment of religion," and no elected official would risk being caught recruiting clergymen in the shadow of the wall between church and state. Chaplains had customarily been whisked through Congress using temporary measures that left no "incriminating" trails.[10]

According to the congressional conventionalities, the antebellum army chaplain was elected to his office by vote of a post's administrative council or the men of its garrison. His principal responsibility was as schoolmaster for the garrison, but his proper title was "chaplain," though this was in no way to be construed as his rank. The crowning irony of this was a complete lack of required religious functions, even though a Protestant minister was specified as the preferred candidate.

Starting in May 1861 an effort was made to convert vague and inconsistent military "customs" into helpful guidelines that meshed one crystal-clear standard smoothly with the next. Although the twentieth century never witnessed this accomplishment, a relatively stable status for the army chaplain, and the rest of the army, was attained by early April 1864, after thirty-five months of effort, a few dozen acts of Congress, and many more War Department missives. The continuing difficulty with army regulations was their frequent and outrageous misinterpretation, especially by the paymaster general. This worked a particularly severe hardship on chaplains. From the first shot of the Civil War through 1864, paymasters were supervised by men born in the eighteenth century, the first of whom was Col. Benjamin Franklin Larned. When the pay of chaplains was reduced on July 17, 1862, Larned took no satisfaction in apparent validation of his views, because he had wanted the army chaplaincy disbanded completely.

The paymaster general took similar swipes at other parts of the army as well. He guaranteed that $5 million would be saved if regimental bands were sent home, and recommended elimination of sutlers because they too often got hold of money that should have gone to soldiers' families. Larned was not overly concerned for those families, however, because he not only demanded that the $2 raise in the pay of privates be repealed, but also that the increases already disbursed be recovered for a windfall of $15 million. Suggesting that generals stop appointing colonels and other highly paid ranks to their staffs because he could not see the reason "that aides and quartermasters and adjutants-general should be brigadiers or colonels," the wizened old weasel of a paymaster then saucily confessed: "I speak with diffidence on this subject, of course, as I may be ignorant of the necessities of service."[11]

Colonel Larned died in 1862, within weeks of seeing regimental bands sent home and the pay of regimental and hospital chaplains cut from $145.50 per month plus three daily rations and forage for one horse, to "$100 per month plus two daily rations and forage for one horse *while on duty.*" To a man, army chaplains accepted the pay cut. Chaplain Daniel P. Cilley of the 8th New Hampshire noted in his diary for August 25, 1862, that the "Army reduced chaplains' pay today but that won't make me leave. . . . I did not come here for money."

What did make many chaplains leave, however, were the three seemingly unimportant words tacked on the end of the salary reduction clause. Their alienation was caused by the persistence of Paymaster General Timothy Patrick Andrews, a contrary Irishman who had fought in the War of 1812 and the Mexican War. His office was certain beyond any doubt that if chaplains were to be paid "while on duty," they were not to be paid while off duty. Though he was obviously wrong, nothing could change Andrews's mind—not the Congress advising him that the law was meant to favor chaplains, not even when the manuscript copy of the law was unearthed and found to have "a comma after the word 'month,' separating the words 'one hundred dollars per month' from the words 'two rations a day while on duty,' and thereby intending that the chaplain should still receive one hundred dollars per month when he was absent."

For twenty months, regimental and hospital chaplains were denied payment for days they were absent, on any sort of leave, until a bill was rammed through both houses of Congress and promulgated on April 9, 1864, which specifically directed that chaplains be paid in the same manner as other officers on legitimate leave. This episode was not just a case of "office warfare," but an awe-inspiring two-part demonstration of the "powers that be" and the army's talent for closing ranks against outsiders. Its first part concerned the irrational intransigence of the paymaster general and how nothing could force him out of his misunderstanding of regulations except a congressional order for the paymaster's compliance. The second part is based on the realization that after the Civil War had raged on for three full years, an act of Congress on April 9, 1864, had to unequivocally enjoin all members of the U.S. Army to treat chaplains in the same manner as other commissioned officers because chaplains were commissioned officers.

Though army regulations said chaplains were to be mustered in a similar manner as commissioned officers, and that chaplains were to be considered equivalent to captains, no official document said chaplains were commissioned officers. As if to underscore this lesson in army obstinacy, Paymaster General Andrews immediately began to appeal to the public and to the courts but was barred by congressional injunction from any further mention of the dispute. Not long after being notified of this ruling, Colonel Andrews died, and the case with him.

The July 17, 1862, acts of Congress seemed to have been instigated by a suspicion of privilege focused upon military chaplains. Though this legislation cut the pay of all chaplains, it sanctioned and codified hospital chaplaincy. Its biggest surprise, however, had been a brand-new rule concerning qualifications. "No person shall be appointed a chaplain in the U.S. army who is not a regularly ordained minister of some religious denomination, and who does not present testimonials of his present good standing as such minister with a recommendation for his appointment as an army Chaplain from some authorized ecclesiastical body, or not less than five accredited ministers belonging to said denomination."

Later in the year, War Department General Orders Nos. 126 and 152 were enacted to complement this requirement for documentation. An applicant for a chaplain's office had to present documentation of the vote or other method used to choose him for appointment. War Department General Orders No. 152 ominously directed "each officer commanding a district or post . . . or a brigade of troops, within thirty days after the reception of the order promulgating this act, to inquire into the fitness, efficiency, and qualifications of the chaplains of hospitals or regiments, and to muster out of service such chaplains as were not appointed in conformity with the requirements of this act, and who have not faithfully discharged the duties of chaplains during the time they have been engaged as such."

Several examination boards were operating in full swing by the end of October 1862. No chaplains were specifically identified as having been dismissed under the regulation; thirty resigned or were discharged for disability during December, whereas an average of twenty chaplains departed the army in each of the first eleven months of that year. Forty-two new chaplains were mustered in during the last month of 1862.

It is important to keep things in perspective regarding the prodigious acts of Congress and canonical-sounding pronouncements from the War Department. Most of these decrees were liable to be ignored or subverted by army commanders who had no use for the politicians in Congress. A colonel usually held absolute authority within his unit, unless some flagrant excesses brought down the wrath of brigade or division commanders.

That was how John Pickell understood his power as commander of the 13th New York, a regiment raised in the city of Rochester and Monroe County. Unit organizer Isaac F. Quinby went west as a newly appointed brigadier general in U. S. Grant's army and left the 13th's colonelcy to Pickell. Initially commissioned in 1822 as a lieutenant of the 4th U.S. Artillery, Colonel Pickell enunciated his name with emphasis on the final syllable so it sounded like anything but a vegetable. Only weeks before Pickell was appointed commander, Pvt. John D. Barnes, a twenty-five-year-old Baptist minister in Company F, had been elected chaplain at a meeting of company officers and had already received his commission from Gov. Edwin D.

Morgan. "Jolly Johnny" Barnes was the apple of every enlisted man's eye and had been christened "The Patriotic Binghamton Boy" by his hometown newspaper, the Broome *Republican*. Barnes accepted the proffered chaplaincy only on the condition he could get back in the ranks with his musket at battles.

Long years in the Regulars, however, had left Colonel Pickell with the "old army" preference for Episcopal chaplains. He therefore installed Rev. John A. Bowman, nearly twice the age of Barnes and for many years a rector in the city of Rochester, as regimental chaplain, complete with a commission backdated to the initial organization of the regiment. Barnes protested, but he was promptly placed under arrest and confined to his tent so the regiment would have "a fair chance to get acquainted" with Chaplain Bowman.[12] Bowman soon went back home, however, and Barnes returned as the 13th's chaplain. Records still omit his earlier muster and show Barnes as the regiment's second chaplain following three months served by Bowman. Reverend Bowman was later commissioned as a hospital chaplain of U.S. Volunteers and served in that capacity through 1865. Poor health forced the resignation of "Jolly Johnny" after seven months with the 13th, but upon recovery he became an agent of the U.S. Christian Commission.

The requirement for written testimonials on behalf of men seeking a military chaplaincy went into effect just as acquaintances of Ezra A. Carman discovered he had been authorized to raise the 13th New Jersey. From that time on, not a day went by that the Carman house was not besieged "by numbers of patriotic persons anxious to do duty as Lt. Col's., Majors, Capt's, Quartermasters, Chaplains, Surgeons, Wagon Masters, Teamsters, etc, etc; but very few privates. It is scarcely to be believed and yet true," wrote Carman, "that for the position of Quartermaster alone I had 87 applicants. For Chaplain, 13 applied—3 Methodist, 5 Baptist, 2 Presbyterian, 1 Roman Catholic, and two I guess of no religion at all. Some graduated at colleges and one of them at the state prison. One (Williams of East Newark) was under indictment for rape and seduction and yet, strange to say, he had recommendations from ten of the Newark clergy."[13] Hoping to have plucked a diamond in the rough from among the clodhoppers, Colonel Carman chose Rev. Theodore R. Beck of New Brunswick. Though he was more than thirty years of age and had just been ordained, Chaplain Beck managed to keep up with the 13th until he resigned after the battle of Gettysburg.

The most entertaining account of a chaplain's election appears in the papers of Chap. Joseph B. O'Hagan, 73rd New York. Born in Ireland, he crossed the ocean to British North America and later entered the Jesuit

Ninth Massachusetts Infantry camp near Washington, D.C. LIBRARY OF CONGRESS

order. Father O'Hagan was thirty-five years old when he took on the role of a regimental chaplain in Gen. Daniel Sickles's Excelsior Brigade. The priest served thirty-five months and even spent one of them in Richmond with Fr. Peter Tissot, chaplain of the 37th New York, and Fr. Thomas Scully, chaplain of the 9th Massachusetts, after they had all been captured at Savage Station. Father O'Hagan gave absolution to Catholic troops during the 1862 battle of Williamsburg and on July 2, 1863, at Gettysburg. He was president of Holy Cross College for six years until his death in 1878.

General Sickles evidently took a populist approach to electing chaplains because Father O'Hagan described votes cast in his election by soldiers of the 73rd New York Volunteers regiment. "Over four hundred voted for a Catholic priest," he recalled, "one hundred and fifty-four, for any kind of a Protestant minister; eleven, for a Mormon elder; and three hundred and thirty-five said they could find their way to hell without the assistance of clergy."[14]

George S. Bradley joined the 22nd Wisconsin at the height of spring 1864, to fill a space left by Chap. Caleb D. Pillsbury's resignation. A year earlier, the regiment had been gobbled up by Gen. Nathan Bedford Forrest at Brentwood, on the rail line between Nashville and Franklin, Tennessee. Because that wily Southern "Wizard of the Saddle" recognized worthy Methodist elders, he released Pillsbury and 19th Michigan chaplain Israel

Coggeshall on their honor to ride to Vicksburg for exchange. Chaplain Bradley lived up to Pillsbury's example and mustered out with the regiment fifteen months later.

In his book, *The Star Corps: Notes of an Army Chaplain during Sherman's Famous March to the Sea,* published during 1865, Bradford said the first adverse circumstance faced by every chaplain was that he came to the army from the narrow path of an obscure life. "The regulations require that a chaplain must be an ordained minister of the Gospel. That means he must have spent several quiet years as a student and probably several more with a peaceful congregation, seeing almost nothing of what he will meet in the army. In camp, all the props of ordinary society are knocked away, and the man must stand alone if he stands at all." Bradford may have known he paraphrased Martin Luther's assertion that "talent is built up in solitude, character in the stream of the world."

Before Reverend Bradford's volume appeared in print, a veteran chaplain of a New York two-year regiment composed his own pithy version of introductory advice for prospective chaplains. "Deacon John" E. Robie had been an owner-publisher of religious newspapers in Auburn and Rochester before settling in Buffalo during 1850. That he had a soldierly bent showed in his service as chaplain of Buffalo's 74th New York State Militia from its 1854 organization. Robie was elected chaplain of the 21st New York, the first of six regiments sent to the war from Buffalo and Erie County.[15]

Having served "with valor and broad humanitarianism," Robie went back to Buffalo in May 1863, at the end of the 21st's term. A year later found him writing about the common routines and basic concerns of a regimental chaplain based on his time with the army. "Deacon John" then submitted his work to the local Methodist newspaper, thinking it "may be of use to some who propose entering the service." On June 2, 1864, Reverend Robie's article appeared in the *Buffalo Christian Advocate* under the heading: "Religious Army Chaplains." Chaplain Haigh, 36th Illinois, would have read it with great envy and a grain of salt. Could anything go so smoothly in the army? Never in Missouri, certainly.

> In order to become a chaplain it is necessary (1) to get a certificate of not less than five ministers of one's own denomination that one is a regularly-ordained clergyman with their recommendation of him as a suitable person to fill the office and (2) to get a certified statement of the vote of the staff officers and commandants of companies electing him to that office in a particular regiment.

With these two papers, he can obtain (3) a commission from the governor of the state.

He will then join his regiment and, with these three papers, will apply to the mustering officer of the division or corps to which the regiment belongs. This officer will muster him into the service of the U.S. and give him (4) a certificate of muster, the officer retaining papers (1) and (2).

The chaplain will then show (4) to the adjutant of his regiment, who will enter his name on the roll of the Field & Staff with the date of muster.

The monthly pay of a chaplain, which begins with the day of his muster, is $100 plus $18 for rations plus forage for one horse.

In active service, his baggage must be comprised in one valise, or carpetbag, and one roll of blankets—say three or four woolen blankets and one India rubber blanket, bound together by a shawl strap with handle. These will be carried in the staff wagon. Besides these, he may carry whatever he chooses on his horse or on his person.

When lying for any length of time in one camp or at a station, or in winter quarters, he may have a trunk and a camp bedstead, which must be stored with the post quartermaster or expressed home when the regiment takes the field.

When on the march and at all times during an active campaign, he will do well to carry on his horse one woolen and one gum blanket, lest at night the wagons should fail to reach the troops. He should carry a haversack. Not one of the showy and expensive things which officers often buy, but the simplest kind of gum or oil cloth to contain his most-necessary toilet articles and sufficient food if he should fail to get regular meals during the day. The regular provisions and cooking utensils and table furniture of his mess will be carried in the wagons. His canteen should be filled at every good stream or spring on the road. The cheap government canteen is better than the expensive and ornamental ones. The shoulder strap of both haversack and canteen should be as broad as possible, so as not to cut the shoulder. A small tin cup may be attached to either canteen or haversack. A bottle of Essence of Jamaica Ginger should always be at hand.

The chaplain's dress is a plain black frock coat with standing collar such as are commonly worn by Episcopalian ministers, except that the ordinary clerical coat has seven buttons and the military coat has nine, covered with cloth. A black felt hat is most convenient. Some chaplains wear a blue sash at parades and reviews, and many wear black velvet buttons.

As the commanding officer will permit, the chaplain should have prayer daily at dress parade, which occurs just before sunset. The best time for the prayer is when the officers have marched to the center and have faced the colonel, and before they march forward to salute him. The prayer should not be more than three minutes long. A form of prayer will ensure the requisite brevity and be in keeping with the formalities of the parade.

While in camp, the chaplain should visit the regimental hospital daily and spend ten minutes—no more—in scripture-reading and prayer. The best time is in the morning, after the surgeon's visit and before the patients fall asleep again. At the close of this short service, he may distribute tracts and papers. Judicious letters from the chaplain to friends of the sick and deceased will be very highly appreciated.

On Sunday, but one service can be held, and that not always. The service, including scripture-reading, singing, sermon or address, and prayers should occupy 20 or 25 minutes—never over thirty. The ordinary time for the Sunday service in the army is ten or eleven o'clock—the period most free from interruptions. The adjutant will have the church call sounded on drum or bugle at the request of the chaplain, but the best of all church calls is the singing of a hymn by the chaplain in a good strong voice. The ability to sing independently is a prime qualification for the chaplaincy. One who can sing can call a congregation together on a hundred occasions where one who cannot sing must forgo the pleasure of preaching. At the close of the Sunday service, tracts and religious papers should be thoroughly distributed. The Christian Commission will furnish them.

On the battlefield, the chaplain should not needlessly expose himself to danger to show his bravery. Least of all, should he undertake to act the soldier, since he is regarded as a non-combatant. Let him assist the wounded and the surgeons who will be [located] where it is shielded from the enemy's fire.

Robie's brief account was a chaplain's ground-level view of the army. Far from an exciting lithograph of a minister-catalyst amid pounding hooves, the flash of gunpowder, and clash of sabers, it was day after humdrum day of uncomfortable outdoor life so uneventful that the sound of the chaplain's breathing was always loud in his ears. Begun with a sarcastic treatment of army red tape that poked fun at an itemized jumble of numbered documents and procedural steps that hopelessly confused the simple procedure of mustering in, "Deacon John's" account went on to a careful review of personal gear.

Painful trial and error "in the field" surely spurred Robie's particular admonition to load saddles with adequate food, wool blankets, and waterproof gum ground cloth because regimental wagons frequently lagged far behind. Likewise his reminder to fill and refill canteens as often as the opportunity arose. The aromatic distillation of Jamaica ginger was indeed a soldier's standby for protection against effects of exposure because it improved the circulation of warm blood through the body and doubled as a remedy for diarrhea. Temperance crusaders of the time denounced Jamaica ginger as a substance abused by habitual drinkers of ardent spirits when they could not obtain alcohol, warning that overdose caused progressive loss of sight and sometimes brought sudden death.

Of greater significance was the even-tempered manner in which Chaplain Robie described pay and allowances, including his matter-of-fact suggestion that prayers and sermons be brief. Though he was in the army when Congress cut chaplains' pay by a third, the current salary was stated without any editorializing. He betrayed not a hint of the caustic wrath many felt over the army's continued refusal to acknowledge the respectability and consequentiality of its chaplains. Robie had apparently seen the writing on the wall and put aside poisonous rumination before it made a casualty of him.

There was also importance in "Deacon John's" having obtained his colonel's approval to read a prayer as part of the daily dress parade. This involvement in the official daily routines of the regiment showed Robie's realization that many young men had "grown up" in the army. Religion had to be part of their orders or the young soldiers adopted by the army would ignore it as irrelevant to their new home away from home.

Obvious roles existed in a regiment for its surgeon and chaplain. Every soldier knew the risk and felt that there but for the grace of God went he, and he wanted to know how long God's grace would hold out. The soldiers, their families, and the military officers all felt better when the self-confident, highly paid surgeon or chaplain could be called in to deal with threatening harm or actual injury to a regiment's bodies and souls. Their ministrations relieved others of the responsibility for deciding what to do. It had never dawned on chaplains or church leaders, however, that the enterprise of war would take men away from consistent routines of religious observance, while these same men would call the chaplain for specific consolation in times of loneliness, illness, or injury. Some chaplains, expecting the army to be somewhat similar to their experiences back home, interpreted small turnouts for weekly worship as signs of their failure to reach their men, and promptly resigned their commissions.

There may have been something in opinions like the one expressed by "JWR" in the November 5, 1864, issue of the *Army and Navy Journal:* "A chaplain is generally a good man and at home was useful; but in the Army he hardly ever has a part . . . in the making of his regiment's moral force. Congress has ordered chaplains into a path which no man is bound to respect in a military sense. He must preach once each week if practicable, but no man is ordered to go and hear him. The regiment is governed by order in everything else but church-going."

Though there was never an armywide requirement regarding compulsory attendance at religious services, plenty of date-specific orders were issued, as well as departmental directives, that soldiers had to attend worship services. During August 1863, for example, in his general field orders for the Army of the Ohio, Maj. Gen. Ambrose E. Burnside stipulated: "Whenever regimental evening dress parades are held, it shall be the duty of the commanding officer to see that the chaplain . . . holds some short religious service . . . with appropriate prayers for the protection and assistance of Divine Providence."

For a number of chaplains, these issues of faulty army guidelines and exclusion from the soldiers' official duties even extended to their uniforms. When Rev. Benjamin T. Phillips accepted his May 1861 appointment as chaplain of the 83rd New York, he asked Col. Michael M. Van Beuren about his duties and uniform. "You are to be pastor of the regiment, and your uniform what would be suitable for a minister of the gospel," was the reply.[16] Although Van Beuren resigned the next day when his 9th New York State Militia entered state service as the 83rd New York, the venerable old veteran's opinion about the regiment's chaplaincy remained through the war as a rule.

Chaplain Phillips adopted a captain's single-button frock of plain black wool with unadorned black pantaloons and hat, which the War Department specified as the official uniform of army chaplains on November 25, 1861. Most army chaplains were satisfied with this uniform. There were chaplains whose denominations shunned any type of ecclesiastical uniforms in protest of the church power structure they implied. To these men, even the prescribed army uniform, severe as it was, must have felt theatrical, stagy, unreal; and yet, all army chaplains doubtless felt a new kind of poise and authority seeping inward to their souls from their clothing.

Many chaplains reported that the intended significance of their black military dress was recognized by soldiers, but, just as there was antagonistic repartee regarding the insufficiency of the chaplaincy's legal base, there were fireworks over the uniform. Past codes and guidelines proved just as useless for uniform precedents as they had regarding the post and duties of army chaplains. The Army Regulations of 1816 called for a "General Staff" uniform, but civilian dress was made the standard in 1821. During 1832, Orders No. 50 of the adjutant general directed chaplains to wear black "citizen's dress" with military buttons, complemented by "a round hat and black cockade with gold eagle." During 1839, General Orders No. 36 added some soldierly variations to the uniform, including a dress sword, optional blue frock, "forage cap of the engineers," and a blue cloak.

Citing the military look of the 1839 uniform as a possible way to overcome their treatment as "fifth wheels on a coach," some chaplains obtained their regimental commanders' approval to wear the blue uniform of captains. They were instantly dubbed "chaplains militant" by their colleagues. In a letter to a friend, Chap. Alonzo H. Quint, 2nd Massachusetts, observed: "The shoulder-straps, gilt buttons, and swords, on some chaplains, have always excited the ridicule of army officers. The less a chaplain assumes to be a military man, the better. His influence is that of a Christian minister. Men expect that, but they do not expect a mere preaching officer. As to rank, due respect, etc, a chaplain needs no military rank, nor exacted salutations. As General Scott told a committee, a chaplain will secure that position his qualities entitle him to occupy; that is, when officers are gentlemen. Some regiments—many—have officers not what they should be; and there the best chaplains find trouble. But the reverse is sometimes true. In this division, we are glad of the new regulation [War Department General Orders No. 102 concerning the chaplain's uniform]. We believe that a chaplain's position is too noble for him to need gilt and tinsel. Andrew Jackson once told a minister applying for office, 'You have a higher office than is in my power to bestow.' So has a chaplain; but it is not a military office; it is that of friend, adviser, and helper, to both officer and private alike."[17]

During the last week of November 1861, the *New York Times* reported on a "convention of army chaplains" at Trinity Church in Washington, D.C. It was held under the auspices of fifteen Northern chapters of the Young Men's Christian Association, which had just met in New York City to organize a "national mission for the temporal and religious relief of Union soldiers." Their "mission" took the shape of a relief agency run by Evangelical Christians called the U.S. Christian Commission (USCC). The chaplain-delegates demonstrated their enthusiastic support for the USCC as a source of religious relief to Union soldiers and as a disdainful answer to the "Godless Christianity of the Universalists," who were prominent in the competing U.S. Sanitary Commission (USSC) organization. It was hoped that the Christian Commission would spark an evangelical revival as strong and invigorating as the first fire felt at Gasper River, Kentucky, back in the summer of 1800.

After their discussion of the Christian Commission, "a resolution came up to appoint a committee which should take measures to secure a legislative act that should fix the rank of a chaplain in the service."

Now he had none whatever, but his pay being that of a captain of cavalry, he was supposed to hold that rank, and hence wore his uniform. This gave rise to an interesting discussion respecting the propriety of chaplains wearing uniforms at all. Quite a portion of the Convention at first seemed to think it was not becoming a minister of the Gospel to be bedizened with military trappings, but on comparing notes, great difficulties were found to arise from wearing the dress of a civilian. One, who had attempted it, found himself very much circumscribed in his movements, being constantly stopped by the guards, and asked for his pass, and because he had none turned back; while another, who had worn the uniform, had been mistaken for an officer and invited by another to take a drink of brandy and water with him.

At length, however, the vexatious question seemed to present itself in its true aspect, when a chaplain gave an account of his own conversion to the propriety of wearing a uniform. His simple, earnest and truthful manner could not fail to win the heart of every listener. He said he could not bring his feelings to consent to wear a uniform, and did not, till one day he encountered General [George B.] McClellan, who was disguised so as to appear only as an ordinary officer. The General halted, and inquired if he had a pass. He replied, "No; that he was not aware it was necessary for a commissioned officer to have one." "Sir," sternly answered the General, "I recognize no commissioned officer without his uniform." He then told him he was a chaplain. The General, touching his cap, begged his pardon, and rode off. "I immediately went," he said, "and got these shoulder straps put on." He, however, made up his mind that nothing should induce him to wear a sword, for such an appendage was wholly unbecoming in one who preached the Gospel of peace. But he found by the army regulations that a chaplain, in a review, was obliged to ride behind his regiment; while an officer riding thus, without his sword, was always supposed to be under arrest. This was a new dilemma, and he finally concluded it would do more harm to be looked upon as a culprit than to wear a sword, so on such occasions, at least, he had made up his mind to carry one. This at once presented the whole subject in its proper, common-sense view, and this Convention resolved it was best to wear a uniform.

When the question arose what that uniform should be, the regulations—or, as one of the chaplains, not quite accustomed to quote new authority, said, "revelations"—prescribed none. It was desirable that the chaplain's character should never be mistaken, but known at once by some definite sign. One proposed, as surgeons wore green sashes, that the chaplains should adopt black ones. A member said that one of the brethren did put on this badge, but the first time he wore it in camp, as he was passing a soldier, the latter stopped, looked at him for a moment, shook his head solemnly, and said, "That looks too much like an undertaker." It would be rather a somber badge on a battle field. A blue one met with more favor. This was an excellent suggestion. The green sash of the surgeon makes him known as far as his uniform can be seen and prevents him from becoming the special target of the enemy. A blue sash would serve the same purpose for the chaplains. A committee was finally appointed to attend to it.

Evidently, the conventioneers were unaware that, while they met, the War Department was promulgating General Orders No. 102, which prescribed the uniform for army chaplains. The only changes made to this uniform were contained in War Department General Orders No. 247, issued in April 1864, which ordered black braid around the black frock's buttonholes and a gold embroidered wreath on the hat or cap. Nothing else happened to the black frock coat and trousers until 1880, when a black velvet shoulder strap was authorized, bearing a shepherd's crook of frosted silver.

The 1864 uniform regulations had no impact during the war. Just as with all other congressional and departmental edicts, plenty of exceptions were made regarding the appointed uniform. Many chaplains thought they

Chap. Thomas G. Brown, 21st Connecticut Infantry. COURTESY OF ROD CODDINGTON

would look less like "fifth wheels" if they wore the blue uniform of other captains in their regiments. Chaplain John S. Inskip wore the "French Chasseur" uniform, which was an emblem of the 14th "Brooklyn" New York State Militia, redesignated in the war as the 84th New York. Chaplain Augustus Woodbury, 1st Rhode Island, wore his unit's pleated smock with captain's shoulder straps. A few men added religious insignias to the blue coat, such as Chap. Louis N. Boudrye of the 5th New York Cavalry, whose history of that unit contains the Frenchman's portrait in a captain's uniform with standard shoulder straps that had a cross of gold embroidery inserted between the two pairs of bars. The blue line officer's frock of Chap. William C. Way, 24th Michigan, was crowned with squarish black shoulder straps unenclosed by gold embroidery, but with a single large Latin cross of gold bullion. Much as the military uniform may have added to the esteem in which his soldiers held him, the chaplain looked like a combatant in the sights of Confederate weapons.

In 1889, "the first battlefield monument to perpetuate the memory of a chaplain slain in battle" was dedicated in front of the Christ Lutheran Church, Gettysburg, in memory of 90th Pennsylvania chaplain Horatio S. Howell. In the class of 1843 at Lafayette College, Easton, Pennsylvania, and an 1845 graduate of New York City's Union Theological Seminary, Howell had been a pastor at Delaware Water Gap from 1853 to his enlistment and had also operated a private school for boys there. He had been seeing to wounded in what was then called "College Lutheran Church," which had been declared a field hospital on July 1, 1863, when Federal units were seen to be moving away from the battlefield in the street outside.

"I had just had my wound dressed and was leaving through the front door just behind Chaplain Howell," recalled Sgt. Archibald B. Snow, 97th New York, "when the advance skirmishers of the Confederates were coming up the street on a run. Howell, in addition to his shoulder straps and uniform, wore the straight dress sword. . . . The first skirmisher arrived at the foot of the church steps just as the chaplain and I came out. Placing one foot on the first step the soldier called on the chaplain to surrender; but Howell, instead of throwing up his hands promptly and uttering the usual, 'I surrender,' attempted some dignified explanation to the effect that he was a non-combatant . . . when a shot from the skirmisher's rifle ended the controversy." Though Chaplain Howell sleeps in Brooklyn's Green-Wood Cemetery, he still speaks through his Gettysburg memorial.

There were many variations on the homely black ensemble specified by the 1861 army regulations. Whereas a pristine example of the prescribed uniform is worn by Fr. William Corby, Roman Catholic chaplain of the 88th New York, in his Gettysburg battlefield statue, the oddest improvised shoulder straps were fabricated by nuns for another Catholic priest: Chap. Peter P. Cooney of the Irish 35th Indiana. From a distance they would have looked like a captain's shoulder straps in the regulation dimensions of four inches by one and three-quarters inches, but they were actually black velvet backgrounds enclosed by gold embroidery with a gold "C" and "N" (first and last letters of the word "chaplain") on either end where the pairs of gold-embroidered bars normally would have been, and a gold cross between them. Cooney wore these straps on his black frock, but also had "gold chords down the sides of my pants." "The buttons on my coat are bright black gutta percha buttons," Cooney continued "and around my hat I wear a gold band with gold tassels . . . Around my waist I wear a blue silk sash about five inches wide with tassels."

Chaplain John L. Staples, "an old-fashioned shouting methodist" from Stroudsburg, Pennsylvania, whose son John S. Staples was President Lincoln's representative recruit, served with the 2nd Capitol District Infantry in a black frock with a pair of gold metal captain's bars pinned to each side of his collar. Whether or not these badges of rank were of any help in the pursuit of status and respect in the army's subculture, they are clearly artifacts with great significance.

Of the 112 regimental chaplains who served for three years or longer during the Civil War, many embraced a willful attitude about succeeding in spite of difficulty. "A chaplain had a position utterly unlike any other person in the army," wrote Henry C. Trumbull, "and it was his own fault if he did not avail himself of it, and improve its advantages."[18] William R. Eastman assumed his position on the first day of 1863 as chaplain of the 72nd New York, and served sixteen and one-half months in Maj. Gen. Daniel Sickles's Excelsior Brigade. He actually saw an advantage in the chaplain's solitary post.

In one word, the significance of the chaplaincy was this: that the government offered to each regiment one man to be a friend to every man. While other officers might be good friends, this man was to make a business of kindliness. Not a commander, not a fighter, not hemmed in by any rules or any rank; left to himself to reach men by their hearts . . . and by their hearts to make them better soldiers; a man to be sought in the hour of need . . . a man to stand for honorable living and hopeful dying; and having done all to stand by . . . Many regiments did not understand and did not care; many commanders found it impossible to secure the man they would gladly have welcomed to such a post; many men who undertook the service fell short of their opportunities; but many also gained for themselves much love and a good name and a share in the final triumph.[19]

Second Massachusetts Cavalry chaplain Charles A. Humphreys cited two bits of poignant advice received from fellow graduates of the Harvard Divinity School. Edward H. Hall, who served as chaplain with the 44th Massachusetts (nine-month), gave Humphreys counsel about being a successful chaplain. "At home, where conventions and customs enclose," Hall wrote, "a man must yield to them somewhat, if he does not get overlaid by them. . . . As a Chaplain, your occasions, your duties, are not—cannot—be limited. You enter a broad and largely untrodden field. In camp, in hospital, on the march, in the field, you must find out some way to do something. Never let soldiers catch you down-hearted or timid." The most highly prized of all the encouragement he received came to Chaplain Humphreys from Rev. James Walker, ex-president of Harvard College. "You have often heard me say," wrote Reverend Walker, "how little confidence I have in the usefulness of chaplains, taken as they rise."

It is not enough that their heart is in the work; they must have a much larger share of practical sense than commonly falls to the lot of ministers, to be able to adjust themselves to their new and strange relations, or make much of their anomalous parish. Ours, you know, is a profession which, unlike law or medicine, *must first make men feel the want of what we can do before we can do it.* Meanwhile you must not give up, or lose heart, if in stormy weather, or a dark night, or a hard chase to no purpose, you sometimes do hear a trooper swear. Believe that a quiet, persistent, tender fidelity always wins the day.[20]

Praise given chaplains by men of their regiments reads like a litany of the best human motives and qualities. In some cases, their descriptions form our only glimpse of a particular churchman's entire life—a few bits of identifying information and then the chaplain simply disappears into the radiant glare of his work. "Though the chaplain's duty in our army is anomalous, many a chaplain having nothing to do and regarded by many as an encumbrance, Chap. Henry E. Parker was an exception," wrote Gen. Gilman Marston, former commander of the 2nd New Hampshire. "He endured every hardship and was a comforter in trouble. In battle he would load his horse with wounded and carry them away to safety only to return again on the same errand."

A memorial tablet honoring Chap. Aaron H. Kerr, erected in 1897 by survivors of the 9th Minnesota, reads: "A faithful preacher of the Word of God, a sympathetic pastor, his ministry in peace and war a constant benison, his presence a benediction, his life an impressive sermon."

High praise came for Lyman S. Chittenden, who was chaplain of the 67th Indiana. "Rev. Chittenden was the right man in the right place, and the boys of the 77th can never forget his kind services," recalled a soldier.[21] "He was faithful in season and out of season—faithful all the time. His work was not confined to his own regiment, but throughout the camp—wherever a soldier, whether sick or well, or dying, needed his service, he was there at the post of duty. With a smile and cheerful greeting, 'Well, boys, how do you do?' and a warm fraternal grasp of the hand, he scattered sunshine wherever he went."

"A chaplain's work," remarked Chap. John Burgess, 30th Iowa, "is enough to fill an angel's heart."[22]

Chaplain Eastman said the "most vital" qualification for the chaplaincy was that he be "a man—of a manly sort; of a kindly sympathetic spirit but not weak, of all things not weak, for that would be failure from the beginning; an intelligent man, but with an eye to read men as well as books, able to know a man when he saw him, whatever his clothes or his rank; a shrewd, discriminating, fair man; one to be trusted; having positive convictions but broad-minded, a man of faith with an enthusiasm for people in this world, laying more emphasis on life than doctrine; not lazy, but energetic and, withal, a man of an adventurous spirit, buoyant, cheerful, careless of hardship, a true comrade ready to stand by and to serve to the uttermost. For this is a place where personality alone will count."

While squabbles over uniform and "turf" contributed to a leitmotif of unproductive pettiness that constantly played in the background as they worked through their days, chaplains furnished many glimpses of courage's distant shore. Civil War army chaplains immersed themselves in the experience of war—its methods, human costs, and moral ambiguities—knowing in advance that they attempted something fundamentally impossible, yet necessary and highly important. To be an army chaplain meant submission to chaos while nevertheless retaining faith in order and meaning. Every day held experiences that tested not only the chaplain's physical stamina but also the beliefs that were the underpinnings of his entire being. Faith and doubt were part and parcel of a chaplain's role—they governed each other like breath let in and let out.

Martin Luther's ideal minister was a preacher and teacher combined, who was sure of doctrine and in full possession of eloquence, wit, memory, and "a voice." Equipped with such armament, this minister was actively to spread God's word despite temptation and threats coming from the world's beauty, wealth, and influence. When confronted by ridicule and insult, Luther's ideal cleric would "not only allow it but patiently tolerate it, though he should know when to make an end of it." Three hundred and sixty-five years later, Disciples of Christ preacher Edgar DeWitt Jones put his own spin on Luther's list of strengths. "An evangelistic preacher," said Jones, "needs a lion's heart, skin like a hippopotamus, a donkey's patience, an ant's industry, and all the lives of a cat."

He especially needed that thick skin, for chaplains did not enjoy universal good opinion in the America of the 1860s. " For most of the soldiers, army chaplains were not as popular as even the sutlers," one veteran later claimed. "Of course, when a fellow was on his back in the hospital with a leg or an arm gone or something like that, he was glad enough to have the chaplain come in and talk to him if only to take his mind off his troubles, but ordinarily there was a great lack of reverence for the cloth among soldiers. Why, I remember one incident that occurred down on the Potomac where even a wounded man was not so darned anxious to see the preacher."

A caustic yarn had been told a thousand times concerning a young soldier who awoke in a hospital, realizing he had fallen asleep on picket duty. Convinced he would be executed, he requested a chaplain, but then a surgeon explained to the boy that he was safe from arrest in the hospital, whereupon the boy exclaimed, "Forget about the chaplain!" This musty old joke still brought guffaws thirty-six years after its debut because part of America did not need much prodding to see churchmen as petty and conniving.[23]

"A Clergyman," according to America's favorite posttraumatic shock casualty, Ambrose Bierce, was "a man who undertakes the management of our spiritual affairs as a method of bettering his temporal ones," and he defined faith as "belief without evidence in what is told by one who speaks without knowledge, of things without parallel."

A purposeful smear campaign aimed at army chaplains by the U.S. Christian Commission during 1861–62 did considerable damage as Evangelicals behind the Young Men's Christian Association tried to use the Christian Commission as a means to establish a strong influence in the Northern armies. To win converts, these Evangelicals hoped to rekindle the prewar blaze of revivalism that had gloriously raged through 1857–58, converting a million Americans in a population of thirty million and renewing the faith of at least a million more.

The first major evangelical thrust came in a letter sent to the secretary of war in July 1861, from the "Army Committee of the New York Young Men's Christian Association." With the most amazing left-handed eloquence, the "Army Committee" told Simon Cameron that "improper persons have been appointed Chaplains," indignantly identifying several false chaplains, particularly pointing out one man who was a "play-actor." The Army Committee demanded that the secretary refuse commissions to "the unworthies" and immediately dismiss the knaves who were already in the field. In words as devious as they were robust, the YMCA agents gushed about army chaplains who they considered "among the most excellent and self-denying men in the ministry." They had never thought to "disparage the usefulness or the honor of faithful chaplains" nor "supersede the Government army and hospital chaplaincy systems." The committee absolved the government of any responsibility for "the sad state of facts pertaining to the army chaplaincy," and moreover proclaimed Washington "helpless to remedy its [the army chaplaincy] evils." Nevertheless, they declared that "the Christianity of the country owes it to the great Head of the Church, to itself, and to a noble army, to meet the emergency [the army chaplaincy] and to meet it NOW."[24]

There came thereafter a steady stream of defamation about military chaplains that found its way into orations or newspapers. These incessant aspersions nurtured a suspicion in the public mind that decades thereafter would equate "chaplain" with "legendary rogue." There was a response to the YMCA attack. "In nine cases out of ten," railed one editor, "all such self-constituted fault-finding committees cater to a morbid appetite for criticism which has its origin either in a disappointed ambition for place or a narrow and bigoted notion of propriety."[25] However, the offensive against the chaplains was much more adept than the defense.

Probably the single most vicious blow came during the winter of 1861–62, when Brig. Gen. Oliver Otis Howard spoke to the House of Representatives. All but hopeless as a general, despite his steady rise in prominence, he was as dogged a religious idealist as any Evangelical. Howard had already received the sobriquet "Christian Soldier," although many took the title to mean he was one-quarter flesh and three-parts holy fool. A high-minded man who was happiest when he could expound upon great virtuous causes, the general would then break into the sunless smile that belied his out-and-out humorlessness. It was no accident nor an exaggeration when, later in the war, Abner Doubleday described Howard's staff as made up of ministers and religious people who were looking out for their own interests.

Mounted squarely on his moral high horse, "The Christian Soldier" unwaveringly told Congress that the army chaplaincy had proved a failure, citing as an example, Maj. Gen. Edwin "Bull" Sumner's Division of the Potomac, to which his brigade was assigned. Of the fifteen regiments comprising the division, only two had chaplains, hinting that Sumner shared some responsibility. Not surprisingly, Howard aspired to Sumner's command as well.

Hard on the heels of General Howard's testimony came an evangelical plan "respectfully urging the voluntary enlistment of at least one minister of the Gospel, of talent, position, and approved adaptation to this special service, for each brigade of the army—say three hundred in all—during a period of two or three months each." The rest of the plan called for laymen to volunteer as chaplains' assistants and the Christian Commission to defray "all expenses of pastor and assistants going to, returning from, and while on the field, and furnish all needed publications, stores, and other means of usefulness."[26]

The stunning efficiency of this ecclesiastic coup d'état was driven by the same vehement energy that had fractured Protestantism before the war, formally dividing the Presbyterian church into "Old School" and "New School" during 1837, the Methodists into Northern and Southern wings in 1844, and the Baptists in 1855. Where there should have been some kind of common ground for all Northern Christians, there was continual fragmenting from within as the Evangelicals of various denominations kept competing with each other for custodianship of moral vocabulary. In the end, there was no wholesale replacement of "bad" army chaplains with evangelical ministers, and nothing at all came of the suggested "brigade chaplains" with three-month terms of service.

The commission's passionate early-war criticism of army chaplains may even have worked against its goals, though General Grant pretty much ordered their acceptance in 1864. While commission leaders relentlessly claimed that huge fundamental chasms separated Christian from Sanitary, they grew more and more alike during the final two years of the Civil War. Thanks to the single-minded concern of the charitable public for what portion of a donated dollar resulted in how much material assistance for the troops, the "Great Commissions" became expert in the collection and distribution of supplemental relief supplies for the army, seeming as though they were grim rivals in attracting and maintaining donations. When the war ended, both the Christian Commission and Sanitary Commission voluntarily dissolved amid thunderous self-congratulation.

One clear goal of the commissions had been to ensure that Union soldiers were brought only Christian comfort and teaching, but not all Yankees were Christians. In the *Jewish Messenger* in 1861, an editor reminded his readers: "The Union, for whose prosperity we ask Divine aid, has been the source of happiness for our ancestors and ourselves. Under the protection of the freedom guaranteed us by the Constitution, we have lived in the enjoyment of full and perfect equality with our fellow-citizens, we are enabled to worship the Supreme according to the dictates of conscience, we can maintain the position to which our abilities entitle us without our religious opinions being an impediment to advancement."[27]

After reading such an exhortation, Michael M. Allen decided to become a Pennsylvania volunteer in June 1861. A thirty-one-year-old native of Philadelphia in 1861, Allen was an Orthodox Jew who became what might be called an "associate rabbi" (chaver) back in 1851 when he completed studies on the basic implications of Jewish law (Shulchan Aruch). Making a comfortable living in the sale of ardent spirits, Allen had gone no further with rabbinical studies when the Civil War first opened, but he was known for his religious interest. Having brought a healthy number of recruits to the 5th Pennsylvania Cavalry, Allen was in line for a captain's commission when the other company officers elected him regimental chaplain.

Though he was not a full-fledged rabbi, neither were many leaders of Jewish congregations in America, and, tricked out in his blue captain's uniform, he looked as zealous as he felt about satisfying government expectations of his role to the letter. So avid, in fact, that he approached downright Protestantism in conducting nondenominational services and preaching inspirational sermons. Michael Allen was soon to become another individual with great historical significance for the army chaplaincy who will not be named on any list of commissioned chaplains.

When the evangelical Protestants, who were woof and warp of Young Men's Christian Associations, began their smear campaign against the U.S. Army's chaplaincy, Allen was high on their list of dramatic examples that would discredit the army. It was no accident, therefore, when a volunteer from the Philadelphia YMCA entered the 5th Pennsylvania Cavalry's camp only to rush out shortly, on his way to spread the appalling news that the "Army of the Lord" had a chaplain who was an "unordained Jew." As if it flew on wings of its own, Allen's story was instantaneously distributed across the North, thanks to prearranged contacts with major newspapers.

It is revealing that the New York YMCA Army Committee made a point of notifying Secretary of War Simon Cameron about the embarrassment to his name due to this affair. It was Cameron's alleged "outrage" that inflated the matter beyond all reasonable proportion. The 5th Pennsylvania Cavalry had the nickname "Cameron Dragoons" for two reasons, neither of which had direct bearing on the secretary of war. The first reason for the nickname had to do with Col. David Campbell and a clutch of Scottish officers who were part of the 5th's original organization. The Crimean War was frequently brought up in conversations during 1861 because it had been the most recent conflict. Many expected the Civil War to look something like the British experience "in the Crimea." Since one of the celebrated regiments in that conflict had been the Queen's Own Cameron Highlanders, the Pennsylvania Scots chose a nickname that linked their unit with the proud history of another Scottish unit. The "Cameron" reference broadened after Bull Run, because Simon Cameron's younger brother, sixty-year-old Col. John Cameron, had not only died in that battle at the head of his regiment but his body also had been lost in the chaos. Colonel Cameron's bones were recovered later in the war and buried with ceremony back in Lewisburg.

"Cameron Dragoons" might have even referred to both Col. John Cameron and his older brother Simon, but no one thought their regimental nickname referred solely to the backslapping main-chance legal trickster Simon Cameron. The Evangelicals of the YMCA, however, managed to ignite Simon's righteous indignation. When administrative circulars began arriving in the headquarters of brigades and regiments, requesting unit commanders to verify that their officers possessed adequate credentials relevant to their assigned duties, Michael Allen saw the writing on the wall and resigned due to "poor health" on September 23, 1861.

Michael Allen's sensationalized story, complete with its lurid mental image of noble national defenders chained to an "anti-Christ" as their source of religious inspiration, was one of approximately a hundred fed to government officials and journalists with the intent of disparaging the U.S. Army as hopelessly profane and impossibly thickheaded. Hidden behind the guileless and openhearted image of the YMCA, Evangelicals who ran the Manhattan and Philadelphia YMCAs looked for something like a public referendum that would sweep the army clean of all its active-duty chaplains and then leave that job in their hands. Only with evangelical chaplains at work inside the army, and the newly organized Christian Commission bringing supplies (religious and material) and extra manpower from outside, would the Union be saved for eternity.

"Much has been said relative to the physical and mental weakness of our armies," wrote a 12th West Virginia lieutenant to the *Wheeling Daily Intelligencer* on December 9, 1862,

> but little is said relative to the moral and religious condition. . . . No nation so universally acknowledges its existence to be given by God as the people of the United States. Yet, in this hour of her peril, there is no nation so slack in the moral and religious discipline of her armies—none so slow to acknowledge God. . . . There is a demoralization in the camp which seems to shroud the prospect of saving our country with everlasting doubt. . . . Whilst we have collected an army capable of striking the world with terror, we have wickedness and profanity enough to damn a universe. . . . Let chaplains enter upon the spirit of their work and visit the objects of their charge, talk to them plainly, talk like Christians, talk in the spirit of Christ; encourage prayer among the men, and much good will be effected.

The ugly side of this shining attempt to reignite revivalism was the Evangelicals' blind determination to batter the current army chaplaincy into oblivion in order to make room for their better system.

Embarrassed and angry that Michael Allen had been railroaded into resigning, the officers of the 5th Pennsylvania Cavalry decided to answer anti-Jewish bigotry with another appointment of a Jewish chaplain. The Board of Delegates of American Israelites recommended Rev. Arnold Fischel as a candidate whose qualifications would stand up under government scrutiny. A Dutch Jew, educated in England, who had recently resigned as rabbi of a New York City congregation, Fischel accepted the officers' invitation and immediately went to work with a will. He first applied to the War Department for a commission as the 5th Pennsylvania Cavalry's chaplain and promptly received what he needed to demonstrate his victimization by religious discrimination—Simon Cameron's official rejection based on the legal requirement that only Christian ministers be appointed as chaplains. This flaming example of civil rights violation brought newspapers from all across the country to Fischel's defense. Editorials insisted that Jewish soldiers who defended the flag must be entitled to a minister of their own faith.

The Board of Delegates of American Israelites got a petition drive under way in early December 1861, and Fischel had surprising success in arranging an interview with President Lincoln on December 11. Based on his encounter with Fischel, Lincoln initiated the changes needed in army regulations, though these were not promulgated until mid-July 1862. In the meantime, Rabbi Fischel gradually established influence with congressmen on the Military Affairs Committee who had the power to amend the Volunteer Act regarding chaplains. He also visited Jewish soldiers at hospitals, posts, and encampments in the capacity of an unofficial, civilian chaplain. While Rabbi Fischel encountered no difficulty in gaining access to these places, he was compelled to pay his own expenses. The Board of Delegates of American Israelites had initially promised to reimburse him for his food, lodging, and travel. Fischel had to rely completely on the board for fund-raising because his own time was completely taken up with his lobbying and ministry.

When the problematic regulation about army chaplains was finally modified effective July 17, 1862, the phrase "ordained minister of some Christian denomination" was changed to "ordained minister of some religious denomination." The Senate claimed to have assumed "Christian" to mean "religious." With this modification, on September 18, 1862, Jacob Frankel of Philadelphia became the first American rabbi commissioned as a military (hospital) chaplain.

Rabbi Fischel was ultimately forced to give up his work with soldiers because only a fraction of American congregations contributed shares requested by the Board of Delegates of American Israelites. In addition to this indifference, there was opposition from Isaac Mayer Wise's Reform movement. Fischel's last hope for a chaplain's commission faded when a bid for his appointment was rejected because an October 1862 investigation by the surgeon general found only seven Jewish soldiers in the 5,000 beds maintained by the military hospitals of Washington, D.C. Fearing discrimination, hundreds of soldiers in the East chose not to identify themselves as Jews. In the Western theater, considerably more Jewish patients were identified and requests made for appointment of a chaplain. Thus Bernhard Henry Gotthelf was commissioned a hospital chaplain to serve military hospitals at Louisville, Kentucky.

Despite large expenditures of his time, effort, and personal funds, in addition to the many derivative accomplishments of his campaign in behalf of a Jewish army chaplaincy, Arnold Fischel ended up with less than nothing. Of course, he savored his hard-won victory when Jacob Frankel and Bernhard H. Gotthelf were appointed as hospital chaplains. And there were the ties he had established with powerful American leaders that gave an inside edge to future generations of his people in the Union. He never received a commission, however, and there were eventually no donations whatsoever to support his work with hospitalized Jewish soldiers. With less in his wallet than when he had arrived, Dr. Fischel sailed for England on August 21, 1864, to rejoin his family. He never returned to America and died in Holland in 1894. Baptist minister Martin E. Harmstead was mustered in Michael Allen's former chaplaincy with the 5th Pennsylvania Cavalry in May 1862, and he remained with his men until he fell victim to typhoid fever on February 1, 1865.

As often happened in a regiment where bitter adversaries refused to relax their adversarial relations, the officers and noncommissioned officers began to leave, leaking away singly or in pairs—Colonel Campbell resigned October 16, 1862, and the ever-popular Col. Max Friedman did the same March 9, 1863. Colonel Robert Mayhew West, a twenty-nine-year-old career soldier, led the 5th Pennsylvania Cavalry through the rest of the war. When the regiment was discharged in 1865, barely two officers remained of those who had command in 1861–62.[28]

A final irony regarding the Jewish chaplaincy was Ferdinand L. Sarner's service as regimental chaplain of the 54th New York from April 1863 through September 1864. Up to April 1862, the 54th had been one of a dozen German infantry regiments in Gen. Louis Blenker's division, known for a legendary supply of lager, singing, three pet dogs for every man in the division, and notorious, outspoken apologists of socialism and other theories that baffled or bored most Americans. Shifted to the XI Corps, the 54th New York fought at Chancellorsville and Gettysburg in the Army of the Potomac. The regiment was then reassigned to the X Corps, part of the force that ringed Charleston, South Carolina, and its harbor.

Born in Lissa, Posen, and graduated from the University of Hesse, Chaplain Sarner had been the rabbi of a congregation in Rochester, New York, when the war started. Though he was the first American rabbi to serve as a regimental chaplain, there was no celebration of Ferdinand Sarner's accomplishment nor did he receive recognition from contemporaries. There has been conjecture that he was worth more as a linguist than a cleric to the "freethinking Dutchmen" of General Blenker's division. In addition to beer and socialists, Blenker's chaplains had been a peculiar collection of skeptics, heretics, and outright atheists, though Sarner was mustered during 1863 after the division had gone through a change. Slightly wounded at Gettysburg, he also had a horse shot out from under him at that battle.

The 54th's chaplain was dismissed October 3, 1864, on charges of his being AWOL. Like hundreds of other officers who required additional time for full recovery, Sarner had to submit a physician's statement of the problem along with a written request for time off. He might have submitted incorrect paperwork, or he may have been less than prompt in sending it to his colonel. It was plain that the chaplain had been hampered by poor health and his illegal absence had not been a demonstration of defiance. When he left the army, Sarner passed into obscurity, except for his death in 1874 at Memphis, Tennessee, during a catastrophic yellow fever epidemic.

And then there was the woman. Abraham Lincoln had the straight and clear touch; he could draw limpid truths from a swamp of error. Though the Civil War was a dirty, demented, and disgusting business that many saw as nothing more than a failure of rational policy, Lincoln gave it meaning, honor, and purpose in the 272 words of his "Gettysburg Address." He called upon the same uncanny knack for succinct summation in his White House office on November 10, 1864, at the close of his meeting with Ellen E. Hobart.

Mrs. Hobart, née Gibson, was a minister, married to a regimental chaplain. She wanted to be an army chaplain herself. Despite the aptitude she displayed in presenting her case, however, Ellen—more often known as Ella—apparently had never imagined she looked for the impossible. In wellnigh eighty years of existence, the War Department had never once considered women suitable material for soldiers, let alone commissioned officers. The president may have tried letting her down easy, telling her that hers was a hopeless application. Yet there she sat, in a somber black dress that was her feminine version of the prescribed chaplain's uniform. A veteran of many political bargaining sessions, Lincoln recognized blind determination in the face of reason when he saw it, and so he finessed the problem with an expedient nick-of-time gimmick.

"This lady would be appointed Chaplain of the First Wisconsin Heavy Artillery, only that she is a woman," he wrote as she watched. "The President has not legally anything to do with such a question, but has no objection to her appointment." He wished Mrs. Hobart good luck with her quest, handed her the note that listed the salient points of their discussion, and directed her to Secretary of War Edwin Stanton. The note with Lincoln's signature should gain her deference and prompt treatment at the War Department.

It was about time that the secretary of war defended some of his halfbaked policies. Army regulations relevant to chaplains were among the vaguest acts of Congress passed during 1861–62, and they had already pro-

voked two troublous disputes. Now the list of offended individuals was beginning to sound like a bigot's tasteless joke—a Jew, a Negro, and a woman.
Rabbi Fischel had returned to Europe three months earlier, defeated. Then
there was the mean-spirited treatment given Samuel Harrison, the third of
seventeen African-American army chaplains who were commissioned as officers during the Civil War (15 regimental, 2 hospital). Pastor of the First Colored Congregational Church of Pittsfield, Massachusetts, he reported for
duty—all six feet, five inches of him—on November 12, 1863, with the 54th
Massachusetts at Morris Island, South Carolina.

Trouble began within a month of his arrival. Properly elected by the
regiment's field officers and company commanders and commissioned by
Massachusetts governor John Albion Andrew, Harrison had borrowed
nearly $1,000 to outfit himself and support his family during his absence.
The army paymaster, however, offered him only $10 per month though his
monthly pay was supposed to be ten times that. The paymaster general had
ordered that he be shortchanged on the basis of a regulation that had nothing at all to do with the army chaplaincy. This one permitted "the employment of persons of African descent for labor on fortifications and for similar
tasks at a monthly wage of [$10]."

After seven and a half months of service, when he should have received
$750 but got nothing, Chaplain Harrison was forced to resign on March 14,
1864. A month after the chaplain's resignation, Atty. Gen. Edward Bates
notified President Lincoln that he had looked into Harrison's case to find he
was due his entire pay as a chaplain. After several warnings, the paymaster
general finally paid Harrison for his time, but it took twenty months from
the day the chaplain had reported for duty in 1863.[29]

Now, after making her way to the War Department building through
hordes of petitioners, aspirants, and claimants sparked to new intensity by
Lincoln's reelection, Mrs. Hobart was courteously presented to Secretary
Stanton. The matter was settled in moments. In the middle of a nasty
catarrhal gag, Stanton sputtered out something unintelligible about not
wanting to "set a precedent," then refused Hobart's request out of hand with
a shrug and a shake of the head. But Ellen (Gibson) Hobart was an outspoken freethinker and feminist trailblazer who would yet be responsible for an
extraordinary chapter in the history of America's military chaplaincy. In the
offing she would take on the War Department, the adjutant general, and
maybe even God.

Just five days after the July 21, 1861, battle of Bull Run, she began
the war by marrying Methodist minister John Hobart in Geneva, Illinois,

a village on the Fox River, west of Chicago. The forty-nine-year-old Hobart had become a spiritualist in 1856–57, after which he received no further assignments to Methodist congregations. Their marriage less than a week after the Federal defeat may be somehow related to that battle. For years, Ella and John had been effective speakers on moral subjects, and they may have decided to see the war through as married delegates of the U.S. Sanitary Commission (neither of them would have been able to abide the Evangelicals of the Christian Commission), but military events had hurried along their plans. Soon Ella was credited with writing a brief inspirational homily called *The Dangers and Temptations of Army Life*. She dedicated the booklet to her husband, though some suggested that her real intent in the homilies therein revealed her frustration at his weakness for ardent spirits.

Both Ella and John eventually got their desired opportunity to work with Union soldiers, but in separate locations. He was elected chaplain of the 8th Wisconsin, a role that took him from Ella's life from January 1863 until he was mustered out September 5, 1865. The 8th's sobriquet was "The Live Eagle Regiment" because of "Old Abe the War Eagle," a luckless animal that was carried into action alongside the regiment's colors, tied to a perch with twenty feet of rope. Hobart served with the regiment through the Vicksburg campaign in 1863 and the Red River campaign during early 1864.

Then, on July 15, 1864, Hobart was practically driven from the 8th's camp on the authorization of War Department Special Orders No. 238, which gave no more of an explanation than "Chaplain John Hobart Eighth Wisconsin Volunteers, being inefficient and unfitted for the position of chaplain, is, by direction of the President, hereby mustered out of the service of the United Sates." On October 10, 1864, he was just as abruptly restored to duty and remained with the regiment for eleven more months.

Meanwhile, from December 1861 through December 1863, Ella's time was completely taken up, in her words, with "organizing Soldiers Aid Societies in Wisconsin, raising funds for the Sanitary Commission, and rendering service in other states in various ways." Even small settlements had their own Soldiers Aid Societies, and these organizations were a crucial foundation for the USSC. Once Mrs. Hobart assembled a reliable core of volunteers, she would start them on the assessment of all wage earners and businessmen in town. The local Soldiers' Aid Society then collected monthly "taxes" ranging from a nickel to a dollar, sending the funds to USSC headquarters. For two weeks starting on October 27, 1863, the Northwest Sanitary fair was held in Chicago, and through the fair Mrs. Hobart made to the Sanitary

Commission a sizable donation, said to have come from her earnings as a writer for "The Truth Seeker."

"It was these two years of faithful service," she said in 1869, "that influenced Governor James T Lewis, Secretary of State Lucius Fairchild, and State Treasurer Samuel Dexter Hastings . . . to give me a paying position. . . . The Governor offered me a commission if any Wisconsin unit would elect me its regimental chaplain. I was recommended as a chaplain . . . to regiments which were recruiting and otherwise organizing at Camp Randall, Madison, Wisconsin."

In truth, Governor Lewis had a soft spot for ladies who expressed an interest in the war. At least once a week the Madison or Milwaukee newspapers contained an item about him presenting a commission to yet another lovely patriot. Although these commissions could have been construed as valid appointments, Lewis believed that none of the flag-waving women would ever take their commissions seriously. But Ella would.

Convinced that support from the governor and other state officials gave her sufficient clout to gain an army chaplaincy, Ella Hobart set out on an arduous schedule of visits to all of Wisconsin's military rendezvous. Her travels would also put her in touch with every regiment being organized in the state. She found that there would not be any new cavalry regiments; and of the fifty-three infantry regiments that would be raised in Wisconsin, thirty-seven had already left the state for duty. Still there would be eight one-year infantry units raised in 1865, and that left eight possibilities for Ella. The regiment that stood as her best bet, however, was the 1st Wisconsin Heavy Artillery.

During August and September, six new "heavy" companies began to fill Camp Randall, and Mrs. Hobart, who resided in Madison, became a frequent visitor. The "heavies" developed an attachment to her, and local newspapers mentioned that "temperance crusader Mrs. Chaplain John Hobart" was becoming "famous for the concern she shows Wisconsin soldiers at Camp Randall." On September 30, 1864, Col. Charles C. Meservey came to Camp Randall to personally complete arrangements for moving his recruits south to the defenses of Washington. Ella Hobart was able to give him a certificate and written testimonial, endorsed by other ministers of the denomination, that verified her to have been a duly ordained minister in good standing with the Religio Philosophical Society of St. Charles, Illinois—an association of Spiritualists located just two miles north of Geneva, where she and John had been wed. "I had never seen the colonel until that day," wrote Ella in 1869, "but he had heard of my labors, and those approving remarks from the volunteers combined with the papers in my possession to influence him to grant me the position of chaplain."

On September 30, 1864, Ella reported, "Colonel Meservey and all his officers in camp committed themselves to me." Meservey left for Alexandria that day after seeing Governor Lewis and obtaining from him confirmation of his promise of a commission for her if she could be elected chaplain of any regiment. Ella felt her service with the 1st Wisconsin Heavy Artillery began that same day, "because from that day I labored particularly for that regiment . . . doing all in my power for the comfort and happiness of the men, just as I did after the November 22 election when I was legally acknowledged chaplain-elect of the regiment."

Whether or not Ella had some earlier plan as a feminist to become the first woman appointed as an army chaplain, there is ample evidence that she worked hard in her role, and that she used her own money to pay her way, assuming that the government would reimburse her now that she believed she would be receiving a genuine commission.

Ella went south with Company K and immediately assumed the duties of a regimental chaplain when she arrived. Her first problem was the separation of her nine companies in their assignments to seven fortifications. Even though Forts Ellsworth, Lyon, O'Rourke, Farnsworth, Willard, and Weed all stood within a space of four miles, the men in one fortification would not be allowed outside of its walls, and services would have to be repeated. "I did all and more than was required of me in the hospital," wrote Ella, "and I held two or three services every Sunday in various barracks, speaking also weekday evenings and conducting funerals. Much was done in the open air as late in the season as December because we had no chapel or place of meeting other than the barracks."

Opinions of Chaplain Ella's efforts soon began to appear in letters from soldiers that were published in hometown papers. The *Wisconsin Journal* for November 5, for instance, contained a short note from a fifer in the 1st Wisconsin Heavies. "Listened to a very practical sermon from our chaplain, Mrs. Hobart, of Camp Randall fame," he wrote, "it seems rather novel to have a female chaplain, but I suppose if Mrs. H is suited, we ought to be."

Meservey appointed Ella to be the regiment's chaplain as supported in a unanimous vote by the field officers and company commanders on November 22, 1864, and published General Orders No. 19, which formally notified his men of her appointment. The colonel also sent word to Governor Lewis back in Wisconsin, because he had promised to authorize a chaplain's commission for her. In a postwar letter, however, Ella bitterly observed that the governor did not immediately issue her commission, but merely wrote to Stanton "inquiring if the Secretary would authorize the mustering providing he *did* commission me." Lewis had altered his promise, telling her now: "I won't commission you, if Stanton won't muster you." At the War Department, Stanton had already told Ella on November 10 that he would not muster a woman. "Even the approbation of President Lincoln, obtained by myself, failed to move him," she complained.

A flurry of activity followed in the ensuing months. Letters were sent to Lincoln and Stanton, signed by every officer of the 1st Wisconsin, asking for the former's help and petitioning the latter to reconsider his rejection of their November vote. "They affirmed they would not elect any other chaplain," Ella proudly recalled, "and I signified my willingness to remain and act as chaplain as long as they were satisfied, without any expense to them or the regiment."

In December, Governor Lewis petitioned the adjutant general with his latest idea about fixing the matter, asking that "if under present regulations she cannot be mustered, can a special law be passed?" In fact, Stanton himself had already contacted Ella after he received the officers' petition, offering his solution to her problem. He advised her to submit through a congressman a bill to obtain the place she wanted by a special act, she later claimed, "which I then did not feel disposed to do." Then, two days before Christmas, the adjutant general's office sent communications to Lewis, the Wisconsin state adjutant general, and the officers of the 1st Wisconsin Heavy Artillery, with a peremptory notification that Ella (Gibson) Hobart would never be mustered, and the matter was ended.

During her final six months in the army, Chaplain Hobart maintained her intense degree of application to duty. In the last week of June 1865, the 1st Wisconsin was discharged and the happy veterans boarded trains headed north. While she would always have the satisfaction of knowing she had measured up to her duties, Ella received no notice that her duties were done, but she had seen other members of the regiment with their discharge papers. She would never receive a discharge certificate because she had never been mustered into the army. She moved to New York City and returned to writing, and divorced John Hobart on August 5, 1868, apparently because of his drinking and/or womanizing during the war.

For the next thirty-seven years Ella would struggle to get from the government the justice and recognition she felt she deserved. Her cause received a boost when Wisconsin governor Lucius Fairchild became an outspoken advocate for her case. In addition, she was able to provide affidavits from Colonel Meservey and other members of the 1st Wisconsin Heavy Artillery who attested to her election and the hard work she had done as their chaplain. When Sen. Henry Wilson lent his influence to Ella's cause, it was not long before a joint resolution of Congress was passed on March 3, 1869, that recognized Ella Gibson's right to receive the full pay and emoluments of a chaplain in the U.S. Army for the time during which she faithfully performed her duties.

In the case of a celebrated claim such as Ella's, however, the government was allowed one more opportunity to scrutinize the case and to determine the exact amount of the award. The official assigned to conduct this final inquiry was none other than Capt. Thomas Vincent, the man in the adjutant general's office in Washington who back in 1864 had been convinced that a little more scrutiny would have discredited Ella Gibson.

Not only did Vincent urge Congress to cancel Gibson's award—a recommendation that was ignored—he used every tactic he could muster to postpone payment of Ella's final award for six years. The payment approved by Congress on March 3, 1869, did not reach her until March 7, 1876. Even then Vincent managed to have the original amount of the award reduced, arguing that she should not be paid from her first day of work on September 30, 1864, nor from November 22, the date of her election. Rather, the pay should start from the time Governor Lewis had the Wisconsin assistant adjutant general write to the War Department in December 1864, regarding the possibility of mustering Ella Gibson. This December letter had been Vincent's first bit of correspondence that started his many years of following the Gibson matter.

The six-year delay before she received her $1,210 award was the hardest blow Ella had to endure, but not the only one. In 1879, claiming that she returned from the war "unable to bear the rigors of the climate or any exposure, and at all times as sensitive to the changes of weather as a sick babe," she filed for an invalid pension, which was never approved. More congressional bills were introduced for Ella's relief, but none succeeded.

She continued her writing, becoming increasingly strident on feminism and more and more confrontational with conventional Christianity. Ella was fond of predicting that a time would come when the King James Bible would not be mentioned "without a blush of shame tingling the cheek of modesty, or referred to except as a textbook obsolete, superannuated, blasphemous, false, pernicious, corrupt, immodest, obscene, and too immoral to be tolerated, even as a past nuisance, ancient, foreign, and worthless."

She died in Barre, Massachusetts, on March 5, 1901. "Mrs. Gibson was a remarkable person, energetic, intellectual, and talented, and had it not been for her eccentricities, inherited and acquired, she would have been a noble and grand woman," said a local obituary. There was no mention whatsoever of her effective stumping for temperance as well as Spiritualism, her soldier relief activities throughout Wisconsin, and especially her service as a regimental chaplain in the Civil War. She had been effectively written out of history.[30]

When he gave a presentation about "The Chaplains in the Volunteer Army" in the District of Columbia in 1892, veteran chaplain James H. Bradford certainly did not have Ella (Gibson) Hobart specifically in mind, but he could have when he commented that "the chaplain was only one in a thousand; yes, more than that, for some regiments had none."[31] More to the point, the wartime total that includes all of the Civil War's Northern regimental chaplains, hospital chaplains, and navy chaplains was 2,398. Divided by what James McPherson calls the "generally accepted" 2.1 million head count of Union soldiers and sailors, it turns out that military chaplains composed only a fraction of a percent within the total force, and that there would have been 876 other Yankee soldiers for every chaplain if everyone had served together for the same amount of time.

Regarding their time in the army as chaplains, of the 2,154 total regimental chaplains, 129 (6 percent) served from half a month to two and a half months, 440 (20 percent) served for three to six months, 223 (10 percent) served for six and a half to eight months, 320 (15 percent) served for eight and a half to eleven and a half months, 109 (5 percent) served a full year, 346 (16 percent) served for twelve and a half to eighteen months, 168 (8 percent) served for eighteen and a half to twenty-three and a half months, 33 (1.5 percent) chaplains served two full years, 110 (5 percent) served for twenty-four and a half to thirty months, 117 (5 percent) served for thirty and a half to thirty-five and a half months, 32 (1.5 percent) served a full three years, 64 (3 percent) served for thirty-six and a half to forty-five and a half months, and 16 (.7 percent) chaplains served for forty-six to fifty-two months. Three of the 2,154 regimental chaplains served four units in succession, 13 served three units in succession, and 179 served two units in succession. Additionally, 47 appointed chaplains (2.18 percent) either never accepted their appointments or their terms of service escaped being recorded.

The average regimental chaplain in the Union army during the Civil War was a Methodist, thirty-eight years and eight months of age, who served thirteen and a half months. Though all averages must be taken with

a grain of salt because of incomplete data and very small numbers of regiments for some states, the average age of regimental chaplains was older
(age forty or more years) in Illinois, Maine, Wisconsin, Missouri, Michigan,
and Tennessee. For denominations, the average Methodist chaplain was age
38.3 and his service 15 months. Presbyterian was 39 years and 15.2 months;
Congregational was 37.8 years, 13.7 months; Baptist was 39 years, 14.7
months; Episcopal was 40.6 years and 13.3 months; Catholic was 34.9 years
and 16 months.

As to ages when mustered as regimental chaplains, 243 individuals were
between the ages of twenty and twenty-nine, 540 were between age thirty
and thirty-nine, 412 were in their forties, 185 in their fifties, and 20 men
were sixty-something. Hospital chaplains Burr Baldwin and Augustus Eddy
were aged seventy-two and seventy-three, respectively, when mustered during 1862, and John McVickar, U.S. Army post chaplain for Forts Wood and
Columbus in New York Harbor, was seventy-four when on duty at the start
of the war. Impossibly old Rev. John Pierpont was mustered as chaplain of
the 22nd Massachusetts on September 12, 1861, though he had been born in
Litchfield, Connecticut, on April 6, 1785. A great-grandson of the founder
of Yale, he had passed the Massachusetts bar during 1812 and was ordained a
Unitarian minister in 1819. A pastor in Boston and then Medford, Pierpont
was an Abolition party candidate for governor and the 1850 Free Soil Party
congressional candidate. He resigned his chaplaincy due to health problems
after serving a month and a half, but soon landed a clerk's position in the
Treasury Department! He died in 1866. One of his sons, a Confederate soldier, is remembered for having written "Jingle Bells."

The youngest regimental chaplain, George F. Pentecost, 8th Kentucky
Cavalry (twelve-month), entered the service at age nineteen, serving from
September 12, 1862, to September 23, 1863. Born in Albion, Illinois, September 23, 1842, to a veteran colonel of the Mexican War, he had attended
Georgetown Seminary in Kentucky from the fall of 1861 through June 1862.
At the age of sixteen, Pentecost had been employed at John Brown's *Herald
of Freedom* in Lawrence, Kansas. After the war, Reverend Pentecost had
charge of many Baptist congregations from Kentucky and Indiana to Brooklyn, New York, and London, England. Charles Wheeler Dennison was
recorded as having been eighteen years of age when appointed from Massachusetts as a hospital chaplain on July 31, 1862.

The tallest had to have been Chap. Charles P. Nash of the 7th Michigan
Cavalry, who was "a monstrous big man" from Holly, who stood six feet, six
inches and "preferred to walk instead of ride due to lumbago." Chaplain
Enoch K. Miller, 25th U.S. Colored Troops, was an Episcopal cleric who had

been born in London in 1840. More than one of his descriptive lists state that he stood four feet, four and a half inches in height. The prize for the longest name must go to the chaplain of the 16th New York Heavy Artillery, a Dutch-Reformed clergyman named Herman Frederick Francis Schnellendreussler.

Chaplain Charles L. Bacon of the 85th New York served the shortest term with a commission—less than a month, while the longest term was the fifty-one and a half months of Congregational minister John R. Adams, who was mustered at age fifty-nine and served with the 5th Maine from January 24, 1861, to July 27, 1864, and then with the 121st New York Infantry until June 25, 1865. At Fredericksburg, Adams had to be ordered out of the first wave of attack boats "because he carried $2,000 in soldier's pay."

"I am in good health and full of hope," he once wrote home, "I have undressed twice this month . . . I sleep on the ground, wet or dry . . . have not removed my boots for six nights because they were so wet I feared not getting them on again." Adams returned home to Northampton, Massachusetts, during June 1865, and died April 25, 1866—"a wartime casualty as sure as if he had been killed by a bullet." Adams's early death after discharge was not an uncommon occurrence. In addition to 73 chaplains who died noncombat deaths while on active duty, nearly another 200 died inordinately young or within five years after discharge.

Methodism was represented by the largest number of chaplains, which was double the size of the second-largest denomination, Presbyterian. The next three in descending order of size were Baptist, Episcopal, and Congregational. Denominations represented by less than 5 percent of military chaplains were, starting with the largest group: Unitarian/Universalist, Roman Catholic, Lutheran, Dutch-Reformed, Disciples of Christ, German-Reformed, and Jewish. This hierarchy reflected the relative numbers of Northern members claimed by these religions.

Methodist	38 percent
Presbyterian	17 percent
Baptist	12 percent
Episcopal	10 percent
Congregational	9 percent
Unitarian/Universalist	4 percent
Roman Catholic	3 percent
Lutheran	2 percent
all others	1 percent or less each

Fort Darling in April 1865, the chaplain's quarters of the 1st Connecticut Heavy Artillery, photographed by J. Reekie. LIBRARY OF CONGRESS

Eleven chaplains were killed in action and another four mortally wounded. The first to die was Navy chaplain John L. Lenhart, a fifty-seven-year-old Methodist minister who disappeared beneath the waves when the U.S. sloop of war *Cumberland* was rammed by the CSS *Virginia*. The next navy chaplains to die would be aboard the *Arizona* and *Oklahoma* at Pearl Harbor. Chaplain Bovell McCall, 13th Tennessee Cavalry, a physician from Jonesboro, is often omitted because he was instantly executed when captured out of uniform during July 1864, near Seaton's Mill, Green County, Tennessee. He was returning to his unit after sneaking through Confederate lines to visit his home. Chaplain Ozem B. Gardner, 13th Kansas, was killed on Thanksgiving Day, 1864, while escorting "loyal refugees to Fort Scott, Kansas[,]" through the Cherokee Nation. Some accounts claimed he was killed by Jesse James. Chaplain John R. Eddy of the 72nd Indiana was nearly obliterated by a "six-pounder" solid artillery round that passed through him in June 1863, after he had been with his unit for only eight days. Chaplain Orlando N. Benton, 51st New York, was badly wounded in action March 14, 1862, at New Bern, North Carolina, and died soon after.

Ninety-seven chaplains were named in after-action reports by their unit commanders for having provided precious care for the wounded and the dead in battle. The largest number of Western chaplains cited was at the horrific battle of Murfreesboro, and the most Eastern army mentions were in regard to Seven Pines. The remaining names are those of chaplains taken prisoner in various situations and the hospital chaplains appointed early by President Lincoln. There are a few chaplains who encountered the enemy while escorting wounded home or carrying soldiers' pay to their families up north. A group of chaplains filed a petition protesting an "easy surrender" made to Nathan Bedford Forrest. Four chaplains would be awarded the Medal of Honor, two for helping wounded under fire and one for leading men in action prior to his appointment, and Chap. Milton L. Haney of the 55th Illinois for stepping into a command vacuum at Atlanta and leading a counterattack.

When completing one of many rounds of forms to obtain an army pension, Rev. Jeremiah W. Marsh explained that he had "remained with the regiment until my health was completely broken," but that he could not complete the full service term of the 28th Maine nine-month regiment. Faced with a blank line on the form but no question, Jeremiah condensed his life to fit the space. "I have had many severe trials thus far on my pilgrimage, having buried a wife and four children; still I feel I have not lived altogether in rain." Indeed he had not, nor had they all.

UNION MILITARY CHAPLAINS NOTES

1. William L. Shea and Earl J. Hess, *Pea Ridge: Civil War Campaign in the West* (Chapel Hill, 1992), 110, 114, 115; U.S. War Department, *War of the Rebellion: A Compilation of the Official Records of the Union and Confederate Armies* (Washington, D.C., 1880–1902), ser. 1, vol. 8 (hereafter cited as OR).

2. Service and Pension Records of William M. Haigh, possession of the National Archives (hereafter cited as NA).

3. Francis A. Lord, *They Fought for the Union: A Complete Reference Work on the Federal Fighting Man* (New York, 1960), 97–100.

4. Roy J. Honeywell, *Chaplains of the United States Army* (Washington, D.C., 1958), 201.

5. William Reed Eastman, "The Army Chaplain of 1863," *Personal Recollections of the War of the Rebellion: Addresses Delivered before the Military Order*

of the Loyal Legion of the United States, New York Commandery (Series 4; New York, 1891–1915), article no. 20, delivered December 13, 1911.

6. *Boston Christian Advocate*, May 23, 1861.

7. Garry Wills, *Under God: Religion and American Politics* (New York, 1990), 208. Curtis D. Johnson, *Redeeming America: Evangelicals and the Road to Civil War* (Chicago, 1993), 184–89.

8. Thomas K. Beecher, Papers from 1863, Thomas K. Beecher Papers, Cornell University.

9. Service and Pension Records of William Y. Brown, John G. Butler, George G. Goss, Henry H. Hopkins, and John C. Smith, possession of the NA.

10. Honeywell, *Chaplains*, 104–25; Rollin W. Quimby, "The Chaplains' Predicament," *Civil War History* 8 (1962): 25–37; Rollin W. Quimby, "Congress and the Civil War Chaplaincy," *Civil War History* 10 (1964): 246–59.

11. OR, ser. 3. All regulations quoted, and statements by Paymasters Larned and Andrews can be found in this series.

12. *Rochester Daily Union and Advertiser*, October 26, 1861.

13. Ezra Carman, 13th New Jersey Volunteers, New Jersey Historical Society.

14. Joseph O'Hagan, " Father Joseph O'Hagan," *Woodstock Letters*, November 11, 1861.

15. References appear in the *Buffalo Morning Express*, the *Buffalo Daily Courier*, and the *Buffalo Commercial Advertiser*.

16. William Todd, ed., *History of the Ninth Regiment, N.Y.S.M. 1845–1888* (New York, 1889), 98–99.

17. Alonzo H. Quint, *The Potomac and the Rapidan* (Boston, 1864).

18. Henry Clay Trumbull, *War Memories of an Army Chaplain* (New York, 1898), 3.

19. Eastman, "Army Chaplain."

20. Charles A. Humphreys, *Field, Camp, Hospital, and Prison in the Civil War, 1863–1865* (1918), 15–23.

21. William H. Bentley, *History of the 77th Illinois Volunteer Infantry* (Peoria, 1883).

22. John Burgess, *Pleasant Recollections of Characters and Works of Noble Men* (Cincinatti, 1887), 398.

23. "Stories of the War Told in the Camps of Peace," *Buffalo Enquirer*, August 25, 1897. This was part of the coverage given the Grand Army of the Republic National Encampment at Buffalo, New York.

24. The "Memorial to the Secretary of War from the Army Committee of the Y. M. C. A." was quoted in many newspapers during the second week of July 1861.

25. *Buffalo Advocate*, July 11, 1861.

26. Edward P. Smith, *Incidents of the U.S. Christian Commission* (Philadelphia, 1869). Howard's February 1862 appearance and the plan offered during March 1862 are described, though not as a unified action by the U.S.C.C.

27. *Jewish Messenger*, December 28, 1861.

28. Betram W. Korn, *American Jewry and the Civil War* (Philadelphia, 1951). All the facts of the above piece came from Korn's work, which still stands after more than five decades.

29. Service and Pension Records of Samuel Harrison, NA; Addison Ballard, ed., *Reverend Samuel Harrison: His Life Story As Told by Himself by Request of Reverend Dr Addison Ballard of New York University* (1899); Samuel Harrison, *An Appeal of a Colored Man to His Fellow-Citizens of a Fairer Hue in the United States* (1877).

30. Much of Ella's story is found in letters written by her that appear in her military and pension files at the National Archives. More good glimpses of her life and ideas can be found in *Women without Superstition*, Annie Laurie Gaylor, ed., (Madison, 1997).

31. James H. Bradford, "The Chaplains in the Volunteer Army," *War Papers Delivered before the Military Order of the Loyal Legion of the United States, Commandery of the District of Columbia* (War Paper 11; Washington, D. C., 1887–1900).

Chaplains of the Confederacy

John W. Brinsfield

I have read a fiery gospel writ in burnished rows of steel.
                                                    —*Julia Ward Howe*

*So the priests blew the trumpets . . . Then all the army went
into the city.*   —*Joshua 6*

The Provisional Government of the Confederate States was literally born a child of war. A month before Jefferson Davis of Mississippi was inaugurated president, South Carolina batteries fired on the U.S. merchantman *Star of the West*, sent by Pres. James Buchanan to relieve Fort Sumter. The same week, in January 1861, Gov. Joseph E. Brown of Georgia seized Fort Pulaski at the mouth of the Savannah River. Thereafter Florida, Alabama, Mississippi, and Louisiana militia units occupied six Federal forts and two arsenals in their respective states.[1] The Confederate Congress, meeting in Montgomery, Alabama, on February 15, resolved that Fort Sumter, South Carolina, and Fort Pickens, Florida, should be taken as soon as possible "either by negotiation or by force." It was intolerable to allow the presence of "foreign" military installations on soil that belonged to the sovereign states of the South.[2]

In delivering his inaugural address on February 18, Jefferson Davis explained to the crowd at the Alabama capitol in Montgomery that these events did not mark a revolution as much as a transfer of ownership. He hoped for peace, but was resolved on independence for the South.

When the Confederate batteries shelled Fort Sumter two months later on April 12, many Southern leaders celebrated the event as the end of subjugation to Northern politics and insults and the beginning of a new Southern nation. On April 15, when President Lincoln issued a proclamation calling for 75,000 militiamen from the remaining states in the Union to put down the insurrection, Virginia, North Carolina, and Tennessee refused to supply their quotas and began discussing joining the Deep South states in secession.

On April 29,1861, barely two weeks into the war, Pres. Jefferson Davis expressed his sentiments:

> We feel that our cause is just and holy; we protest solemnly in the face of mankind that we desire peace at any sacrifice save that of honor and independence; we ask no conquest, no aggrandizement, no concession of any kind from the States with which we were lately confederated; all we ask is to be let alone.[3]

The war from Davis's perspective was just, because it was defensive. Many Southerners complied with the official position that the attack on Fort Sumter was not an aggressive act, but an invitation to the president of the United States to withdraw his soldiers from sovereign territory, not unlike the first shot fired at Lexington in 1775. The real cause of war was Lincoln's invasion of the South. In a sermon preached to the General Assembly of Georgia, Methodist bishop George F. Pierce reiterated to the legislators that "the triumph of our army is the triumph of right and truth and justice. The defeat of our enemies is the defeat of wrong and malice and outrage."[4] Not all believed that, but most of the people did believe that they had to defend their homes from the invading Federal armies.

After Virginia seceded the next month, former congressman Lucius Q. C. Lamar of Mississippi, speaking in Richmond in June 1861, told an assembly of patriotic citizens: "[T]hank God! We have a country at last . . . to live for, to pray for, to fight for, and if necessary, to die for."[5] Thomas R. R. Cobb of Georgia wanted to call the new nation The Republic of Washington, recalling that George Washington was one of the first great American rebels. Some newspaper editors suggested the term "Commonwealth" or "The Allied Republics," which might in time come to include states in Central and South America.[6]

Religious leaders in the South reacted to the news with caution. As churchmen, they represented the only truly national institutions apart from the government. Although the Methodist Episcopal Church, South, the largest Protestant denomination in the eleven states that would compose the Confederacy, had separated from the Methodist Episcopal Church in 1845, her bishops were not yet ready to embrace state secession before it could be properly assessed.[7]

Many of the Southern Baptists, who had also split from their Northern Baptist brethren in 1845, were much more enthusiastic about a new government for a new nation. The state Baptist conventions of Alabama, Mississippi, and South Carolina officially declared for secession in December 1860.

The Presbyterian General Assembly in November 1860 condemned "political intermeddling by professed Ministers of the Gospel," and sought to keep the churches focused on purely spiritual matters. Eleven months later, however, following the lead of the South Carolina Synod, the Southern members of the General Assembly met in Augusta, Georgia, to form the Presbyterian Church in the Confederate States.[8]

The Episcopal Church's bishops in the South, William Meade of Virginia and James Otey of Tennessee in particular, initially urged moderation with regard to supporting secession and requested all clergymen to pray that national wounds would be healed. When Louisiana seceded, however, Bishop Leonidas Polk, who had graduated from West Point early in his life, suggested that the church conform to a territorial principle. The Northern Episcopal dioceses would minister in the United States, while the Southern dioceses would do the same in the South. Bishop Thomas Atkinson of North Carolina declared that political and ecclesiastical boundaries were not coterminous and that the secession of the states had no bearing on the church.

However, in July 1861, Polk, supported by Bishop Stephen Elliott of Georgia, issued a call for Southern delegates to meet in Montgomery, Alabama, to form a separate Episcopal Church. Virginia, Tennessee, Texas, and North Carolina were not represented at the convocation, but the delegates from Louisiana, Georgia, Alabama, South Carolina, Mississippi, and later Arkansas and Florida formed the Protestant Episcopal Church in the Confederate States. Delegates from seven states adopted a new constitution in October 1861 at Columbia, South Carolina.[9]

Roman Catholic clergy were few in the South and the membership was small, composed in part of immigrant groups, and largely poor. The church did not split North and South, but the Catholics gave support to the people and soldiers of the Confederacy when it re-formed based on the same territorial principle the Episcopal bishops discussed. This principle of subordination of the church to the state dated, of course, from the sixteenth century. Bishop John McGill of Richmond was enthusiastic about the Southern cause, and promoted enlistments, procured priests for the chaplaincies, and offered other aid where possible. Bishops Augustine Verot of Savannah and Auguste Martin of Alexandria urged secession. However, most of the eleven Catholic bishops, including Bishop James Whelan of Nashville, viewed secession as something to be endured rather than embraced.[10]

Although many Southern leaders, including church leaders, hoped that actual war could be avoided, the Confederate government began making immediate preparations for purchasing arms and organizing a Provisional army for the Confederate States. Louisiana had obtained more than 47,000 small arms from the Baton Rouge Arsenal; Georgia had nearly 23,000 at Augusta; and South Carolina and Alabama had smaller amounts at Charleston and Mount Vernon, a small town twenty miles north of Mobile. Southern agents also traveled north to buy weapons from Northern manufacturers, Col. Samuel Colt among them.[11]

Josiah Gorgas, head of the Confederate Ordnance Bureau, gave his undivided attention to the procurement of ammunition. The Confederate Congress, mindful that there were no cannon factories, shipyards, or ships owned by any Southern state, gave subsidies to businesses, including the Tredegar Iron Works in Richmond, for transformation to wartime production of arms, munitions, and eventually iron plate for ships.[12] Including arms taken from Federal troops in Texas, the Confederacy had approximately 190,000 arms for use by the summer of 1861.[13]

Against this backdrop of emergency military preparations was the problem of organizing the Provisional army. The War Department reserved the right to establish geographical military departments.[14] The senior rank would be lieutenant general, followed by major general, brigadier general, and colonel. Divisions, following the organization of the U.S. Army, would consist of brigades, which in turn would be made up of two or three regiments of approximately 1,000 soldiers each when fully manned. Within the regiments, companies of approximately eighty to one hundred soldiers would be alphabetically designated, beginning with "A" Company.[15] Individual soldiers were numbered and placed in one of four squads in each company, each squad in the charge of a noncommissioned officer.[16]

Regimental staff officers included a lieutenant colonel, a major, an adjutant, a surgeon, an assistant surgeon, and a quartermaster. Company grade officers included captains, first and second lieutenants, and cadets if available. Cadets were established by law as apprentices "until a military school shall be established by the Government for their instruction."[17]

In most particulars, the Provisional army of the Confederate States mirrored the organization of the U.S. Army with one notable exception. In its first formulation, the organizational tables for regiments, brigades, and divisions contained no positions for chaplains.

Providing for the spiritual welfare of soldiers was not a high priority for three reasons. First, there had not been a strong emphasis on chaplains in the U.S. Army for the forty years preceding the Civil War and therefore not a strong precedent for including them in the Provisional army. As an economy measure, the U.S. Congress had passed an act on April 14, 1818, that reduced the size of the Regular army and eliminated positions for surgeons, judge advocates, and chaplains. Thus, from 1818 to 1838 there was but one chaplain on active duty in the U.S. Army—the U.S. Military Academy chaplain at West Point, who was also the professor of geography, history, and ethics.[18]

When the Mexican War started, in 1846, there was a total of thirteen chaplains in the army.[19] These chaplains were not allowed to deploy with tactical units such as regiments or brigades, but were permitted by an 1838 congressional authorization to serve only at military posts. Although there were plenty of chaplains in militia units, when President Polk called for volunteers, he did not request the mobilization of complete militia units as such. Therefore, because entire militia units were not mobilized, the staffs on which chaplains served did not report for active duty. The chaplains who did go to the war zone were volunteers from outside the Regular army. Among the nine chaplains who eventually volunteered and served in Mexico, Texas, or California during the war, two were Roman Catholic, four were Protestant, and three were Mormon elders.[20]

The second reason chaplains were initially omitted from the organization of the Provisional army was that Pres. Jefferson Davis's attitude toward them was lukewarm at best. Although Davis attended Episcopal services regularly, he had not been impressed with the chaplains he knew at West Point or with the few he may have encountered later as an officer in Mexico and as secretary of war.[21] Indeed, Rev. Thomas Warner, chaplain at West Point when Davis was a cadet, was forced to resign over a dispute with Gen. Winfield Scott.[22] Of the five chaplains who served at West Point from 1813 to 1837, three resigned and two were discharged—not a good model for obedience to the discipline of army life.

Finally, both Davis and James Seddon, who eventually became secretary of war, were more concerned with filling the ranks with properly equipped soldiers than with Bible-toting chaplains. One correspondent for the *Macon (Ga.) Christian Index* reported that Seddon "persists that he is unwilling to convert good officers or soldiers into chaplains, since they do a higher and holier work in their present position."[23] The opinion among those who did want to expend valuable resources for a marginal position was that there would be plenty of lay preachers in the ranks to minister to their fellow soldiers.

➤─◆─○─◆─◄

When it became apparent that there were no authorized positions for chaplains in the army, there were protests from ministers seeking to apply and from several church bodies. The first official proposal for the inclusion of chaplains in the Provisional army came from Secretary of War Leroy P. Walker. In a report to President Davis on April 27, 1861, Walker wrote:

> I cannot more appropriately conclude this report than by urging upon Congress the passage of a law empowering this Department to appoint Chaplains for the Service. Military experience demonstrates the importance of religious habitudes to the morality, good order, and general discipline of an army in the camp or in the field. If we expect God to bless us in our struggle in defense of our rights—to terminate, in all probability, only after a protracted and bloody war—we must recognize Him in our actions.[24]

Walker's brief arguments for good order and discipline and acknowledgment of God's Providence were mirror images of an order Gen. George Washington had issued in 1776 to the Continental army commending the ministry of chaplains. "The blessing and protection of Heaven are at all times necessary, but especially so in times of public distress and danger," Washington wrote, ". . . and as a chaplain is allowed to each Regiment, see that the men regularly attend divine worship."[25] Washington thought that only a righteous army led by the Providence of God could prevail against the powerful British fleet and soldiery. Whether Walker, who was a jurist from Alabama, deliberately or coincidentally used the same rationale for including chaplains in the army as had the Founding Fathers, there was no doubt that his argument struck a sympathetic chord with Davis.

Moreover, on the same day that Walker issued his report, the Virginia Convention for Secession and for the "Adoption and Ratification of the Constitution of the Provisional Government of the Confederate States" passed an ordinance "that the Governor shall appoint one chaplain for each Brigade, who shall be entitled to the same pay and emoluments as a Major of Infantry."[26] Five days later, on May 2, Confederate congressman Francis S. Bartow reported a bill to provide for the appointment of chaplains in the army. After the required three readings, the bill passed and was engrossed.

An Act to Provide for the Appointment of Chaplains in the Army

Section 1. The Congress of the Confederate States of America do enact, that there shall be appointed by the President such number of chaplains, to serve with the armies of the Confederate States

Portrait of Lt. Bartley P. Bynum, C.S.A.,
also chaplain in the Confederate army. LIBRARY OF CONGRESS

during the existing war, as he may deem expedient, and the President shall assign them to such regiments, brigades or posts as he may deem necessary; and the appointment made as aforesaid shall expire whenever the existing war shall terminate.

Section 2. The monthly pay of said chaplains shall be eighty-five dollars; and said pay shall be in full of all allowance whatever.[27]

This law was a "bare bones" piece of legislation. It did not prescribe duties or provide for rations, a horse, forage, supplies, quarters, or a uniform, items that the chaplains must presumably provide for themselves. Moreover, the salary of $85 a month was far below the $150 a month paid militia chaplains in both Virginia and North Carolina. The salary pegged the chaplains exactly midway between a first and a second lieutenant, though chaplains of course had no command authority. Two weeks after the law was passed, it was amended by Congress to lower the pay of chaplains to $50 a month, $30 more than a first sergeant but $30 less than a second lieutenant.[28] With rations computed at $.25 per meal, chaplains could afford to eat for a month with about $1 a day left over.

Many church leaders and editors were dismayed at such treatment and condemned the impoverishment of clergy appointed to the army. The editor of the Richmond Daily Dispatch suggested that the legislation be entitled, "An act to abolish the office of chaplain in the Confederate army." The Army and Navy Messenger asserted that chaplains' pay was "utterly inadequate." Indeed, on such meager support, married clergy would not be able to stay long in the army. One editor wrote: "It was barely possible, at the high rates of living prevailing throughout the country, for a gentleman to support a family on this amount in the rural districts, and quite impossible in a city."[29] Resignations after a short period of service would be routine for chaplains who were family men.

Eventually, in the spring of 1862, after the Georgia Conference of the Methodist Church and the "Ladies of Richmond" petitioned Congress, the pay of chaplains was increased to eighty dollars a month.[30] Another bill previously passed allowed chaplains the same rations as privates. In 1864 chaplains were authorized forage if they owned a horse and a stationery allowance for writing letters. Some unit commanders allowed chaplains to draw fuel in the winter; others permitted a cloth or clothing issue. With these few privileges, most chaplains were able to avoid begging for food at farmhouses, or raiding berry patches and apple orchards, practices common among the enlisted soldiers.

Chaplains were appointed by the president of the Confederate States, confirmed by the Senate, and received a commission as "Chaplain" from the secretary of war. The process usually required the endorsement of a regimental or brigade commander forwarded directly to the secretary of war. This requirement ensured that there was indeed a vacant position and that the commander approved the candidate for a commission. Most regimental commanders solicited opinions and even accepted petitions from their own soldiers and company grade officers before sending their endorsements to Richmond. Within a couple of months, depending on couriers and mail as it existed, a commission signed by the secretary of war for the president would be presented to the chaplain by the regimental commander. At that time the chaplain would be recognized as a commissioned officer without command, but also without fatigue details, stable or guard duties. All Confederate chaplains had the same rank, determined by their pay, although some served at higher echelons in the armies at brigade and even at corps headquarters.

The standardized wording of the notification from the War Department in Richmond offered the nominee a choice of whether to accept or decline the appointment.

You are hereby informed that the President has appointed you

Chaplain

(regiment supplied)

In the Provisional Army in the service of the Confederate States: to rank as such from (date supplied). Should the Senate at their next session advise and consent thereto, you will be commissioned accordingly.

Immediately on receipt hereof, please to communicate to this Department, through its Adjutant and Inspector General's Offices your acceptance or non-acceptance of said appointment; and with your letter of acceptance, return to the Adjutant and Inspector General the Oath, herewith enclosed, properly filled up, subscribed and attested, reporting at the same time your age, residence when appointed, and the state in which you were born.

Should you accept, you will report for duty to (commander's name supplied).

James Seddon
Secretary of War[31]

(Addressee's name)

The oath of office simply promised obedience to the Confederate States of America and to the president and superior officers according to the rules and Articles of War.[32] Although approximately twenty ministers and missionaries declined chaplain commissions during the war, more than 1,300 soldiers and ordained clergymen accepted them.

⊱─┥◆┝─○─┥◆┝─⊰

There was no problem in finding ministers, priests, or pious soldiers who were eligible to serve as Confederate chaplains during the first two years of the war. Half of the population of the United States in 1860 was under the age of 21, and in the Southern states approximately 6,000 young men under age 35 were licensed or ordained preachers.[33]

Nevertheless, many chaplains had to be recruited because ministers who held appointments as pastors of churches were exempt from the 1862 Conscription Act. Ministers therefore had to volunteer to serve as chaplains because they could not be drafted into the army.

No ecclesiastical or denominational endorsements, certification of special training, experience, or ordination was required by the government to commission a chaplain. Since there was but a handful of Protestant seminaries in the South, the majority of the Methodist and Baptist preachers received their ministerial education as apprentices to older ministers or by studying under the supervision of their church leaders.[34] The course of study "for the itinerant Probationers and Deacons of the Methodist Episcopal Church, South," lasted four years and required yearly examinations by conference examining committees. The subjects included study of the Bible, the church discipline, the hymn book, Wesley's sermons, English grammar and composition, rhetoric, church history, logic, pastoral theology, moral philosophy (ethics), systematic theology, and sermon and essay composition.[35]

Southern ministers who could afford formal educations attended Oglethorpe, Emory College, Louisville Baptist Seminary, Mississippi College, Oakland College, Washington College, Randolph-Macon College, or one of the other existing Southern colleges or state universities. Presbyterian ministers and Episcopal priests, many of whom had previously attended the University of Virginia, Hampden-Sydney, or Davidson, received their ministerial education at Columbia Theological Seminary in South Carolina, Union Theological Seminary in Richmond, or the Theological Seminary of Virginia in Alexandria. Roman Catholic priests had a small seminary in New Orleans, but many were educated in Ireland or in Europe. About a dozen ministers who became chaplains went outside the South for their education—including attendance at Yale, Georgetown, Brown, Amherst, Rochester Baptist Seminary, Dickinson, Columbia, or the University of the City of New York. None, as far as is known, went to Harvard, although Rev. Samuel Strick, later Episcopal chaplain of the 59th Tennessee, was a graduate of Christ Church College, Oxford.

The churches that furnished chaplains to the Confederacy were grouped in ten denominations: Methodist, Presbyterian, Baptist, Episcopal, Roman Catholic, Cumberland Presbyterian, Lutheran, Disciples of Christ, Missionary Baptist, and Congregational Churches. There were no Jewish or female chaplains, although there was at least one Cherokee Christian who served as a religious leader without commission for the North Carolina Cherokee Battalion, and one black "honorary" chaplain in Forrest's Cavalry, perhaps the first black chaplain to serve in the Civil War.[36]

Church membership in the eleven Confederate states has been estimated at 25 percent of the population of 11 million white and black souls.[37] The Methodist Episcopal Church, South, counted 537,136 white members, 207,776 black members, and 4,160 Indian or Native American members for a total of 749,072. Baptists estimated their membership at 450,000, Presbyterians about 117,000, and Cumberland Presbyterians approximately 100,000.

A tabulation of church accommodations from the year 1855 for worship, rather than membership, however, shows a worshiping population of 7 million, or about 64 percent of the whole population. The Methodist Church claimed 2.7 million worshipers, while Southern Baptists counted 2.4 million.[38] There were 829 Disciples of Christ Churches, 513 Episcopal Churches, 217 Lutheran Churches, about 150 Roman Catholic Churches and one Roman Catholic seminary, but accurate membership figures for all of the denominations have not been compiled.[39]

Of the 938 Confederate chaplains whose denominations are known, 47 percent were Methodist, 18 percent Presbyterian, 16 percent Baptist, 10 percent Episcopalian, 3 percent Roman Catholic, and less than 1 percent each for the other five denominations. The Southern Baptist Domestic Mission Board, however, sent seventy-six missionaries to the Confederate armies during the war. Presbyterians sent both missionaries and commissioners, whose job was to recruit chaplains from the ranks to fill vacancies.[40] In all, approximately 14 percent of the eligible clergy in the South served as Confederate chaplains.[41] Of the chaplains whose ages are known, 48 percent were thirty years old or younger in 1861. Ten Confederate chaplains were known to have been twenty years of age or younger, and one was sixteen when he was elected chaplain of the Washington Artillery of New Orleans.[42]

In spite of the large pool of eligible ministers, the response to the call to minister in the armies of the Confederacy was slow. The Methodist Church, which would eventually furnish 448 chaplains for the Confederacy, appointed only 61 chaplains in 1861. Twenty-two of these were from Tennessee, traditionally a "volunteer" state, where a true "civil war" was raging in the eastern counties and where Gov. Isham Harris had raised 22,000 troops loyal to the Confederacy by July 1861. Interestingly, another seventy-two ordained Methodist ministers from twenty-four state conferences received appointments from their bishops in the same year to serve as officers or enlisted men in the ranks.[43] These were the largest group of "fighting clergy" since the American Revolution. Clearly, in the period before the Geneva Conventions, the Church Militant was alive and well, as the majority of the Methodist clergy in 1861 in the South seemed to prefer fighting to preaching.

The Baptist churches also appeared to dally in furnishing ministers for the army, possibly because the process of securing a commission was somewhat vague. Reverend J. William Jones, later Baptist chaplain in the 13th Virginia, wrote to the *Religious Herald* in Richmond that "it is a common mistake that anybody will do to preach to soldiers; and hence the chaplaincies are generally filled by young and inexperienced men. But a moment's reflection will suffice to convince, that since we have in the army the flower of the country, we ought to have the best preaching-talent of the country."[44]

>-+-+>-+-O-+<+-+-<

The motivation for ministers to volunteer for a ministry in the armies of the Confederacy was complex and varied from one individual to another. The great majority of chaplains left no written record of their thoughts or feelings when they first reported for duty. A few, however, did provide some insights in their diaries, journals, letters, and even by way of family members and friends, in oral tradition.

The greatest number of ministers and priests volunteered for duty as chaplains because they loved their communities and their people and were bonded to them. The churches and clergy of the South were embedded in the daily lives of their congregations. As pastors, they baptized or consecrated infants, taught Sunday school and catechism classes, confirmed young people into membership, performed weddings, led revivals, visited the sick, and buried the dead. It was not unusual for Protestant pastors, over time, to minister to several generations of their members, including some of their own relatives. When the young men of their churches went to war, many pastors went with them.

Reverend Charles T. Quintard, M.D., Episcopal rector of the Church of the Advent in Nashville, was one of those who joined the army at the petition of the men of his church and his community. Quintard was an unlikely candidate to be a chaplain in the field. He was born in Stamford, Connecticut, and educated at Columbia College and the University of the City of New York, where he earned a medical degree. In 1851 he accepted the chair of physiology and pathological anatomy at the Medical College of Memphis, Tennessee, but left three years later to study theology under the direction of Episcopal bishop James Otey.[45] In 1856 he was ordained a priest and became rector of the Church of the Advent and also of the Church of the Holy Trinity in Nashville.

While rector of the Church of the Advent, Quintard was elected chaplain of the "Rock City Guard," one of the local militia units. He had no "fondness" for the military life and regarded himself as "chaplain only by courtesy."[46] Indeed, he preached a sermon that he regarded as "a strong plea for the Union" when Lincoln was elected president. When the "Rock City Guard" was mustered into the service of the state in Spring 1861, however, the men signed a petition asking Quintard to be their chaplain in what would become the 1st Tennessee Volunteer Infantry Regiment. He wrote simply,

> On the 10th of July 1861, orders were received by the regiment to repair to Virginia. Being very urgently pressed by members of the Rock City Guard and their friends in Nashville to accompany the regiment as chaplain, I resolved to do so. This, of course, made it necessary for me to break up my household. I moved my family to Georgia, left my parish in the hands of the Rev. George C. Harris, and prepared to join my regiment in Virginia.[47]

Quintard's family was safe enough, but in March 1862, when Nashville was occupied by Union forces and became the headquarters for Brig. Gen. Andrew Johnson, President Lincoln's military governor of Tennessee, Rev. George C. Harris left Nashville as well and joined the Confederate army as chaplain of the 26th Tennessee.

Hundreds of other ministers had the same experience because recruitment to fill Confederate regiments occurred not only at courthouses and in public squares, but also in churches and in colleges. Fifteen members of the Sweetwater Baptist Church of Paulding County, Georgia, joined Company F of the 40th Georgia in 1862 and took their pastor with them as their chaplain.[48] When several of the elders of the First Presbyterian Church of Oxford, Mississippi, went to war, their pastor, Rev. Thomas D. Witherspoon, enlisted with them in the Lamar Rifles. Witherspoon soon became a chaplain, eventually to three Mississippi regiments during the war. Father P. Emmeran Bliemel petitioned his Roman Catholic superior, Bishop James Whelan of Nashville, for a year to allow him to become chaplain for the 10th Tennessee, which contained seven companies of Irish Catholics from his parish. When Bliemel did receive permission, it was because his vicar general, Rev. Henry V. Browne, formerly chaplain of the same regiment, supported his petition.[49] Elder Joseph D. Pickett, a Disciples of Christ minister and a professor at Bethany College, taught his students until the college recess in 1861. Then he joined the Kentucky Orphan Brigade as a chaplain "to minister to the spiritual wants" of the boys.[50]

Father John B. Bannon, Roman Catholic priest of St. Louis and a chaplain in the Missouri militia, may have had the largest number of appellants for his services. When some 1,800 Catholics in the Missouri State Guard joined Gen. Sterling Price's Confederate forces, they did not complain about anything except the absence of Father Bannon, their chaplain. Accordingly, to support his militia parishioners, Bannon joined Price's army in January 1862, even though he did not receive his chaplain's commission until February 1863. When he was finally included on the army's pay roster, he was $1,000 in debt.[51]

Another path to service lay through the personal appeals or recruitment of church officials, army commanders, and friends. Father James B. Sheeran of Louisiana was one of the first Roman Catholic priests recruited by the Catholic Church for Confederate service. Born in County Longford, Ireland, in 1819, Sheeran emigrated to Canada and thence to New York, Pennsylvania, and Michigan. He worked as a tailor, studied law, and taught in a Catholic boys' school. Sheeran married and had two children, but when his wife died in 1849, he began to contemplate the priesthood. In 1855 he joined the Redemptorist Congregation and was ordained a priest in 1858. He was subsequently sent to the Redemptorist Church in New Orleans, where, over the next three years, he became an ardent advocate of the Southern cause. When his father provincial asked for volunteers to act as chaplains for the Confederate army, Sheeran responded immediately and was assigned to the 14th Louisiana on September 2, 1861.[52]

Chaplain Thomas W. Caskey of the 16th Mississippi Cavalry, a Disciples of Christ minister, twice declined to enter the army. He preferred his charge as pastor of the Christian Church in Jackson. But he could not turn down the appeals of his friend, cavalry commander Gen. Wirt Adams. Caskey left some revealing insights in his *Recollections* about his feelings toward the war.

> I enlisted in the army as a preacher of the gospel and was assigned the duty of a chaplain. It was the hardest place to fill in the whole army. I was expected to cut my sermons to fit the pattern of our occupation as soldiers. It was expected that my preaching, prayers and exhortations would tend to make the soldiers hard fighters. It was difficult to find even texts from which to construct such sermons. I soon discovered that I would have to close my Bible and manufacture my ministerial supplies out of the whole cloth.
>
> Some of my preaching brethren told the soldiers that our cause was just and that God would fight our battles for us. I never did feel authorized to make any such statements. I believed our cause was just, of course, but I could see as clear as a sunbeam that the odds were against us, and, to be plain, I gravely doubted whether God was taking any hand with us in that squabble. I told some of the preachers who were making that point in their sermons that they were taking a big risk. I asked them what explanation they would give, if we should happen to get thrashed. I told them such preaching would make infidels of the whole army, and put an end to their business if we should happen to get the worst of the fracas. I wanted to do my duty as a preacher in the army, but I didn't want to checkmate the ministry in case we should come out second best. I think a preacher should always leave a wide margin for mistakes when it comes to interpreting the purposes of God beyond what has been clearly revealed in the Scriptures. It is not good policy for a one-horse preacher to arbitrarily commit the God of the universe to either side of a personal difficulty anyhow. I told the soldiers plainly that I didn't know exactly what position God would take in that fight. The issue was a personal matter between us and the Yankees, and we must settle it, as best we could, among ourselves.
>
> It became clearer to me every day that one good soldier was worth a whole brigade of canting chaplains so far as insuring the success of our army was concerned. If I must preach to others so as to make them good fighters, why not give them an object lesson on the battlefield myself?
>
> So I asked for a gun, took a place with "the boys" and was dubbed the "fighting parson."[53]

Interestingly, even as a fighting parson, Caskey was averse to killing other human beings. Therefore he planned to shoot at the legs of his adversaries. Not only was this plan more humane, in Caskey's mind, but it also required two more soldiers to carry the wounded man off the battlefield.

In consonance with this philosophy, Caskey spent a good deal of his time ministering to his own wounded soldiers and improving hospital conditions for them. He so impressed his superiors that he was invited to address the Mississippi legislature on the subject of improving military hospitals. At the conclusion of his address, the legislature gave him $100,000 with which he subsequently built four hospitals.[54]

The account of the Reverend Dr. Alexander D. Betts of North Carolina also indicates that the decision to undertake a ministry in the army was not an easy one even when friends appealed.

> One day in April, 1861, I heard that President Lincoln had called on the State troops to force the seceding States back into the Union. That was one of the saddest days of my life. I had prayed and hoped that war might be averted. I had loved the Union, and clung to it. That day I saw war was inevitable. The inevitable must be met. That day I walked up and down my porch in Smithville . . . and wept and suffered and prayed for the South.[55]

Betts did not immediately volunteer for the army, however. He continued on his preaching circuit until a number of his former parishioners in the 30th North Carolina, a Lt. L. D. Cain among them, wrote to say that the officers of the regiment had selected him to be their chaplain. Betts recalled that he "prayed over it a few days and wrote to Governor Clark that I would accept." On October 25, 1861, Betts's commission came from the governor. He served in the Army of Northern Virginia until March 1865, when he received a furlough. While on leave, he heard of Lee's surrender at Appomattox. Betts then reported to the Army of Tennessee and remained on duty until Gen. Joseph E. Johnston surrendered on April 26 at the Bennett House, nine miles from Betts's home at Chapel Hill.

Many ministers volunteered to serve as chaplains in the armies from a sense of adventure and patriotic obligation. The prospect of war was advertised as a great event in local communities, a war for Southern independence on par with the American Revolution. There was a large pool, at least 6,000 in number, of young farmers, mechanics, and manual laborers in the South who were also lay preachers or deacons in their churches. The war gave them an opportunity to move from lives routinely spent to lives of adventure, added responsibility, and public notice. The war, if it came, would surely make heroes and martyrs, though it would be better to be in the former rather than in the latter category.

Most ministers and priests of various denominations could recall sixteen years earlier in 1845, when the Methodist and Baptist Churches in the South had separated from their Northern counterparts. The two largest denominations in the South had been independent churches for almost a generation. The Presbyterian and Episcopal Churches in the Deep South followed suit in 1861. With the advent of secession, the majority of young Protestant preachers were already primed by their respective church traditions to regard the possibilities of political separation from the United States without undue anxiety.

The notion of going to war as an adventure was, of course, a very idealistic and uninformed concept. At the outset, the paradigm of the American Revolution seemed inspirational for the 1861 generation. Relative casualties during the Revolution, seen in the warm glow of heroic history, seemed light and the rewards of victory seemed to have been monumental. The same could be said of the War of 1812 and of the Mexican War. Yet had the average farmer or laborer known the true figures, the rosiness of war might have paled. In the period from 1775 to 1848, the U.S. Armies sustained 19,978 deaths and 14,845 wounds among their military personnel—about one and a half times the number of troops Washington commanded during most of the American Revolution.[56] Nevertheless, the call to duty and the peer pressure of the thousands of young men who were marching off as neighbors from their home counties overcame cold analysis.

Chaplain George G. Smith of Phillips's Legion, who was wounded while rallying his regiment at the 1862 battle of South Mountain, Maryland, recalled that it was the enthusiasm of youth and the prospect of victory that caused him to leave his church near Macon, Georgia, where he served as a deacon, to seek a commission in the chaplaincy:

> The state had seceded from the General Government . . . and it became evident that we would become seriously involved perhaps in war. I had always been most ardently attached to the Union and the previous election had voted for Bell & Everett with the hope of saving it but there seemed to be now no choice between the Abolition of slavery and Secession. To secede might but would not we thought involve war. When however the step was taken and when

it was too late to retrace it, it became apparent that we were to be driven into the most desperate strife. I of course felt as a southern man and when the war was declared I determined to take my part in it. The result was that I left my little church and entered the Army as Chaplain in August, immediately after we had won the battle of Manassas. I cannot think now I acted prudently I cannot think that I would have so hastily if I had the same circumstances around me now but I was young and ardent and as such I acted on the impulse of the hour.[57]

Chaplain James M. Campbell of the 1st Georgia was another case in point. Campbell grew up in modest circumstances near Gaylesville, Cherokee County, in northeast Alabama. As a twelve-year-old boy, he worked as a farm laborer for fifteen cents or a peck of corn a day. At age fifteen Campbell was converted and joined the Oak Bowery Methodist Church, three miles from town. With the strong Christian influence and support of his father, he gave much thought to the ministry. In 1853, at the age of twenty-three, he was "admitted on trial" into the Alabama Conference with eleven other young preachers.

For six years Campbell struggled with a limited education to be a good preacher and pastor. He was appointed to eight churches or circuits in six years. When one church refused to have him, Rev. Stephen F. Pilley, district presiding elder, changed his appointment to the Geneva Circuit, where he remained for a short tenure.

When the call for soldiers came, Campbell offered himself for service as a chaplain. "The soldiers need the Gospel and I can preach to them, do good and fight for my country," he wrote his mother. Interestingly, Pilley, who had been his mentor, sent two of his sons and one son-in-law into the army at the same time. Two were church deacons and one was a schoolteacher. All three, along with Campbell, eventually became chaplains in the Confederate forces.

Campbell remained in his position as chaplain of the 1st Georgia for a year, spending most of the time in Virginia. In April 1862, he heard from his family that a friend, Rev. F. T. J. Brandon, had recruited men for Company E of the 47th Alabama. Brandon promised Campbell a captaincy if he would come home and join the unit. Campbell decided that he "wanted to do more" in the army than serve as a chaplain, so he resigned that commission and received another as captain in the 47th Alabama.

Campbell was an outstanding officer, popular with the troops, and appointed major on the regimental staff within a few months. The 47th Alabama was attached to Gen. "Stonewall" Jackson's forces early in 1862. Campbell was wounded at Cedar Mountain but recovered to fight at Antietam, Fredericksburg, and (as acting regimental commander) at Gettysburg. Late in 1863 he was present with James Longstreet's corps at Chickamauga and in the campaign at Knoxville.

On May 11, 1864, Major Campbell was killed by a sharpshooter at Spotsylvania Courthouse. Reverend Frank T. J. Brandon, his friend from Cherokee County, who was a missionary to the Army of Northern Virginia in 1864, conducted his funeral. Thirty years later, in 1895, Gov. William Oates of Alabama, formerly a regimental commander in Hood's Division wrote:

> Now as to Maj. Campbell of the 47th Regiment . . . I knew him well. I heard him preach in my town of Abbeville, Ala. Before the war began. Then I knew him in the army and was looking at him when he was shot dead. I was about 60 yards away from him, but my attention happened to be called in that direction and I saw him standing near the left of his regiment. . . . It was about one mile northwest of Spotsylvania Courthouse. There was no battle going on, but occasional exchange of shots by sharpshooters. Maj. Campbell, I think was shot through the head, and of course never knew what hurt him. He was a good officer and a very gallant man. He did his whole duty manfully and well.[58]

Brandon noted in a letter to the family, as well, that Campbell had really served in two positions in the 47th Alabama. At the time of his death he was both a major and acting chaplain of the unit, in his ultimate attempt to "do good" and fight for his country.[59]

＞━◆〉━○━〈◆━＜

In practice, many chaplains were ordained ministers and provided letters of recommendation from other ministers, associations, or bishops attesting to their good standing and qualifications.[60] However, if a regimental or brigade commander forwarded a request for a specific individual to fill the position of unit chaplain, regardless of the candidate's education or experience, the secretary of war usually issued a commission. Those soldiers who desired to be commissioned as chaplains directly from the ranks had an easier time get-

ting approval at the beginning of the war than toward the end when manpower was ebbing.

The routes to a chaplain's commission were generally four in number.
First, a minister or priest from a civilian church could be nominated or apply
to the secretary of war for a direct commission. Many of these clergy were
first recommended to a regimental or higher commander by their church
superiors in order to assure support from the army for such an application.
Roman Catholic, Episcopal, and ordained Methodist chaplains usually
served with the approval of a bishop as well as with the commission of the
government.

The second route was through recognition of a previous state commission as a militia chaplain or chaplain of a home guard unit. Six of the thirteen Georgia militia chaplains, in Gov. Joseph Brown's Army of Georgia in
1861, for example, became Confederate chaplains in this manner.[61]

The third route was by commission from the ranks. At least half of all
Confederate chaplains served in the ranks as enlisted men or as officers
before they were commissioned as chaplains. A list of Georgia chaplains
identifies their enlisted rank and the company they were in before they were
commissioned to serve as chaplains in their own regiments.

> Robert B. Lester, private, Co. A, later chaplain, 3rd Georgia
> J. O. A. Sparks, private, Co. A, later chaplain, 4th Georgia
> Jacob E. Dodd, private, Co. H, later chaplain, 5th Georgia
> David C. Stokes, private, Co. A., later chaplain, 7th Georgia
> William C. Dunlap, private, Co. D, later chaplain, 8th Georgia
> Joel C. Burnham, private, Co. D, later chaplain, 9th Georgia
> J. C. Camp, 3rd sergeant, Co. E, later chaplain, 10th Georgia
> Asa M. Marshall, private, Co. G, later chaplain, 12th Georgia
> William F. Robinson, private, Co. K, later chaplain, 15th Georgia
> William Flinn, private, Co. H, later chaplain, 16th Georgia
> John N. Hudson, private, Co. B, later chaplain, 17th Georgia
> William E. Jones, private, Co. G, later chaplain, 22nd Georgia
> G. R. Edwards, private, Co. D, later chaplain, 23rd Georgia
> Augustus B. Fears, private, Co. H, later chaplain, 30th Georgia
> Bannister R. Bray, private, Co. D, later chaplain, 40th Georgia

Chaplains in this category were generally elected by the company grade
officers for the regimental commander's approval. The regimental commander would then forward his recommended candidate to the secretary of

war. The list of chaplains who served first as line officers is even longer because many clergy who volunteered to be chaplains found that the positions were filled or not available when they requested commissions.

Fourth were a few cases of chaplains who were detailed into the position or who received the equivalent of "battlefield commissions" from commanders. Private R. C. Armstrong, performing the duties of an "acting chaplain" for the 9th Texas Cavalry in 1863, so impressed his commander, Col. David W. Jones, that he was commissioned a chaplain in October of that year. Thomas H. Davenport of the 3rd Tennessee was allegedly appointed a chaplain "without his knowledge" by the colonel of his regiment. Likewise, Mrs. Ella Hopson asserted after the war that her husband, William H. Hopson, a Disciples of Christ minister in Kentucky, "without his desire, knowledge, or consent . . . was made General John Morgan's chaplain five months before he found it out."[62]

Private John V. Pointer of the 9th Texas Infantry received his on-the-spot commission for an extemporaneous devotional. Just before his regiment was to meet the enemy at Allatoona, Georgia, in October 1864, Pointer called his fellow soldiers together and preached to them about the "Grace of God." The division commander, Maj. Gen. S. G. French, was visiting a brigade commander and overheard Pointer's sermon. The next day Pointer was appointed chaplain to the regiment pending approval from Richmond. He was commissioned on October 31, 1864, and served as chaplain of the 9th Texas until he surrendered on May 20, 1865.[63]

In addition to chaplains, there were other religious leaders sent to minister to the soldiers. Some churches, especially Baptist congregations, objected to the government paying chaplains' salaries as a violation of the separation of church and state. Other Baptist churches furnished missionaries instead of chaplains to the Confederate army, although there were more than 160 Baptist and Missionary Baptist chaplains commissioned in the Confederate armies as well.

A missionary, or "missionary chaplain" as they were sometimes titled, differed from the commissioned army chaplains in that missionaries were paid, at least in part, by the churches and had more freedom of movement. A missionary could return home after completing a short preaching or evangelistic tour and then return to the army at a later time. Some of the missionaries, designated "evangelists," might visit the soldiers for a week or two and then return to their civilian parishes or to a hospital ministry. Others, such as Rev. J. P. McMullen, a Presbyterian missionary with Baker's Alabama Brigade; Rev. John B. McFerrin, Methodist missionary with Palmer's Brigade, both in the Army of Tennessee; and Rev. J. William Jones, formerly the Baptist chaplain of the 13th Virginia, and later missionary to A. P. Hill's corps in the Army of Northern Virginia, shared the soldiers' daily hardships and dangers for the duration of the war or for the duration of their lives—whichever was shorter.[64]

Colporteurs were ministers or laymen who distributed Bibles, testaments, church newspapers, and religious tracts from churches and church publishing houses directly to soldiers in the field. Reverend Sterling M. Cherry, chaplain of the 37th Georgia, became one of the most successful colporteurs in the Army of Tennessee during the last year of the war. In Cherry's monthly reports during the 1864 Atlanta campaign, he said that he distributed 225 Bibles, 4,917 testaments, 46,890 religious newspapers, and 284,000 religious tracts to the 40,000 soldiers of the army while also serving as a chaplain for various hospitals near Atlanta. During this same period of time, Cherry preached at least eighteen times, joined 2,500 soldiers attending services, and witnessed the baptism of 300 of the troops.[65]

Finally, there were bishops, superintendents, and other church leaders who supported the cause, the chaplains, and the soldiers in their work. Methodist bishop James O. Andrew of Alabama sent money, appointed preachers as chaplains or missionaries, and forwarded letters of encouragement to the army, as did the five other bishops of the Methodist church.[66] Roman Catholic bishop Patrick Lynch of Charleston went to Rome with a letter from Pres. Jefferson Davis seeking the endorsement and support of Pope Pius IX. Episcopal bishop Leonidas Polk of Louisiana became a major general in the Army of Tennessee.[67] Dr. J. L. Burrows, pastor of the First Baptist Church of Richmond, served as a member of the "Richmond Ambulance Corps." Dr. Moses D. Hoge, pastor of the Second Presbyterian Church in the same city, served at various times as a chaplain at Camp Lee, a colporteur, and a blockade-runner to secure Bibles from England.[68]

Because there was no formal organization to supervise, support, or promote chaplains in the army, many chaplains served in several roles during their time in service. It was not at all unusual for a minister to enlist as a private, be commissioned as a regimental chaplain, transfer to a post or hospital chaplain's position, resign his commission after a year or two, and return to the army as a missionary or evangelist.

J. William Jones of the Army of Northern Virginia served successively as an enlisted soldier, chaplain of the 13th Virginia, and Baptist missionary to Lt. Gen. A. P. Hill's III Corps. Reverened L. C. Vass, a Presbyterian minister, was chaplain for the 27th Virginia before accepting the position of post chaplain at Petersburg. Chaplain Charles T. Quintard served in the 1st

Tennessee until 1864, when Episcopal bishop Stephen Elliot of Georgia appointed him permanent missionary to the Army of Tennessee. The Episcopal missionary's salary was $3,000 per year as opposed to $960 for a regimental chaplain.[69] By 1864, many chaplains needed extra income and extra time to recuperate from their labors. If one could secure a church salary, even in Confederate money, both of these objects could be achieved.

>─ ◆─○─◆ ─◄

Although chaplains were commissioned, they had no authorized uniforms, rank, chaplain insignia, or command authority. On one hand, the lack of legislation or regulations for such basic elements of the military life might seem self-defeating. On the other hand, the absence of guidelines gave chaplains a considerable amount of freedom.

The traditional attire for ministers serving as chaplains, reflected in U.S. Army regulations, consisted of a black frock coat, dark trousers, and eventually a kepi, a cap with a round top sloping toward a short bill in the front. The initials *U.S.* in silver script within a gold wreath could be sewn on the front of the cap above the bill. Ministers and priests were also allowed to wear the vestments of their denomination, if any, when conducting services. In 1862, the U.S. Navy prescribed angled crosses to be worn on the cuffs of chaplains' uniform coats, but the U.S. Army did not adopt this insignia during the Civil War.

Confederate chaplains did not like the somber, black dress. Chaplain Oscar M. Addison of the 13th Texas wrote the secretary of war that "the dark clothing usually worn by the ministers too closely identified them in appearance with the deep blue of the Yankee troops to make it either desirable or safe."[70]

When left to their own devices, however, some of the chaplains designed uniforms that were definitely bizarre. One chaplain reported to a North Carolina regiment wearing bearskin leggings, perhaps the only pair in the army. Another, Chap. Franklin H. Wood of the 22nd North Carolina, sported a beaver hat until the soldiers ridiculed him out of it. Another insisted upon wearing his clerical robes on a daily basis.[71] One chaplain appeared on the battlefield of Manassas in a full-dress uniform complete with a sash, side arms, and an ostrich feather in his hat. Brigadier General T. H. Holmes told him: "Go back, sir, this is no place for you: Take off that sash, retire to the grove, and besiege a Throne of Grace."[72]

Chaplains in the Army of Tennessee "considered the best and cheapest uniform, under the circumstances, to be gray cloth, with black facing, and trimming, like the surgeon's uniform."[73] They proposed a Maltese cross an inch in diameter to be worn on each side of the collar like a major's star. The chaplains of the II and III Corps of the Army of Northern Virginia agreed with gray uniforms, but they wanted to use as a chaplain insignia the letter "C" within a wreath of olive leaves worked in gold bullion on a background of black velvet, the total being about two and a half inches wide.[74] One Virginia minister suggested "a small open Bible—or perhaps—half enrolled scroll—with the words 'Godliness is profitable unto all' (I Timothy 4:8) engrossed upon the open leaf."[75] There is no evidence, however, that the Confederate government ever approved these suggestions or that chaplains were ever officially furnished the insignia they had designed.

In practice, chaplains wore whatever they could buy, borrow, or manufacture. Many wore gray frock coats with staff officer buttons and assumed the rank of captains, though they were paid less than first lieutenants. For use on the battlefield, Father Bannon of the Missouri State Troops devised a white armband with a cross on it, not unlike those medics would wear in later wars. Chaplain Lyman B. Wharton of the 59th Virginia had an elegant gray uniform made with black lapels. On each lapel he put a Latin cross, an insignia the U.S. Army would eventually adopt.[76] By contrast, Chap. James H. McNeilly of the 49th Tennessee Infantry left the following description of himself after the battle of Nashville in 1864.

> My hat was of brown jeans, quilted; my jacket of gray, with wooden buttons, had suffered sadly in the battle. I had thrown it off so as to better help a wounded comrade. As it lay on the ground a shell burst over us, and a spark fell on the middle of the back and gradually burned a round hole in the cotton fabric. My shirt of checked Osnaberg [rough cotton cloth] would not button at the collar. My pantaloons were scorched from standing too close to our fires and were in strings from the knees down, and my semistockingless feet were encased in a pair of brogans that let in air and mud through the gaping chinks.[77]

Although McNeilly did not comment on a chaplain insignia for his own uniform, he did report that he saw "a brass or silver imitation of a Bible" on the collar of some chaplains and "quite a number who had a large cross of braid on the shoulder."[78]

Aside from small allowances for daily rations, writing paper, fuel, and denim to make trousers late in the war, the only other allowance chaplains were authorized was forage for a horse, if the chaplain had a horse. Since transportation was essential for chaplains to visit soldiers and hospitals as well as headquarters, the lack of horses or wagons put a severe strain on many. The simplest solution, and one adopted by Chap. Charles J. Oliver of Georgia's Troup Artillery, was to secure a Yankee horse after a battle. The soldiers reasoned that since horses were apolitical, it would not make much difference to them who was in the saddle.

One chaplain, however, decided to commandeer a horse in Virginia from a farmer who was loyal to the South. His possession was brief, as related by one army correspondent:

> The chaplain rode into the presence of his superior officers, and was asked where he got the horse? The chaplain says, "Down on the road there." The officer remarked: "You had better take him back again." The chaplain says: "Why Jesus Christ, when he was on earth, took an ass from his owner, whereon to ride into Jerusalem." The officer replied: "You are not Jesus Christ; this is not an ass; you are not on your way to Jerusalem; and the sooner you restore that horse to its owner, the better it will be for you."[79]

Actually the chaplain was lucky, for in a similar incident involving theft, a chaplain assigned to an Arkansas regiment had been sent to the guard-house.[80]

As far as is known, any other equipment chaplains needed had to be scrounged from captured supplies or dead bodies on the battlefield, furnished by churches back home or colporteurs in the field, built by hand, or bought with scanty funds. Chaplain Charles J. Oliver, who spent time as a private as well as a chaplain in the Troup Artillery in the Army of Northern Virginia, captured a horse and found tentage after several battles. He walked to various farmhouses to beg his supper, at times offering a dollar in Confederate money. He hunted for fruit trees and berry bushes, and in the winter of 1863–64 built a small cabin with the help of two other soldiers. He did send and receive mail from his family through the adjutant, and after he was commissioned a chaplain he was able to take the train to Richmond to visit soldiers in the hospital there. When he received a furlough to go home to Athens, Georgia, in the winter of 1864–65, to see his family, he was not able to return and was paroled at home.[81]

Sitting around a campfire at night usually led a soldier to dream of loved ones back home. HARPER'S WEEKLY ILLUSTRATED NEWSPAPER

Confederate regulations prescribed duties for chaplains in the army. Article XXIV of the *1863 Regulations* read simply: "The posts at, and regiments with, which Chaplains may be employed, will be announced by the War Department, upon recommendations made by the commanding officer of posts or regiments, and the pay of a Chaplain will be $80 per month."[82] Other provisions specified that pay accounts of post chaplains were to be certified by the post commander. If a garrison was withdrawn from a post, the pay of the chaplain would cease.[83]

Chaplains were therefore allowed to fashion their own ministries, but always under the watchful eye of their commanders, fellow officers, and soldiers of the line. The soldiers themselves had expectations for their chaplains, as a North Carolina cavalryman, of unusual insight, reported to the *North Carolina Presbyterian* in June 1862:

One word as to a soldier's ideas of what a chaplain should be. Presuming his orthodoxy, he should be a man whose life is the incarnation of his theology, his creed should be no mere mortal elaboration, he should be taught of the things of God by the Spirit of God that is in him. He should be largely possessed of that cardinal virtue charity. . . . He should have strong convictions of the

righteousness of the war, that he might add to the ordinary suggestions of patriotism, new incentive to fight courageously and endure
with fortitude. You see we want no ordinary man of Christian experience; nor yet any of these extraordinary orators who are more
applauded for the exclusive character of their congregations than
beloved for the number of their children in Christ.[84]

An Episcopal soldier from the 28th Mississippi Cavalry pled for just one
"sensible" chaplain:

There is not a chaplain—no, not one, among us. By little prayer
meetings held by a few members (of different churches) in the regiment, evidences have been given of a willingness to submit to the
Divine Will. Each regiment composing the brigade has lost upward
of one hundred men in battle since May 17. Many of these souls
have been prepared. I know that outside the abuse heaped upon us,
my arm of the service is supposed to be the most godless and reck-
less; thus the greater need for God's word. It matters not what
denomination he be, we only ask for a sensible man, who preaches
the Gospel of Christ; let the road be called by any name, so it lead to
the True Portal. One active minister in the brigade would do. For his
maintenance several have expressed their willingness to contribute
one day's rations per week—thus seven can maintain a preacher. I
appeal to you, who have the most influence, to send us aid speedily,
for what soldier can count on the rising of another sun?[85]

J. William Jones, the outspoken chaplain of the 13th Virginia, wrote to
the *Religious Herald* in Richmond: "Send us the names of *good men;* and here
I repeat, we want *none others*—our object being not merely to fill up the
regiments with nominal chaplains, but to fill up the vacancies with *efficient,
working* men. We want *effective Gospel preachers*, whose burden shall be
Christ and Him crucified."[86]

Colonel A. E. Reynolds, commanding the 26th Mississippi, wanted a
chaplain who was not afraid to fight. In a November 14, 1864, letter to Rev.
C. K. Marshall, Colonel Reynolds discussed his requirements:

I have been exceedingly unfortunate with my chaplains, none have
done me any good; all have become indolent and neglectful of
those duties they could make themselves most careful in; hence I

persuaded them to resign and go home. For two years I have had
none preferring to be without rather than have one who does not
command the respect of my men. At this period of the war no official will be respected in camp unless he is a working man. A man
should not be afraid to fight if necessary; always be ready to wait on
the sick and administer to the distressed and should ever be at the
right place at the right time.[87]

The essential goal of the chaplains' ministries was to prepare soldiers for
battle—to fight the enemy with courage and conviction, and to endure
defeat, disfigurement, disease, or death if necessary. The path to this goal
was to "do the work of an evangelist," as St. Paul had written in his Second
Letter to Timothy, one of the books in the New Testament treasured for
advice to ministers.

Evangelism was important because only about 25 percent of the Confederate soldiers were members of a church at the beginning of the war.
Another estimated 25 percent were barely literate and had trouble reading
the Bible for themselves. Two-thirds owned no slaves and were prone to
grumble that this was "a rich man's war, but a poor man's fight," especially
after April 1862, when the Confederate government allowed paid substitutes to be provided for the draft.[88] A letter from a Georgia private, Joseph
Cowan, to his cousin, written December 1, 1862, reflected the feelings of
thousands just like him.

I am a poor harted sinner and got no chance to be no other way, for
I ain't got no Bible. Yankees want us to lose our soles, same as our
lifes. It is aggravashun for brexfus, dinner, and supper.[89]

For such soldiers, chaplains brought a gospel message of individual
worth, hope, encouragement, and faith in God. Chaplains also provided
Bibles, tracts, newspapers, visits to the sick, and a willing hand to help the
men write to their families back home so their families would know what
had happened to them. On occasion, when there was time and bodies could
be recovered, they conducted funerals.[90]

The chaplains' work of preaching and teaching was usually tied to
weekly Bible studies or prayer meetings.[91] In civilian communities, the pattern for worship in a typical country church would include Sunday school
and two preaching services on Sunday, usually with dinner on the church
grounds brought by church families. On Wednesday evenings there was a
prayer meeting for specific needs of the congregation. Other meetings, for

administrative discussions involving deacons, wardens, stewards, or elders, frequently followed worship services or prayer meetings.

In the Confederate armies the basic schedule of preaching services on Sundays, if there was no fighting, and prayer meetings during the week followed the civilian pattern—minus the Sunday church dinners. Sunday school classes and the observation of communion, or the Lord's Supper, was sporadic because literature and elements were scarce. Baptisms, often in rivers or creeks, were numerous and mostly followed extended preaching services by a battery of preachers of different denominations.[92]

Hymns sung by soldiers frequently reflected both their fears and their faith. Just before the battle of Chickamauga in 1863, chaplains in the Army of Tennessee urged the soldiers to remember the promises of God.[93] But many of these soldiers, especially from James Longstreet's corps, had also been at Fredericksburg and Gettysburg. They remembered the horrific casualties that one day could bring. The hymns they sang, "Rock of Ages, Cleft for Me, Let Me Hide Myself in Thee"; "Jesus, Lover of My Soul, Let Me to Thy Bosom Fly"; "There is a Fountain Filled with Blood, Drawn from Emmanuel's Veins"; and "Sinners Plunged beneath That Flood Lose All Their Guilty Stains," were hymns not only of faith but also of hope.

⊱⊶⊷⊙⊶⊷⊰

The preponderance of Confederate chaplains focused on evangelical sermons that stressed the importance of individual salvation and Christian morality as revealed in the Scriptures. Most did not preach on the righteousness of secession or offer "just cause" arguments for the war in sermons. They realized that discussing politics in the field produced few converts. Chaplain John C. Granberry of the 11th Virginia wrote:

> Chaplains and visiting ministers determined not to know anything among them save Jesus Christ and Him crucified. It was always assumed that the cause for which they contended was righteous; on it was invoked the divine blessing, and the troops were exhorted to faithful service. But the grounds of the war were not discussed; constitutional and historical questions were passed by, except a certain local coloring, such as illustrations drawn from active military life and appeals based on the perils of war. . . . Eternal things, the claims of God, the worth of the soul, the wages of sin which is death, and the gift of God which is eternal life through Jesus Christ our Lord— these were the matter of preaching.[94]

Sermons by the chaplains varied widely, but the majority stressed what became known as "God's Plan of Salvation," taken directly from the Scripture: A) " For all have sinned, and come short of the glory of God" (Romans 3:23); B) "Christ died for our sins according to the scriptures; And that he was buried, and that he rose again the third day" (1 Corinthians 15:3–4); C) "I acknowledge my sin unto thee and mine iniquity have I not hid" (Psalm 32:5); D) "But as many as received Him, to them gave He power to become the sons of God, even to them that believe on his name" (John 1:12). For soldiers who could not read, the verse from John 3:16 might be sufficient: "For God so loved the world that he gave his only Son, that whosoever believes in him should not perish but have eternal life." For those who did not know if they would survive the next battle, baptism was offered and even church membership.[95]

In addition to the four Gospels and the letters of Paul, the Book of Revelation was popular for sermons because it held both the exhortation, "Awake, and strengthen what remains and is on the point of death, for I have not found your works perfect in the sight of my God" (Revelation 3:2), and the promise: "he who sits upon the throne will shelter them with his presence" (Revelation 7:15). The first text from Revelation was a popular one for Chap. J. William Jones of the 13th Virginia, the second for Chap. Charles J. Oliver of Cabell's Artillery Battalion.[96]

If political ethics were not favored, basic Christian morality was. Gambling, drinking, swearing, profaning the Sabbath, and other sundry sins became favorite topics for discourses and sermons. Soldiers were reminded that "we have little to hope for, if we do not realize our dependence upon heaven's blessing and seek the guidance of truth."[97]

Baptist chaplain Ransdell W. Cridlin of the 38th Virginia convicted gamblers very effectively by using religious tracts to shame them:

> I entered a tent and found two young men engaged in a game of cards. At first they seemed ashamed, then they braced up their failing courage (if courage it was) and continued the game. I kindly asked if I could take a hand. Waiting for my turn, I first threw down *Evils of Gambling;* then *Mother's Parting Words to her Soldier Boy.* I found that the game was mine. At the sight of the word "mother," the tears rolled down their cheeks as they both exclaimed: "Parson, I will never play cards again!"[98]

Excessive consumption of alcohol was a harder nut to crack since whiskey was abundant in the Confederate armies and was used frequently by surgeons as an anesthetic if none other were available. Chaplain William W. Bennett of Richmond cited figures of massive proportions for the production of whiskey: 50,000 bushels of grain consumed monthly in one county in Virginia by the distilleries there; 150 distilleries in operation in one South Carolina district; 64,000 gallons of whiskey manufactured *daily* throughout the Confederacy in 1862.[99] Drunken soldiers were dangerous, profane, and often useless, not to mention frequently out of rational control of themselves.

General Braxton Bragg issued a general order attempting to control the vice: "Commanders of all grades are earnestly called upon to suppress drunkenness. . . . [T]he largest portion of our sickness and mortality results from it; our guardhouses are filled by it; officers are constantly called from their duties to form court-martials in consequence of it; inefficiency in our troops, and consequent danger to our cause is the inevitable result."[100]

President Jefferson Davis was more direct. On March 1, 1862, he prohibited all distillation of spirituous liquors within ten miles of Richmond, and directed that the distilleries be forthwith closed and the establishments for the sale thereof closed.[101] Nevertheless, there were testimonies of chaplains in the summer of 1864 who found Confederate soldiers wounded on battlefields with canteens filled not with water, but with whiskey.[102]

⊱⊶⊙⊷⊰

Unquestionably there were many chaplains who took up arms and fought as regular soldiers during the heat of combat. There were no regulations or written instructions with regard to the chaplain's place of duty during a battle, and no Geneva Conventions as yet in effect. Both the Union and Confederate armies regarded chaplains as noncombatants when they were captured because most chaplains reported to field hospitals to pray for the wounded and comfort the dying during battle.[103] About a half dozen, in fact, were dual professionals, trained as surgeons or assistant surgeons and also commissioned as chaplains.[104]

The major battlefields of the Civil War were often described by the chaplains as "fearful sights for Christian eyes."[105] A doctor of the 2nd Tennessee, Joseph Cross, pictured what he found among the cedar trees at Stone's River:

"Prayer in Stonewall Jackson's Camp."
THE MUSEUM OF THE CONFEDERACY, RICHMOND, VIRGINIA

Here is a foot, shot off at the ankle—a fine model for a sculptor. Here is an officer's hand, severed from the wrist, the glove still upon it, and the sword in its grasp. Here is an entire brain, perfectly isolated, showing no sign of violence, as if carefully taken from the skull that enclosed it by the hands of a skillful surgeon. Here is a corpse, sitting upon the ground, with its back against a tree, in the most natural position of life, holding before its face the photograph likeness of a good-looking old lady, probably the dead man's mother. Here is a handsome young man, with placid countenance, lying upon his back, his Bible upon his bosom, and his hands folded over it, as if gone to sleep saying his evening prayer. . . . Dissevered heads, arms, legs are scattered everywhere; and the coagulated pools of blood gleam ghastly in the morning sun.[106]

At Chancellorsville, Fr. James B. Sheeran of the 14th Louisiana said that the line of battle extended for eight miles and "for that distance you could see the dead bodies of the enemy lying in every direction," including those who had been burned to death by a wildfire that broke out in the underbrush.[107] These were just the human casualties, for the thousands of dead horses were just rolled into ditches or trenches or pulled to ravines.

Clearly these battlefields demanded close teamwork from the chaplains, litter bearers, and surgeons just to save a few lives. Chaplain Sterling M. Cherry of the 37th Georgia reported on the work of chaplains in the hospitals after the 1863 battle of Chickamauga:

> Dr. McFerrin was at Cleburn's Division hospital, where his son was, slightly wounded, and his nephew, Rev. John P. McFerrin, severely wounded, working with the sufferers. Dr. Cross, chaplain on Gen. Buckner's staff, was on the field and at the hospital. Bros. Mooney and Miller were at Stewart's Division hospital, active and industrious in attending to the wounded and dying. Dr. Petway came in good time to render efficient aid in the double capacity of surgeon and minister. Chaplain Willoughby was with the dying and superintended the burial of the dead of our division.[108]

In all, Cherry counted thirteen chaplains and two missionaries in two division hospitals, transporting wounded on stretchers, performing surgery, praying for the wounded and dying soldiers, taking last requests, and burying the dead.

It would seem from references in letters and diaries, however, that there were a sizable number of those who held chaplain commissions who did not hesitate to take up arms in the ranks or even to lead other soldiers in assaults in addition to their other duties. Some of these "fighting parsons" had served first as enlisted soldiers and were accustomed to loading and firing weapons. Some wanted to demonstrate their patriotism, their dedication to their soldiers, or, at times, to build or maintain their reputations as Christian warriors not unlike their leaders, Gen. "Stonewall" Jackson, Bishop Leonidas Polk, Rev. William Pendleton, or Robert E. Lee.

John J. D. Renfroe, Baptist chaplain of the 10th Alabama, stated that he usually went with the regiment to their battle line, said what he could to encourage them, and then went "to his station" at the field hospital. At Salem Church and at Gettysburg, Renfroe waited too long and was pinned down in the shooting.[109] In 1863, Dr. Joseph Cross, Methodist chaplain of the 2nd Tennessee, got caught in a retreat and was pushed into Chickamauga Creek before his regiment could fight its way out. His colonel later reminded him that his place was at the field hospital.

One additional motive for "fighting parsons" to take up arms was that in the smoke, explosions, groaning, yelling, and screaming, it was not hard to get caught up in a kind of heroic mass hysteria. Father Sheeran recorded the emotions of his soldiers in their counterattack at Cedar Mountain in August 1862:

> The Irish Battalion of Jackson's old Brigade, and a few regiments were in the advance on the Left. . . . The Yankees pressed upon our advance with overpowering numbers. The enemy now confident of victory over our Left wing advanced rapidly after what they supposed our retreating columns, until they were within fifty yards of the woods where the greatest part of Jackson's old Division were concealed. It was now our turn to charge. As they advanced yelling furiously, they were hailed by a tremendous volley of musketry that mowed them down by regiments. Our boys with a victorious hurrah! which echoed along our lines, start after the retreating enemy shooting them down in great numbers and taking some seven hundred prisoners. Thus ended at about sunset the celebrated infantry contest at the Battle of Cedar Mountain.[110]

At the battle of Shiloh, in the same year, Isaac T. Tichenor, chaplain of the 17th Alabama Infantry, "killed one colonel, a captain, and four privates" with his repeater rifle. In a letter to Gov. Thomas H. Watts of Alabama, Tichenor wrote that "during the engagement we were under a cross fire . . . [u]nder it the boys wavered. I had been wounded and was sitting down, but sprang to my feet, took off my hat, waved it over my head, walked up and down the line . . . reminded them that it was Sunday, that all their home folks were praying for them. . . . I called upon them to stand and die, if need be, for their country. . . . Every man stood to his post . . . every eye flashed and hearts beat high with desperate resolve to conquer or die."[111]

Andrew J. Potter, a Mexican War veteran and chaplain of the 26th Texas Cavalry, seized a rifle at a battle near Bayou Bluff, Louisiana, and rode to the front to take part in the fighting. Thomas L. Duke, chaplain of the 19th Mississippi, was cited for "gallant conduct" at Chancellorsville because he "remained in front of his regiment with his musket during the series of engagements and mainly directed the movements of the skirmishers of that regiment."[112] After one engagement, William P. McBryde, Cumberland Presbyterian chaplain of the 5th Mississippi, found bullet holes in his shoe, his haversack, the back of his coat, the front part of his vest pocket, his sleeve, and his Bible—yet he was not wounded.[113]

Others were not so fortunate. Lucius H. Jones, Episcopal chaplain of the 4th Texas Cavalry, was wounded while ministering to a dying soldier at Glorietta Pass, New Mexico. Chaplain Edward Hudson of the 6th Texas Cavalry was hit while carrying a wounded man off the field at Newnan, Georgia. Father P. Emmeran Bliemel was killed at Jonesboro, Georgia, in 1864 while ministering to the mortally wounded Col. William Grace of the 10th Tennessee. Benjamin T. Crouch, chaplain of the 1st Tennessee Cavalry, was killed "while gallantly leading a regiment in the memorable battle of Thompson's Station." Chaplain M. Leander Weller, Episcopal chaplain of the 9th Mississippi, was killed at Shiloh, and Chap. Benjamin F. Ellison of Madison's Texas Cavalry, was mortally wounded fighting in the front rank at Monett's Ferry, Louisiana.[114]

Possibly one of the most ironic engagements from a casualty standpoint was during the 1864 battle of Resaca, Georgia. There Presbyterian missionary J. P. McMullen, with the 18th Alabama saw his son killed in the first fire, so he buckled on his son's sword and led the men on "a piece further" until he too was killed.[115] Opposite the 18th Alabama was the 3rd Wisconsin, whose chaplain, John M. Springer, was also killed the same day on the same field fighting to repel the Confederate attack.

In all, some forty-one Confederate chaplains are known to have died during the war, thirty-two of them from exhaustion or disease.[116] Of those who died, seventeen, or almost half, expired in the years 1861–62. An additional twenty were wounded during the war, but survived their wounds. Only one, Dr. John P. Richardson, physician and chaplain of the 4th Mississippi, died as a prisoner of war—at Camp Chase, Ohio, in March 1862. Of the forty-one chaplains who died while on duty, twelve were Methodists. Ten, of various faiths, were from Mississippi regiments. The Army of Northern Virginia lost a total of fifteen, the Army of Tennessee, eleven, and the Army of Mississippi, six. The rest of the casualties were hospital chaplains and chaplains from units in other regions of the South.

By 1864 recruitment of chaplains for the armies had declined. Several states simply had no churches or church conferences free of occupying Federal forces, and therefore no way to recruit chaplain replacements. The Baltimore Conference of the Methodist church reportedly appointed fourteen ordained members of their body to serve as chaplains in 1864, but there are few if any military records for this group. The Methodists, Baptists, and

Presbyterians did, however, increase the number of missionaries appointed to the armies. These included chaplains who had been wounded but who volunteered to return as missionaries, such as John C. Granberry of the 11th Virginia, those who had become increasingly involved in colporteur work, such as Sterling M. Cherry of the 37th Georgia, and those who had not served as chaplains but who volunteered to serve as missionaries late in the war. The Southern Baptists furnished about seventy-six and the Methodists about thirty-two missionaries during the war.

The Presbyterians resolved in 1863–64 to put at least one chaplain or missionary in each brigade in the Confederate armies. In 1864 the Presbyterian Committee on Domestic Missions had 130 chaplains or permanent missionaries in the field, more than a quarter of the total number of ministers in the church—the highest proportion of clergy that year of any denomination in the South. The ministers were distributed throughout the armies, with thirty-six in the Army of Northern Virginia, twelve in the Army of Tennessee, nine on the coast of South Carolina, twenty-two in hospitals in Virginia, Georgia, and Mississippi, and the rest scattered in units and hospitals from North Carolina to Florida. Moreover, the blockade-running Dr. Moses D. Hoge of Richmond was able to bring 15,000 Bibles, 50,000 Testaments, and 250,000 copies of the Gospels and Psalms from the British and Foreign Bible Society through Wilmington, North Carolina, to the soldiers of the Confederacy.[117]

CHAPLAINS OF THE CONFEDERACY NOTES

1. E. Merton Coulter, *The Confederate States of America* (Baton Rouge, 1950), 34–35.
2. Ibid.
3. Ibid., 43.
4. As cited in George G. Smith, *The Life and Times of George Foster Pierce, D.D., LL.D.: Bishop of the Methodist Episcopal Church, South* (Sparta, Ga., 1888), 467.
5. Coulter, *Conferedate States*, 57.
6. Ibid., 59.
7. Frank Hieronymus, "For Now and Forever: The Chaplains of the Confederate States Army" (Ph.D. diss., University of California, Los Angeles, 1964), 12.
8. Ibid., 24.

9. Ibid., 32–36.
10. Ibid., 38.
11. Coulter, *Confederate States*, 199, 201.
12. Ibid., 199, 202.
13. Ibid., 200.
14. Confederate States War Department, *Regulations for the Army of the Confederate States* (Richmond, 1863), article VIII.
15. Ibid., article XII. The State of Georgia passed *An Act to Amend the Military Laws of This State* on December 18, 1861, which designated a company of infantry at between fifty to eighty rank and file. State troop units were therefore slightly different before the Confederate army was reorganized and somewhat standardized in 1862.
16. Ibid., article XIII.
17. Ibid., article IV, paragraph 21.
18. Herman A. Norton, *Struggling for Recognition: The United States Army Chaplaincy 1791–1865* (Washington, D.C.: 1977), 19.
19. Ibid., 65.
20. Ibid., 64–76; Daniel Tyler, "History of the Mormon Battalion of the Mexican War," manuscript copy in the Military History Institute Library, Carlisle, PA.
21. "The Religion of Jefferson Davis," *Confederate Veteran* 35 (1927): 374, as cited in Norton, *Struggling for Recognition*, 131.
22. Norton, *Struggling for Recognition*, 34.
23. Herman Norton, "The Organization and Function of the Confederate Military Chaplaincy, 1861–1865" (Ph.D. diss., Vanderbilt University, 1956), 67–68.
24. U.S. War Department, *War of the Rebellion: A Compilation of the Official Records of the Union and Confederate Armies* (Washington, D.C.: Government Printing Office 1880–1902), ser. 4, vol. 1, 252. (hereafter cited as *OR*.)
25. John W. Brinsfield, "Our Roots for Ministry: The Continental Army, General Washington, and the Free Exercise of Religion," *Military Chaplains' Review* (fall 1987): 26–27.
26. Norton, "Confederate Military Chaplaincy," 24.
27. Ibid., 25.
28. Ibid., 26.
29. Ibid., 28.
30. Ibid., 30.

31. Military records of John A. Chambliss, National Archives Microfilm 277 (hereafter cited as NA), Consolidated Service Records of Confederate Generals and Staff Officers, Georgia State Archives.

32. Ibid.

33. In 1860 the Methodist Episcopal Church, South, for example, had 2,615 fully ordained ministers and 5,353 lay preachers, or one minister for each 95 members. The great majority of the lay preachers were young men studying for ordination. See *The Minutes of the Annual Conferences of the Methodist Episcopal Church, South, 1855–1865* (Nashville, 1878), 293.

34. The course of study for lay preachers seeking ordination in the Methodist Church lasted four years and required periodic examinations and two written sermons. The twenty-five books in the course of study for Methodist lay preachers are listed in the Georgia Conference *Minutes of 1864*, 11, Candler School of Theology, Emory University.

35. Ibid.

36. Unaguskie, Christian son of a Cherokee chieftain, as cited in the *Richmond Religious Herald*, June 5, 1862. See Charles F. Pitts, *Chaplains in Gray: The Confederate Chaplains' Story* (Nashville, 1957), 48, and Sidney J. Romero, *Religion in the Rebel Ranks* (New York, 1983), 202. The African-American honorary chaplain in Forrest's Cavalry was Louis Napoleon Nelson, whose grandson, Nelson Winbush of Kissimmee, Florida, is a member of the Sons of Confederate Veterans. Mr. Winbush has pictures of his grandfather, "Uncle Louis." See Pitts, *Chaplains in Gray*, 48–49 for a fuller discussion.

37. Hieronymus, "For Now and Forever," 2.

38. Ibid., 5.

39. Ibid., 3–5.

40. Southern Baptist Convention, *Annual Report, 1866*, in the Southern Baptist Historical Library and Archives, Nashville, Tennessee.

41. Hieronymus, "*For Now and Forever*," 3 and appendix A, 341, as well as the Consolidated Service Records of Confederate General and Staff Officers, microfilm drawers 277, 278, Georgia State Archives. Total clergy under age forty-five counted (with a few estimated, based on known numbers of congregations) at 9,079; total known Confederate chaplains by name, 1,307.

42. Marcus B. Chapman of the Washington Artillery was born in 1846. He entered service in 1862. Two other chaplains, Robert Holland of

Buford's Kentucky Cavalry and Felix R. Hill of Forrest's Cavalry, were born in 1844 and were commissioned at age eighteen.

43. A survey of the *Minutes of the Annual Conferences of the Methodist Episcopal Church, South, 1855–1865* (Nashville, 1878), shows that the 6 Methodist bishops appointed 318 fully ordained elders (ministers) from all conferences to serve as Confederate chaplains or to serve "in the CS army." Of these, 189, or 59.4 percent, received commissions as chaplains, while 20, or 6.3 percent, appointed to be chaplains have no surviving military records. Some 109 ordained elders, or 34.3 percent, appointed to "the CS army" served as line officers or soldiers, but not as chaplains. In 1864 an additional 14 ordained elders from the exiled Baltimore Conference volunteered to serve as chaplains, but their service records have not survived except in their obituaries. Another 259 Methodists who were deacons, local preachers, or lay preachers without full ordination also served as commissioned chaplains in the Confederate armies. The total number of commissioned Methodist chaplains with known service records is therefore 448, 42 percent of whom were ordained elders. Of the 209 ordained elders who were appointed to serve as chaplains, Tennessee contributed 47, Virginia 26, Alabama 25, Georgia 24, South Carolina 24, Arkansas 22, North Carolina 17, Texas 9, Mississippi 9, Florida 5, and Louisiana 1. See also William W. Sweet, *The Methodist Episcopal Church and the Civil War* (Cincinnati, 1912), 219–22 for rosters of some of the appointees.

44. Pitts, *Chaplains in Gray* 46.

45. Arthur Howard Noll, ed., *Doctor Quintard: Chaplain C.S.A. and Second Bishop of Tennessee* (Sewanee, Tenn., 1905), 5.

46. Ibid., 10.

47. Ibid., 12.

48. Gary R. Goodson, Sr., *Georgia Confederate 7,000: New Research* (Shawnee, Colo., 1995), 19, 20, 24.

49. Peter J. Meaney, O.S.B., "Valliant Chaplain of the Bloody Tenth," *Tennessee Historical Quarterly* 41, no.1 (spring 1982), 43.

50. Edwin Porter Thompson, *History of the Orphan Brigade* (Louisville, Ky., 1898), 531.

51. Norton, "Confederate Military Chaplaincy," 51.

52. James B. Sheeran, *Confederate Chaplain: A War Journal* (Milwaukee, 1960), ix.

53. John K. Bettersworth, ed., *Mississippi in the Confederacy: As They Saw it* (Baton Rouge, 1961), 233.

54. Rex B. Magee, "Chaplains Played Vital Roles during Civil War," *Jackson (Miss.) Clarion Ledger,* July 10, 1963.

55. A. D. Betts, *Experience of a Confederate Chaplain* (Greenville, S.C., 1904), 6–7.

56. John W. Wright, ed., *New York Times 2000 Almanac* (New York, 1999), 165.

57. George G. Smith Diary, entry for July 13, 1864, Emory University.

58. Edmund Lee Rice, comp., "Civil War Letters of Major (Chaplain) James McDonald Campbell," Georgia Department of Archives and History, 9.

59. Ibid., 24.

60. The best estimate is 57 percent for ordained ministers and priests of the 938 chaplains whose denomination is known. This assumes all Roman Catholic, Presbyterian, Episcopal, Lutheran, Congregationalist, and Disciples of Christ chaplains were ordained ministers and not laity elected from the ranks, as was the case with some Methodists and Baptists.

61. State of Georgia, Office of the Adjutant General, Index, Book of Commissions, Georgia State Archives.

62. Norton, "Confederate Military Chaplaincy," 72–73.

63. *Minutes of the Louisiana Conference of the Methodist Episcopal Church, South* (Nashville, 1880), 160; NA Service Record for Chap. John V. Pointer, Consolidated Service Records for Confederate Generals and Staff Officers, Georgia State Archives. In the fighting at Allatoona, Georgia, on October 5, Pointer's immediate commander, Brig. Gen. William H. Young, was wounded and captured. It was the sixth time Young had been wounded in the Civil War.

64. Rev. J. P. McMullen was killed fighting along side his son at the battle of Resaca, Georgia, in 1864. The other two, McFerrin and Jones, remained with their soldiers until their units surrendered. Pitts, *Chaplains in Gray,* 102.

65. J. William Jones, *Christ in the Camp* (Richmond, 1887), 583.

66. Marion E. Lazenby, *History of Methodism in Alabama and West Florida* (Nashville, 1960), 343.

67. Dumas Malone, ed., *Dictionary of American Biography* (New York, 1933), xi, 522.

68. Jones, *Christ in the Camp,* 264.

69. Noll, *Doctor Quintard,* 102.

70. Norton, "Confederate Military Chaplaincy," 42.

71. Ibid.
72. Romero, *Religion in the Rebel Ranks*, 19.
73. Norton, "Confederate Military Chaplaincy," 43.
74. Romero, *Religion in the Rebel Ranks*, 19.
75. Norton, "Confederate Military Chaplaincy," 40.
76. Chaplain Wharton's uniform was on display for many years at the Fredericksburg National Military Park Headquarters in Fredericksburg, Virginia.
77. Pitts, *Chaplains in Gray*, 45.
78. Norton, "Confederate Military Chaplaincy," 40.
79. Felix G. DeFontaine, comp., *Marginalia; or, Gleanings from an Army Note Book* (Columbia, SC, 1864), 57.
80. Norton, "Confederate Military Chaplaincy," 84.
81. Charles James Oliver Papers, entry for December 13, 1864, Emory University.
82. *Regulations for the Army of the Confederate States, 1863*, 22.
83. Ibid., 110–11.
84. Norton, "Confederate Military Chaplaincy," 74.
85. Pitts, *Chaplains in Gray*, 48.
86. Ibid., 46.
87. NA, Consolidated Service Records of Confederate General and Staff Officers, Microfilm 277–59, record of Chaplain Marcus B. Chapman, 26th Mississippi, Georgia State Archives, Atlanta.
88. "Persons not liable to duty may be received as substitutes, under such regulations as the Secretary of War may prescribe." Edward McPherson, *The Political History of the United States of America during the Great Rebellion* (Washington, D.C.: 1865), 118.
89. Pitts, *Chaplains in Gray*, 32.
90. As in the case of Lt. Gen. Leonidas Polk's funeral, conducted by Chap. Charles T. Quintard at St. Luke's Episcopal Church in Atlanta in June 1864, see Noll, *Doctor Quintard*, 98.
91. Jones, *Christ in the Camp*, 468.
92. Ibid., 469.
93. Sam R. Watkins, *Co. Aytch: A Side Show of the Big Show* (New York: 1962), 103. Watkins of the 1st Tennessee had both critical and laudatory comments about Confederate chaplains.
94. Jones, *Christ in the Camp*, 15.
95. Ibid., 525.
96. Ibid., 469.

97. Ibid., 42.

98. Ibid., 479.

99. W. W. Bennett, *A Narrative of the Great Revival Which Prevailed in the Southern Armies* (Harrisonburg, Va., 1976), 37.

100. Ibid., 38.

101. McPherson, *Political History*, 121. This was a slightly ironic order from Jefferson Davis since he was court-martialed as a cadet at West Point and almost expelled for consuming spiritous liquors.

102. Milton L. Haney, *The Story of My Life* (Normal, Ill., 1904), 201. Chaplain Haney, of the 55th Illinois, was awarded the Medal of Honor for heroism during the battle of Atlanta. He wrote that Gen. John B. Hood "ordered whiskey barrels to be opened that the boys might fill their canteens, for this was their last battle and they would drive the Yanks out of the country."

103. For a fuller discussion of the fluctuations in regulations regarding chaplain prisoners of war, see Norton, "Confederate Military Chaplaincy" 44–47.

104. Charles T. Quintard of Tennessee, John P. Richardson of Mississippi, and Ferdinand S. Petway of Alabama were three of these.

105. Jones, *Christ in the Camp*, 542.

106. Ibid.

107. Sheeran, *Confederate Chaplain*, 44.

108. Bennett, *Great Revival*, 327–28.

109. Hieronymus, "For Now and Forever," 155–56.

110. James B. Sheeran, *Confederate Chaplain*, 3, 4.

111. Hieronymus, "For Now and Forever," 157–58.

112. OR, ser. 1, vol. 25, pt 1, 873.

113. Hieronymus, "For Now and Forever," 155.

114. Ibid., 163–64.

115. Pitts, *Chaplains in Gray*, 98.

116. Hieronymus, "For Now and Forever," 161. The total of 41 came from examination of 1,307 individual service records.

117. Ernest Trice Thompson, *Presbyterians in the South* (Richmond, 1973), ii, 47.

In Their
Own Words

A s men whose profession was founded on a book, chaplains were by definition men of words. They had to use them to comfort and inspire their flocks, to bring hope to the suffering, and comfort to the bereaved at home. Not surprisingly, they were more literate than the average run of the soldiery, and both during and after the war they put their experiences and thoughts in writing. In the excerpts that follow, fragments from several Confederate chaplains' letters and diaries are compiled to present a first-hand picture of their service, while one Union chaplain's postwar memoir is offered as emblematic of the experience of many of his brethren.

Confederate Chaplains
in Their Own Words

Complete recollections by pastors in gray are considerably fewer than for their Yankee counterparts, yet a few exist, and even more of their diaries and letters survive. What follows is a compilation from several sources that reveals a typical portrait of chaplains in gray. It begins with a brief memoir written in 1910 by Rev. Ransdell W. Cridlin of Virginia. Before the war he had been a carriage maker and lay preacher studying for the Baptist ministry when the sectional crisis came to a head. As he explained later, he was forced then to make a choice. His memoir is currently in the possession of James I. Robertson, Jr.

During the year 1860 I was colporter under Dr. A. E. Dickinson in Amelia County and Manchester, Virginia where I now reside. I continued in my work in Amelia until I was advised by the officers of that county that it was not safe for me to remain there and for the following reason: At the time the war cloud was seen rising in the North. About this time it was stated in some paper that Spurgeon, the great preacher of London, had said, "that he would rather commune with a murderer than to commune with a slave owner". I had some of Spurgeon's sermons in my stock of books for sale. Those who had any of his sermons threw them in the fire and said if I continued to sell such books I would have to suffer for it. So, I thought it best for me to leave the field, which I did in good order. Then I continued my colportage work in Manchester until I entered Richmond College in September 1860. While I was sorry to leave my dear classmates and friends at Green Plain, I was glad to get back to Richmond and to enter Richmond College with enlarged opportunities opening up before me. I entered the college with some degree of pride, finding that I was further advanced than some of my young friends from Leigh Street Church who started Richmond College when I entered Green Plain. I am still of the opinion that a good, well conducted preparatory school, such as I had at Green Plain, is far better for a young man than the college, until he is well prepared for advanced work.

I soon became acquainted with many fine young men and I was able to maintain myself well in my classes. As the war fever was prevalent throughout the whole country we were very much interrupted in our studies. Early in the Spring the Secession Convention met in Richmond and its sessions were very stormy. We soon discovered that war was inevitable with the North and soon the students began to leave college for the service of their state. As I had no military aspirations and having some fear of Yankee bullets, I made up my mind to be in no hurry to leave the quiet halls of college life for the battle field. I think I was among the very last to leave college. These were days I can never forget. The Proclamation of President Lincoln for troops from Virginia to crush the secession of her Southern sisters stirred every heart in every man, and the people rushed to the front in defense of what they thought dear to every Southern heart. I shall never forget the arrival of the first soldiers from South Carolina. The whole city was stirred. I hardly knew what to do. I did not care to join the army as a soldier as my five brothers had already enlisted in the Southern Cause. I accepted a position as a missionary among soldiers and continued in this work, laboring among the hospitals and camps until June 1863 when I became the Chaplain of the 38th Virginia Regiment, Armistead's Brigade, Pickett's Division, Army of Northern Virginia. Very often I was exposed to danger, but not as much as those in the ranks. I could go and come as I wished.

I labored among the soldiers on the Potomac River, Mathias' Point and other places. I spent some time among the hospitals and camps in and around Norfolk and Portsmouth. At the evacuation of Norfolk, after having spent some time at Yorktown and Williamsburg in the hospitals, I took the last steamer that left Jamestown for Richmond. After getting to Richmond I was assigned to work in the Chimborazo Hospital, situated on the hill overlooking Rockets, known as Chimborazo Park. There were thousands of sick and wounded soldiers in this extensive place. This became greatly crowded during the Seven Days Battle around Richmond and we often buried as many as fifty in one day at Oakwood Cemetery. I frequently made trips to the army in the field and preached for them. Three of my brothers were in the 30th Virginia Regiment, one in the Salem Artillery and one in the Government Department in Richmond, though he died in July 1861 of fever.

My other brothers, though two were wounded and one taken prisoner, survived the war and lived for years, though only one besides myself is left now, John N. Cridlin, Jonesville, Lee County, Virginia. He is four years older than I. On June 9th, 1863, at the earnest request of the officers and private soldiers of the 38th Virginia Regiment, I was appointed Chaplain and entered at once on my duties. We were then at or near Suffolk, Virginia. We had a severe battle there and lost some of our best men. From that time on I followed my command in all their marches and battles. I started with them to Gettysburg, but was taken sick at Edenburg, Shenandoah County and was there when the great battle was fought. While I suffered very much, yet it seemed providential that I was not at Gettysburg, as my regiment was cut up, losing many of the best men in the army. As soon as I was able, I came back to Richmond and spent some time in Amelia County with a dear friend, Mr. Pleasant Wilkinson, who was not only a friend, but a father to me during the war, as I made his house my home. I had a very strong inducement to go there as I became engaged to his oldest daughter, Miss Mary, in 1862, in the month of March, and continued this engagement until the close of the war when we mutually parted and we were ever strong friends. There are many incidents that I might relate but it will not be necessary to my object in giving just an outline of my life. I had become licensed to preach by my church, the Leigh Street Church in Richmond in 1860, though it was not until 1863 that I was ordained, as follows: The council of ordination consisted of the following ministers, Rev. T. Hume, Sr., J. B. Hardwick, T. O. Keen, John M. Butler and William M. Young. Rev. T. Hume, Jr., who was not at this time ordained, was present. Rev. Joseph F. Deans, well known as the president of Winsor Academy after the war, was ordained at the same time, with the same council and exercises. I was at this time Chaplain in Pickett's Division and our command was stationed near Petersburg. My certificate of license to exercise my gifts in public was given by my church July 30th, 1860. In that day no one was expected to enter the pulpit and speak from a text until he was authorized by his church to do so. So far as I know at this time, April 18, 1910, every minister who composed my ordaining council has passed over the river and is waiting on the other shore for those left behind. During the war I had the opportunity of preaching to the soldiers in camp, hospitals and during the winter we built rough chapels of logs and had our services.

There were many gracious revivals during the war among the soldiers and you will find much of interest in this subject in Dr. J. W. Jones' admirable book, "Christ in the Camp". You will find some extracts from my work in that book. I baptized a great many and some times under the guns of the enemy. On one occasion on the lines near Chester, Virginia, I had my servant on Saturday afternoon preparing a pond to baptize the next day, but the enemy, thinking I was throwing up breast works, began to shell me. We sought shelter in a nearby bomb-proof place, in a wagon or cook yard and hid until the firing ceased, but I never baptized those candidates. Just before this, in the same pond, I had baptized several, among whom was Capt. Charles F. James of Co. F, 8th Regiment, Hunton's Brigade. He, after the war, became a noted preacher, author and college president in Danville.

I think my best work for the Master was done through the war. Until 1863 when I was commissioned as Chaplain, I was under the S.S. and Colportage Board of which Rev. A. E. Dickinson of Richmond was Superintendent. He was my warm personal friend and I was greatly indebted to him for many favors. I continued with my regiment until the surrender April 9th, 1865 at Appomattox and was paroled by General Grant. I remained in camp there until Thursday morning, and then I went with some of my men to Danville and that neighborhood and spent some two or three weeks, then returned horseback to my home at Mr. Wilkinson's at Amelia, hoping to renew my pleasant relations with my betroth, Miss Mary, his daughter. But the excitement of the close of the war and the unsettled condition of the people brought about certain changes in my plans I may revert to later on. There are many incidents that occurred during the war which may be of interest to my dear children, who perhaps will be the only ones who read these pages. During our encampment below Chester Station in Chesterfield County, Virginia we had our hospital at Chester and I spent part of my time there with the sick. While there, one afternoon, I saw two pretty young ladies get off the train from Richmond and as no one met them, I offered my services. They were Misses Mary and Annie Burgess, whose home was in the hands of the enemy near the Hundreds and they were then living above Chester about seven or eight miles. They missed connection with the Clover Hill train and had no way to get home. I placed them at the agent's house and rode up to their father's and had a servant bring a carriage for them. As it was then dark, I went with them and spent the night at their home and there began a friendship with Miss Mary and myself of which I will speak later. Of course, there are many things which happened while on these lines of much interest, but I will mention but a few. Having remained with my regiment through all the dangers, they wished to express their appreciation and some friend raised in the Regiment and Brigade, $1,200. with which they bought me a nice horse, saddle and bridle as a present, which I most highly valued and kept them until some time after the war. My men were very kind to me. I believe God greatly blessed my labor as their Chaplain.

Once the chaplains like Cridlin went off to war, they faced all of the experiences of camp life from imminent battle to the boredom of seemingly endless garrison duty, as was the case for Chap. James M. Campbell of the 1st Georgia Infantry. His first assignment was to the forces at Pensacola, Florida, opposite Union-held Fort Pickens. It was a position that was rather like the old jokes about the vice presidency—everything in potentiality, and nothing in reality. The war could have started either at Pensacola or Charleston. Confederate authorities chose the latter, and Fort Sumter, making Pensacola a permanent backwater. Still, as Campbell's April 27, 1861, letter to his sister reveals, a chaplain in this war would find that no place was a backwater to his God. Campbell's letters were published as Civil War Letters of James McDonald Campbell *by Edmond Lee Rice in a limited edition for family and friends, a copy of which is in the holdings of the Georgia Department of Archives and History.*

Warrington, Fla.
Saturday night April 27th/61

My Dear Sister,

I wrote you a note a few days since, but as I am thinking of home, I will write again. It is now nine o'clock at night, and all without is dark, except the frequent flashes of lightning that are followed by more intense darkness. The monotony of the falling rain is broken by the artillery of heaven that proclaims the power of "Our Father". There is nothing that recalls the scenes of home and home scene more than the flashing lightning and pattering rain. How well I remember the days of yore, when I sat quietly on the door sill, and watched the serpentine light as it streamed across the wilkin, then waited in silent awe, for the sound of nature's note then touched by nature's God. And as the house jarred around me, I wondered what kind of being God was, and how our little sisters and brothers looked in heaven, and if there were any clouds there. Now I think of heaven as a place where there is no clouds and not only the home of two little brothers and a sister, but two sisters and our dear father. Oh may we all who are left join them. I find I have filled a page with my musing, enough of that now.

I have told you this is a dark night and I believe I told you in a former letter that I pass two or three sentinels between my boarding home and my room. This being a dark night and expecting rain every moment, I hastened to my room and that I might not blunder on a sentinel, I kept up as much noise as convenient by clearing my throat and spitting. Having reached my "sanctum" and lit a lamp, I walked to the door and looked out upon the darkness, when a bright flash of lightning revealed a beautiful boquet, I picked it up and coming to the light found the flowers fresh and wet with the falling rain. Attached was a note which read thus, "From a friend, keep it near your heart." How I should keep it near my heart, I did not understand.

You want to know something about the war, well I can't tell you much more about it. As soon as one battery is completed, another is commenced, Gen Bragg is a sort of battery miser, but I suppose he will stop when he has enough. If we are not attacked in ten days we will be inpregnable. Let us pray to the God of battles for victory, and for the souls of our army. Pray for me, I am trying to save souls. Good night.

Your brother

James

Sooner or later, of course, almost all Confederate chaplains would see action, and then inevitably came surely the most painful and disagreeable duty of all; notifying the next of kin of a loved one's death. In the course of the war a chaplain might have to do so hundreds of times, knowing that each letter to a parent or wife was a unique document of pain and suffering, however similar it might be to all the others he had to write. Victorians had well-defined expectations of death and how it should be remembered, and the chaplains were quite sensitive to what families wanted to hear. Above all, they always made certain, as did George B. Overton of the 2nd Kentucky Infantry, that the bereaved knew that faith was uppermost in the dying man's thoughts before he made the greatest journey.

Overton's letter that follows appeared in the 1917 Annual Conference Minutes of the Louisville, Kentucky, Conference of the Methodist Episcopal Church, South, published in Louisville in 1918.

Camp Near Murfreesboro, Tenn.,

December 13, 1862.

Mr. and Mrs. Maddox—*Dear Sir and Madam:* It is my painful duty to announce to you the death of your son, Thomas Maddox, a sergeant of Second Kentucky Regiment.

He was killed in the battle of Hartsville, December 7, 1862. One ball entered his arm, another his breast, and a third his mouth, which being partly opened did not in the least disfigure his face.

I have known Tom well and intimately ever since he entered the army. I never knew a better boy nor one whom I loved more. The contamination of camp life never reached his pure and lofty spirit. I never knew him to do a wrong. I never heard him speak an unkind word. He lived in the fear of God and kept his commandments.

He was as brave as the bravest, and a smile of heavenly sweetness rested on his countenance in death.

As sure as the Bible is true and religion a divine reality, his spirit rests with the sacramental host of God's elect. I bid you not sorrow as those who have no hope, for he shall live again when the light of the resurrection morn illumines the earth. Death shall restore him immortal. May this blessed hope console your hearts in your sad bereavement! May the God of all grace comfort your hearts as only he can!

Yours respectfully,
G. B. Overton,
Sometime Chaplain Second Kentucky,
Now a Lieut. of Co. E.

Then came battle itself. In the Special Collections Department of the Robert W. Woodruff Library, at Emory University, resides the wartime diary of Charles J. Oliver, and in it he gave brief yet graphic descriptions of his experiences on the battlefields of Lee's Army of Northern Virginia. Here he confronts the horrors of a battle on a Sunday, in the turmoil of Chancellorsville in May 1863.

May 1st, 1863

I look out from this position (to which we were ordered this morning at day break) upon beautiful meadows fertilized with blood, upon the distantly pretty but unhappy town of Fredericksburg. In front a balloon hangs over the Yankee camp & on the left over the battlefield, as [we] have our hopes rise and fall with ever[y] thunder shock of artillery, hangs poised like an eagle another of these aerial spies.

Who will tell us what a day will bring forth? But I think there is bloody work to do.

Waiting for a fray near Fredericksburg, Va May 7th /63

I fear that I cannot now recall in their proper order the events of the past few days. War is such a strange thing. Here we are gay, careless, jocular, yesterday we ran for our lives across this very field, while death dealing shot were sweeping over its hills. Today some of us laid the shattered remains of our brave comrade T. E. Dillard in a soldier's grave; at this moment though the sun shines so brightly, & the breeze kisses our cheeks so kindly; yet are we now in the midst of a great terrible battle. The roar of cannon & rattle of musketry tell that the work of death is going on. Sun 3rd Up before light & were soon banging away. There was some sharp work our boys singularly cool & brave. The double fight & double flight are over, & I am yet alive—unhurt. It seems almost strange. Why did I not fall with body cut in two, heart pierced, or brains dashed out? Surely God's hand was over me. The dread of entering into these fearful scenes increases with their repition [sic] so my coolness & skill—I had almost said pleasure—in the fight increases. I think we left the breastwork about eleven o'clock and in fifteen minutes were in position at Leaches. I could not from my position see the enemy. I was cooler than in the other engagement for I was absorbingly employed nevertheless I heard every shell that howeled [sic] over my head. My own piece was checked and withdrawn. I think I must have been getting ammunition for the howitzer when Tom Dillard was shot. I did not see any of the wounded but W. J. whose cries attracted my attention as I caught sight of Dillard's mutilated form—not then knowing where it was—I should have gone to him but for J. The pouring forth of whose gratitude would bribe me to walk quietly thro any iron storm. All this day I have been oppressed with the thought that it was the Sabbath. After helping Jennings with the horse sent for him I called at Mr. Owen's house. They were all packed up & ready to move & soon passed us on the road going they knew not whither. Poor people of Fredericksburg first attacked by the furay [sic] of one army and then another. Now between the two houses riddled with shot, fences burnt, ground trampled down, roads obliterated, and woods consumed. I am sorry for you & your abounding hospitality does you infinite credit—Miss T. has a sweet face lofty, preposs[ess]ing, and kind. A dull evening—a hard bed & a cold night, closed the history of this memorable day.

A few weeks later in June 1863, on the eve of the Gettysburg campaign, Chaplain Oliver and his unit, the 2nd Georgia Infantry, passed by the Chancellorsville battleground, making him muse yet again on fate and war.

Culpeper

We passed Chancel[l]orsville This morning—were too much hurried and wearied to see, that is, examine much. Saw the smoked walls of Mayor Slaughters new bought mansion and in it the charred bones of some of these who were burnt in it, some say the number was large I think not though.

Feet and hands without owners were still lying about. Some of our men going to the back of the house found a dry well, perhaps ice-house which had filled with Yankee dead and slightly covered up with earth an exhalation like smoke was rising from it. I am tired but have suffered nothing from the march. Camped within 2 miles of Raccoon ford.

Moved up a little and cooked rations.

Started late. crossed the ford—halted and waited sometime in the road showers of rain falling—at length moved on Took the right near Culpeper camped at Stevensburg.

7th Got underweigh early—passed through Culpepper and taking the left proceeded a few miles along the Winchester road halted and unpacked the wagons—had scarcely done so when orders came to return. The impression obtained that we were going to meet the enemy—we returned to the vicinity of C. and after much circumlocution camped at last in a place as little desirable as any other place in any other field.

Held prayer meeting with the Howitzers.

8th Have slept half the day. Large bodies of troops are passing up the Winchester road. I want to moove again. Afternoon. In the graveyard at C[ulpeper].

How quiet! How calm! Death around me but how different from the battlefield! If I should survive the war the prospect of death will seem more sweet than ever but I do shrink from the mutilation of the battlefield and the ditch in which my body may be thrown away from the cherished spot where my loved ones sleep.

Almost inevitably, more chaplain accounts survive from Gettysburg itself than any other engagement of the war. Charles Oliver was there, and yet like so many others, for him the greater horrors came after the battle, during the long retreat to Virginia with trains of wounded and an army shocked by defeat.

Sunday June 28th 1863
Marched at 9 am passin through Chambersburg where we met sour faces tho some of them were pretty Two miles beyond we halted and remained there all day—a cheerless sky—a dirty camp—a sleepy crowd—and a dull time generally Nevertheless we had a prayer meeting at night. Mailed a letter to father.

Mon 29 Marched eastward to Fayetteville halted 6 miles Just beyond remained all day—very showry weather—could not stay in camp tho. Saw some fine farming country and saw, I am sorry to say, abundant evidence that many of our men are base as any Yankees, threatening, plundering, etc.

Wed July 1st We started toward Gettysburg at 1 pm. I had spent the morning, as the previous afternoon, in rambling about the country—got an old dutch woman to make some bread for the mess, which tasted better than it looked. We passed thro a gap in the South Mountains (Blue Ridge) by the Caledonia iron works which had been destroyed by our cavalry—Began about this time hearing firing in front—proceeded through Cashtown and camped late in the night 4 miles from Gettysburg

Thurs 2nd Up soon after daylight—sat by the roadside and watched Hood's division pass

Went over the N.C. hospital saw many horrid sights and much enduring courage—We saw but little indications of the fight. After halting a while we passed at double quick round the town some three miles beyond and there went into position The battalion was along the crest of a hill The firing was very warm N. Hemphill was badly wounded he staggered down toward the limber with his life clasped in his hands poor fellow I hope he will recover but don't expect it.

Late in the afternoon our division charged the battery I was anxious to see it but could not They drove the enemy from his position and took three guns in the orchard to our left Hood also took three guns I do not know that any others were taken having been separated from the guns when they moved I wandered down the pike conversing with our wounded men—went to Kershaws hospital and sent after some of L's wounded then went up to the position of the yankee batteries axcessioned [sic] a forsaken limber counted half a dozen dead Yankees lying round found one poor fellow number one at his piece who had been shot in the back while spunging [sic] out his gun. The air bubbled thro the wound with every inspiration of his breath I gave him some water picked up some blankets and made him a bed and pillow poor fellow blessed me and I gave him some good advice (I believe many of these poor fellows perished from neglect between the armies) I picked a couple horses—but in a tale full of furys—helped to plunder a yankee house and after many adventures found myself at daylight within two hundred yards of the battery not having closed my eyes during the night.

Fri 3rd This is a day long to be remembered early in the misty morning we went into position a mile to the front and left our former position. We were not fired upon in going in but in shifting position shortly afterwards they either fired upon us or a battery going in behind us tearing those to pieces killing Hop Adams and stunning McConnell. (I was but too gay over my breakfast with death so near a [——]

Detail was digging the grave for poor Adams. All the morning the drivers were digging them pits subject of the joke then and congratulation afterwards. In the afternoon pickets division came in and formed in line of battle. Just below our guns soon afterward the batteries opened. There was in round numbers 100 guns in each side and firing was terrific probably there never was such firing of field artillery before in the world's history of war

Gettysburg (continued)

It seems strange that such a storm should leave a single survivor, but by God's grace most of us escaped. I was knocked down at the caisson together with Hill Swan but I was able immediately to resume my work. The shell cut of[f] a horses leg near the caisson and I had to shoot him. Our ammunition was nearly exhausted I had to get out the damaged shell from our rear chest. Then strip the second caisson transfer what remained in it to ours and then sent it to the rear for more. Late in the afternoon when the firing was slack Capt Carlton was knocked down by something too much spent to hurt the flesh but it did break his arm above the elbow. It made him very sick we carried him down to the stone wall and I mounted a horse and went in search of some spirits. The first surgeon I found gave it to me grudgingly and I rode back a mile through the dying and wounded of Pickets division a ghastly procession—met the Cap. and Lieu. Jennings, shot in the knee, The pieces had moved forwarded. I believe it was the proudest moment of my life. I realized the danger—thought it doubtful I should live to recross the hill but commending my soul to God I ascended the hill at an easy trot and when I reached the crest and saw the flash of the guns on the other hill I sang and shouted with delight. I[f] I was ever proud of being a member of the Troop Artillery, it was then Tho there was but few of them there.

Our guns had ceased firing when I reached them, and the enemy fired only occasionally. By order of Gen. Lee we remained there till after nightfall and some skirmishers were advanced to our line—

—At this point in my narrative I was summoned by Orderly Hughes To the battlefield once more, from the hospitable house of Mrs. Fiery upon whom and Laura and Jennie and Linda may God's blessing rest for they are all Kind, The soldiers friends.

[July, 1863]

In Camp Bunker Hill July 17th

And now, having past through greater sufferings than the battle ever brot to me, I resume my account. I was weary I could have fought on but I was too tired to be idle I lay upon the ground and slept. When it was dark we mooved off the caissons without interruption, Thence to the vicinity of Pitzers house and parked again in the clover field.

Sat 4th It began to rain in the morning and was a miserable day—went to Pitzers house, thoroughly dismantled now, and there spent the day Went to the camp after dark and lay down but we were soon roused and hurried across the run with strange pricipitancy [sic]. Then camped again in the tall wet grass. I don't think I had got to sleep before we were ordered off again my old yankee horse had been turned loose by order and I had to tramp it through the mud—It was pitch dark raining a little mud over the shoes—marched or halted in the road all night.

Sun 5th Passed thru Millerstown (I think) soon after began to ascend The South Mountain The weather had improved a little—could see artillery firing in our rear long after night fall wearied and worn out we reached the summit of the mountain where we found a large hotel "Monterey house" and camped round it I got into the piazza and slept there.

Mon 6th Started late passed thru Frogtown reached Hagerstown about dark all was excitement on account of the cavalry fight they had just had in the streets—helped to put a dead man in the engine house—went down to Miss Claggett's sat in piazza and told her of the Captains mishap—went down to camp near the old place.

Tu 7th Started early with H. to visit Ms. Fiery—found that our camp was on their farm—were kindly received—got a good breakfast and some fowls cooked and as the battery did not move stayed dinner also poor Mrs. F. was nearly run to death and giving away everything she had

July

Wed 8th Still at the same place—done a little work today Took tea with Mrs. F. and two or three of us spent the evening with Laura had some music and enjoyed ourselves.

Thurs 9th Have been busy today done all my washing and some things for W. H. straightened up his Knapsack and mine. Bathed and went down with K. & F. in the evening to see Laura again passed the time pleasantly.

Fri 10th Firing began early this morning in the direction of Funkstown packed up and harnessed about noon I was at Fiery's house writing up my Journal when news came that the battery was mooving My leave taking was brief—how uncertain is a soldiers life—I thought I should see them again. I followed the battery down toward Funkstown. we were there but a few minutes when we were sent to join Woffords brigade—travelled 6 or 7 miles very rapidly, the heat was very oppressive—Took position near St. James College 3 miles from Williamsport 8 from Sharpsburg watched the scirmishers [sic] all the evening Slept hard having no blanket Two of Manly's one of Frazier's men were killed today We learn that Cap Frazier is dead. Sergeant Dunn was taken prisoner and Lieu Payne had a narrow escape

Sat 11th Have just awakened from a sweet refreshing sleep on the stone wall. Our men are fortifying here—visited the house of Mr. Brothod *secesh*. The heat is oppressive beyond anything I ever experienced. It has been altogether one of the moast weary days of my life but this evening I found relief in gathering blue berries and a plentiful supply of cherries. Took a walk about dark—

Chaplain Francis M. Kennedy of the 28th North Carolina Infantry was also at Gettysburg, and left an even more fulsome diary account of what he saw and felt, from the time Lee's army crossed into Pennsylvania until its retreat brought it back through Maryland on the way home. A typescript of Chaplain Kennedy's diary is in the George Department of Archives and History.

Saturday, June 27th
Passed the Pennsylvania line about 1 mile from last night's camps. Policy prevents many of these people from looking as sour as they did in Maryland. Passed through Waynesboro and purchased with Confederate money a number of things I needed. I felt that they were taking the money more a[s] a "military necessity" then because they liked to. The next village we passed was Quincy, then Funkstown. This country abounds in villages, in fact we seem to be passing through one continuous village all the time. The farms are in a perfect state of cultivation, and the wheat which seems to be the main crop, is vastly superior to any I have ever seen before. Timothy grass and clover grow luxuriantly and our horses are indeed "in clover". I have gotten my horse's back sore and I fear I will have trouble with it. We are camped about 1 1/2 miles from Funkstown near a fine clover field in a large oak grove.

Sunday, June 28th
The orders are that we remain where we are today and that the men wash their clothes and clean their guns. We learned this morning that the

men committed many depredations yesterday afternoon and last night, going to houses and taking whatever they could lay their hands upon. Such practice, intrinsically wrong and indefensible will, I fear, unless promptly stopped, so demoralize the army as to bring disaster upon it. Stringent orders from Gen'l. Lee have just been published which it is to be hoped will arrest the evil. Most of our men were on Picket this morning, and those left in camp were busy washing, cleaning their guns so that I could not preach until afternoon, when I addressed a pretty good congregation from I John 2nd Ch., 17th Verse. I took occasion to talk plainly to them on the subject to taking what did not belong to them from unarmed inhabitants of the country. A mail came to the Brigade today and almost everybody got a letter but me.

Monday, June 29th

We had orders to march at 5 o'clock this morning, and ate our breakfast about 4 o'clock, when we were instructed to wait for further orders before moving. In the afternoon we were ordered to be ready to move at a moment's warning, send cooking utensils back to the wagons, return rations, etc., and then about the time this order was complied with, another came revoking it and ordering the rations for three days to be cooked. There is some excitement, but none of us know what it is. Bennick held service for me this evening. Our foraging parties do very well getting provisions, but are very unsuccessful about horses. The people have driven off their . . . horses that have been gotten are in the main very inferior. Yesterday we learned "Bushwhackers" captured a party of 20 Artillery-men with their horses, who were out searching for horses—this was rather a losing trip on our side.

Tuesday, June 30th

We left our camp near Funkstown at 5 o'clock this morning and marched 12 miles, turning off from the road to Chambersburg which we thought was our destination, and taking the turnpike toward Gettysburg. On the road we passed the smouldering ruins of extensive iron works, the property of the notorious Abolitionist Thaddeus Stephens, which had been totally destroyed by order of Gen' l. Ewell. This man Stephens was the author of "Yankees' Confiscation Bill" and preparer of the plan of colonizing the South with free negroes, illustrating his theory, I believe by a practical experiment in that portion of Florida which is held by the Yankees. The only unpleasant feature about the destruction of the property is that a considerable number of operators are left without employment. But upon inquiry among them I learned there was no danger of women and children suffering. We have today crossed the Blue Ridge Mountains.

Wednesday, July lst, 1863

Left our camp in the mountainside and marched towards Gettysburg. Passed Graffenburg Springs, Cashtown and New Salem. When we reached the last named place we could hear the sound of battle. Cannonading and musketry. In the course of a few miles we came in sight of the battle, and from a commanding position, I for the first time, *saw* a battle in actual process. Our Division was at once formed in line of battle and advanced. Only two Brigades of Pender's Division became engaged during today—Scales and McGowan's—and they suffered severely. Heth's Division first encountered the enemy, and bore the brunt of the fight, so far as our part of the field was concerned. Our Reg't. had six or eight men wounded, two of them severely. We have driven the enemy several mile[s] and the City of Gettysburg which was stoutly defended by the enemy is occupied tonight by Rhodes' Division of Ewell's Corps.

Thursday, July 2nd

Rode over the battle-field and witnessed some hideous scenes, the most revolting of which were two men torn in two by a shell with their heads turned completely back upon their heels. The morning passed off quietly, save continual firing between the skirmished and an occasional shell. I rode into town and saw some of my friends of Ramseur's Brigade.

About 3 o'clock or 4 the most fearful cannonading of which I ever conceived commenced. The earth fairly shook with the explosions of the guns. The enemy occupied a position of great strength. Longstreet attacked their left about 4 o'clock and Ewell their right. Hill attacked them in the center. The fighting has been fearful, and we have no means of ascertaining tonight the result of the conflict, but we all feel confident of success. Gen'l Pender was disabled this afternoon by a shell wound on the thigh, not serious. Gen'l. Lane is now commanding Pender's Division, and Col. Avery our Brigade.

Friday, July 3rd, 18[6]5

We learned this morning that our success would have been complete but for the bad conduct of Posey's Brigade last night, which gave way, causing a panic, which resulted in the falling back of the whole line. Today a general attack was made on the enemy's position, resulting in a failure to dislodge them and a fearful loss on our side, what it was on the side of the enemy, we don't know. Our Brigade suffered very heavily, my Regiment losing a great many in killed and wounded. I occupied an eminence upon which Gen'l. Lee was stationed, from which I had a very good view of the battle. The cannonading was fearful—the scene terribly sublime. I rode my horse this afternoon trying to find a new hospital which was established today. By some means the Medical Department was badly managed today causing a good deal of unnecessary pain and trouble to the wounded.

Saturday, July 4th

I slept but little last night being very busy with the wounded who were brought in by scores. Our Brigade suffered heavily, as indeed did the entire army. The enemy had an impregnable position, and we attempted to storm it, charging *one mile and a half* over an open field right in the face of scores of cannons. The men came within a few yards of the enemy's entrenchment but had to fall back for want of men enough to hold them. This day's work is *the mistake* of the campaign and it will be well for us if our repulse does not grow into our disaster. Our wounded were all moved 3 miles back and, while there was no fighting, everything looked like a retrograde movement. This afternoon all the slightly wounded, and such others as transportation could be provided for were started back in the direction of Cashtown. The Division Commissary and Quartermaster trains have also gone that way. About sundown we received orders to start with the medical train in an hour by another road.

Sunday, July 5th

I was in the saddle all last night, and in a pouring rain, thoroughly wet all night. Our progress was greatly impeded by the multitude of troops, artillery and wagons along the road, so that when we stopped about 8 o'clock this morning, on this side of a little village called Fairfield, we had only traveled about 8 miles. I was quite sick when we started last night, the road was exceedingly rocky and muddy, my horse had one shoe off, and everything conspired to render it the most *disagreeable night* I ever spent. I had my feelings sorely tried when telling the officers and other men good-bye who were so seriously wounded as to disqualify them for traveling. They will necessarily fall into the . . . near Fairfield until about 1 o'clock and then started forward on our backward course. It has rained on us most of the day. Late this evening we heard cannonading, front and rear, indicating that the enemy has discovered our withdrawal from their front and were also disputing our passage through the Blue Ridge.

Monday, July 6th

Passed a very unpleasant night. Didn't travel very far, but was in the saddle nearly the whole night, not knowing when the train stopped, but it would be in motion again in a moment. We were crossing the Blue Ridge and the road was I think, the most rugged I ever passed over[.] My horse's bare foot made it extremely unpleasant riding. We reached the top of the Ridge this morning about 7½ o' clock and got a very good breakfast at a mountain farm. One of the girls was quite spicy in her chat with some of the boys, indicating pretty plainly that she thought we had been badly whipped and were afraid of meeting the Yankees again. In company with Drs. Holt, Higgenbotham and Mayo, I rode on to the camping ground of the troops. Found our Regiment with 100 men. At 3 o'clock we commenced marching in company with the troops, passed through Waynesboro and camped within a mile or two of Hagerstown. But few of the people showed themselves as we went *forward* through Waynesboro. As we came *back*, we saw the whole population.

Tuesday, July 7th

Started early this morning and marched a few miles, going into camp about 1½ miles this side of Hagerstown. I understand that we stopped so soon for the fact that the recent rains have made the Potomac *too deep for fording*. I rode into Hagerstown hoping to make some purchases but the place was crowded with soldiers and the stores all guarded by sentinels. I am informed that stores were broken open this morning and robbed. Gen'l. Lee is trying hard to prevent incidents of that sort but I am sorry to say he has not been successful. If we meet with disaster before getting back upon our own soil, it will be a Providential visitation for the misconduct of the men. I have tried to do my duty in preventing such misdemeanors, and I think in our Reg't. there was less of it than in most commands. I held services tonight with the small remnant of the 28th which is left. It was a melancholy service to me, and the men seemed to feel very sad.

For those Confederate chaplains who saw service through to the end of the war, the shock of defeat and surrender was just as great as it was for the soldiers to whom they ministered. Having labored for so long with helping the men sustain their morale and composure in the face of hardship and death, some of the chaplains could no longer keep their own when confronted by the end. Chaplain A. D. Betts of the 30th North Carolina kept a sparse diary in which he vented his anguish, first at news of Lee's surrender, and then even more with the surrender of his own Army of Tennessee in North Carolina several weeks later. In 1904 his son W. A. Betts edited and privately published his father's diary as Experience of a Confederate Chaplain, 1861–1864. *A copy now resides in the Woodruff Library at Emory University.*

March 25 [1865]—Brigade moves and I start home on "leave." It was my last furlough, though I had no idea that I was to see the soldiers and Chaplains no more. How tender would have been the leave-taking, if I had known it was my last sight of those with whom I had been so long associated.

March 26 (Sunday)—Heard Rev. Christian preach at Clay Street in Richmond in a. m., and start to N. C. at 6 p.m. It was the last sermon I was to hear in Va. during the war. All night on the railroad.

March 27—Get to Durham and spend night.

March 28—Reach home and find all well. How happy to be with my wife and little ones. My oldest son had but lately given his heart to God and joined the Church.

March 31—Ride thirty miles horseback and spend night with my brother, A. N. Betts.

April 1, '65—Walk five miles to see my mother in the home of Allen Betts. Visited sister Jane Betts, widow of my brother, Andrew, who was captured as captain of his company on R. Island in 1862, and reached home on parole to die. He took his eldest son with him. He died in prison. Spent night with C. H. Cofield, who was my guardian for ten years of my boyhood.

April 2 (Sunday)—Preach at Myatt's schoolhouse. Spend night with my youngest brother, Archibald. "When shall I see my mother again?" Those words were written with the expectation of returning to Lee's Army in a short time.

April 3—Return to Chapel Hill with sick horse. Spent week at home gardening. Receive bacon and lard I had bought on the Harnett line, thirty miles away. Hurrying up to be ready to return to the Army.

April 9 (Sunday)—Heard Brother Willson preach. During this week heard that Lee had surrendered! Sad news. Johnston's Army passed through Chapel Hill. We knew Sherman would soon be in. I did not wish to meet him. I told some of my friends I was going with Gen. Johnston's Army. Rev. Dr. Charles Phillips tenderly told me to go on and my friends would take care of my family. After midnight I kissed my wife and children and mounted a mule and rode away, thinking I might not see them in months or years. I rode all night, crossing Haw river, overtook Johnston's Army, and reported to Brig. Gen. Hoke, who assigned me to duty as Chaplain to 17th N. C. Regt. We camped a few miles from Greensboro for two or three days till we heard we were to be surrendered. I rode to Greensboro one day and met Rev. Dr. John B. McFerrin of Nashville, Tenn., at the home of good Mrs. F. M. Bumpass. The night following the tidings of our contemplated surrender was a still, sad night in our camp. Rev. W. C. Willson, the Chapel Hill pastor, was with us. We had preached a few times in that camp; but that night we made no effort to get the men together. In little, sad groups they softly talked of the past, the present and the future. Old men were there, who would have cheerfully gone on, enduring the hardship of war, and protracted absence from their families, for the freedom of their country. Middle aged men were there, who had been away from wives and children for years, had gone through many battles, had lost much on their farms or stores or factories or professional business; but would that night have been glad to shoulder the gun and march forward for the defense of their "native land". Young men and boys were there, who loved their country and were unspeakably sad at the thought of the failure to secure Southern Independence.

Rev. W. C. Willson and I walked out of the camp and talked and wept together. As I started back to my tent—to my mule and saddle, I should say, for I had no tent—I passed three lads sitting close together, talking softly and sadly. I paused and listened. One said, "It makes me very sad to think of our surrendering." Another said, "It hurts me worse than the thought of battle ever did." The third raised his arm, clenched his fist and seemed to grate his teeth as he said, "I would rather know we had to go into battle tomorrow morning." There was patriotism! There may have been in that camp that night generals, colonels and other officers who had been moved by a desire for worldly honor. Owners of slaves and of lands may have hoped for financial benefit from Confederate success. *But these boys felt they had a country that ought to be free!* I wish I had taken their names. And I wonder if they still live. They are good citizens, I am sure.

Next day I mounted my mule and started to Chapel Hill, intending to surrender there. I took along a negro servant and horse for a friend. At sunset we met an old man at his spring near his house. I politely asked to be permitted to spend the night on his land. He objected. I said, "Boy, take off our saddles and halter our horses." The farmer quickly said, "If you will stay, come up to the house." I slept on his porch.

My First Interview with a Federal Soldier on Duty

I had seen many of them dead, wounded, or prisoners. Near Chapel Hill one rode up to my side. The Blue Coat and the Grey chatted softly and sparingly. He kindly offered to show me the way to headquarters. I thanked him and told him I would ride to my house and see my family and report myself later. The town was full of Federals. Each home had a guard detailed by the commanding General. My guard was a faithful, modest fellow. In due time I called at headquarters and was paroled.

A Yankee Chaplain Remembers

William R. Eastman

On December 13, 1911, New Yorker William R. Eastman addressed members of the New York Commandery of the Military Order of the Loyal
*Legion of the United States, a veterans' organization of former Union officers,
and looked back half a century on his days as an army chaplain. His words were,
as one would expect after such a passage of time, reflective, somewhat romantic,
and almost wholly lacking the horror they might have revealed if written within
months of his war service. Yet they are representative of the Union chaplains'
experiences as a whole, and moreover of their attitude toward their service in after
years. Chaplain Eastman's recollections were published as "The Army Chaplain
of 1863,"* in Personal Recollections of the War of the Rebellion, *published in
1912 by the New York Commandery of the Military Order of the Loyal Legion of
the United States.*

One Sunday afternoon in May, 1861, I was at a recruiting station in this
city at the Assembly Rooms, so called, on Broadway near Grand Street.
Men were being enrolled for the first two regiments of the Excelsior Brigade
and some five hundred were paraded by companies. Their commander, General Sickles, said to them, "Men, I have called you up to present your chaplains who now stand before you, the Rev. Dr. Buckley of the first regiment
and the Rev. Dr. Twichell of the second. They represent," he said, "the great
Commander. Respect them. They are good men and they will do you good.
You will do well to heed their teachings." Each chaplain, thus introduced,
spoke in a few short ringing sentences holding up the fear of God as presenting a soldierly ideal which, when attained, would make it quite unnecessary
to fear either man or devil.

The name chaplain is significant. He is the *chapel* man. He does not need a church. Gothic arches, pulpits, robes, high altars, choirs, responses are without meaning in his work. He is a man who can take with him a great consciousness of the divine presence and speak and act in view of that in any place and in any emergency. It is of the essence of his service that he is always there and always ready. Moving with the column, exposed to heat and storm, sharing every privation, not very far from the battle line, wherever a man, with hurt or pain, may chance to need his help, that spot is his chapel and there he must minister.

In the first order issued by the Adjutant-General of New York, April 18, 1861, naming the officers of volunteers, chaplains are not mentioned. An order of May 1st says that a chaplain shall be appointed for each regiment by the Commander-in-Chief, that is, by the governor, on nomination by the field-officers. An order of the United States War Department, May 4, 1861, gives the full plan for organizing the volunteer force. The chaplain is not named among the regimental officers, but in a memorandum dealing with miscellaneous matters such as musicians and a sutler, etc., the order adds, "There shall be allowed to each regiment one chaplain appointed by the regimental commander on vote of the field-officers and company commanders . . . who shall be a regularly ordained minister of some Christian denomination." This language, for substance, was copied afterwards in state orders. It fixes the standing of the chaplain as an "allowance." The War Department, July 13, 1861, ordered that "Chaplains of volunteers be duly mustered into the service in the same manner as prescribed for commissioned officers." This implies that they were not officers and might not be commissioned; although they certainly were commissioned afterward.

An Act of Congress, approved July 22, 1861, repeats the above provisions for appointment, provides that a chaplain's pay shall be that of a captain of cavalry, bringing then about $1400 a year, and adds this as to his duties. "He shall be required to report to the Colonel commanding, at the end of each quarter, the moral and religious condition of the regiment" (a truly serious task) "and such suggestions as may conduce to the social happiness and moral improvement of the troops." This provision of the law explains, with reasonable clearness, the popular impression of the purpose of a chaplain to promote "social happiness and moral improvement."

The chaplain's uniform of plain black "without ornament" was prescribed by an order of November 25, 1861. The appointment of hospital chaplains by the President was authorized by Act of May 20, 1862. After July 17, 1862, a chaplain could not be mustered without credentials and recommendation from an ecclesiastical body or from five ministers in good standing. In an order of July 26, 1862, we read this: "The principle being recognized that chaplains should not be held as prisoners of war, it is hereby ordered that all chaplains so held be immediately and unconditionally discharged." This defines the character of a chaplain as a non-combatant, entitled to the privileges and subject to the obligations of such a position.

It was not strange that in the general confusion of the first few months of recruiting, some regiments were accompanied to the field by theological students not yet ordained or even by nominal chaplains, friends of the colonel, who did not even profess to be religious men. But, with duties undefined it was left to each to make the most of his opportunity. And what more could any man ask?

Colonel Higginson, in writing a memorial of Chaplain Fuller, says that the position of chaplain is one in which "the majority of clergymen fail," and he adds, "In a little world of the most accurate order, where every man's duties and position are absolutely prescribed the chaplain alone has no definite position and no prescribed duties. In a sphere where everything is concentrated on one sole end, he alone finds himself of no direct use towards that end and apparently superfluous." He cannot succeed without both "moral energy and tact." And he puts it even more strongly in saying that "nine out of ten are useless."

Without regard to the regulations, there were certain qualifications for the chaplaincy of a most vital sort. It called for a *man*,—of a manly sort; of a kindly sympathetic spirit but not weak, of all things not weak, for that would be failure from the beginning; an intelligent man, but with an eye to read men as well as books, able to know a man when he saw him, whatever his clothes or his rank; a shrewd, discriminating, fair man; one to be trusted; having positive convictions but broad-minded, a man of faith with an enthusiasm for people in this world, laying more emphasis on life than doctrine; not lazy, but energetic and, withal, a man of an adventurous spirit, buoyant, cheerful, careless of hardship, a true comrade ready to stand by and to serve to the uttermost. For this is a place where personality alone will count.

The men who offered themselves for this service differed greatly in age, temperament, and power of adaptation as well as in church connections. Some were pastors expecting a short campaign; some I suppose were men out of a place seeking employment; some were students and some were assigned by their ecclesiastical superiors. Before many months had passed chaplains began to resign. The life was rough. The older men found it too hard. The tangible results were slight. In January, 1863, when I first knew the Army of the Potomac, half of the regiments had no chaplains and it was also true that nobody was very much concerned about it. As campaign followed campaign the regiments grew still smaller and one or two chaplains to a brigade were enough.

Now it was obviously impossible for any man to organize in any regiment a religious body who would look to him as their leader. A regiment with three fourths Roman Catholics was not unlikely to have a Protestant chaplain. A Methodist or a Baptist or an Episcopalian would be in camp with men who were decidedly not of his way of thinking. He might recite a collect on dress parade, but compulsory public worship was out of the question. He might invite the men to a Sunday service but who cared to come? He might bring around him a handful of men for Bible study and occasional worship, but they were few. So he was obliged to fall back upon a common humanity broader than denomination and look about to do kindnesses to individual men. It was his business, as it was his pleasure, to be on terms of cordial sympathy with them all. Received among officers as an equal, he was no less a friend of the humblest private. Any one had the right to claim his attention. Sometimes they would try to take advantage of him. I remember one fellow of a rather hard reputation who took occasion for a week or two to visit my tent daily and there bewail his many sins, falling upon his knees and praying the Lord to forgive him, and, of course, I kept hoping that this was real until he finally revealed his true purpose by saying that he needed a furlough and he thought that I could help him—if properly approached.

The chaplain would frequent the hospital, talk with the sick and write letters for them and get them delicacies from the Sanitary or Christian Commissions. When the paymaster came, the chaplain had express envelopes in which to send money home for the men. Any such office of kindness naturally fell to him.

At the same time preaching and prayer were not forgotten. On Sunday mornings a few men, twenty or thirty sometimes, would come to the Cook tent for service. On Sunday evenings a crowd would gather around a fire to sing hymns.

In the winter of '63 to '64, the Christian Commission lent a large canvas to cover any log chapel that might be built and there were several brigade chapels that winter near Brandy Station, each seating more than a hundred men. The men of the New York Engineer regiment built an elaborate and artistic log church in the works before Petersburgh. These chapels were occupied night after night not only for religious services, but also for lectures and entertainments. Visiting clergymen from the North often found sympathetic and deeply interested audiences.

The men who learned the church-going habit under camp conditions showed an uncommon earnestness. A church fellowship that looked forward to certain decimation in the first week of the coming campaign took their religion seriously. I recall one evening on which our chapel service had been led by a pastor well known in New York. Half an hour later I took him with me to a prayer-meeting in one of the company streets. The men were living in huts under shelter tents. Six men crowded a hut. Twenty more were packed close around the entrance. We went behind the tent and listened. The language of the prayers betrayed a rather rude simplicity, but they fairly burned with a flame of blood earnestness and my companion said to me, "If I could hear my Fifth Avenue saints praying like that, I should know that a great revival was coming in New York."

Of course there were occasions of a public character such as a holiday celebration or a flag raising when the chaplain would come to the front to speak, but usually he was in the background with a small following, waiting for the time when he would be wanted. That time came when the army marched and the battle was on. He was distinctly not a fighter and his place was not on the firing line; although I knew a chaplain who once was caught unexpectedly by an attack of the enemy while visiting his men, and deemed it better to stay behind a good breastwork than to retire; and then so forgot his place as to busy himself in loading rifles for the men, and singing "Rally round the flag, boys!" at the top of his voice.

But in battle, the chaplain had no orders and went where he could do the most good. He seemed naturally to belong with the doctors. He could render intelligent help in bandaging wounds and at the operating table, and his opportunity of service to individual sufferers was absolutely without limit. It was his hour of duty. Some of the surgeons were posted well up toward the front to give first aid. More of them were in the large field hospitals of division in more secure places at the rear. The chaplain might be at either place or at both by turns. Some made a point of watching for any wounded man who might come staggering back, who perhaps could be helped up into the saddle and ride back to the hospital. When the demand for help became urgent the chaplains were nurses. As the rows of wounded men grew longer, chaplains went from man to man to see what could be done to relieve their pain, perhaps to take a message or write a letter. All day and far into the night this work would continue. A drink of water, a

loosened bandage on a swollen limb, a question answered, a surgeon summoned, a whispered word of comfort marked their course. While surgeons
and nurses were busy and weary, the chaplains gleaned after them. Each
night at sundown the men who had died during the day were buried, with a
short prayer, side by side in one shallow common grave, each in his uniform
with canvas wrapped about his face and a strip of paper giving his name and
regiment in a bottle buttoned under his blouse.

It was my fortune, one week after the fight at Chancellorsville, to go
back to that field under a flag of truce with a considerable company of surgeons and nurses, taking a wagon load of medical stores. We had left 1200
wounded in the hands of the enemy who had no means to care for them
properly. When each disabled prisoner had given his parole, the other army
were as glad to give them back to us as we were to take them. Such a week
as the wounded had passed had brought on that condition of neglect, suffering, and despair which gives to war one of its peculiar horrors. A few of our
surgeons were among the prisoners, but they lacked supplies. One chaplain,
Thomas L. Ambrose of the 12th New Hampshire, had chanced to be caught
and left within the enemy's lines and had been busy, day and night, to the
limit of his strength, in nursing, preparing food, comforting, and serving in
every conceivable way. For six days we were all busy in the same fashion. At
Dowdall's Tavern, where Colonel Stevens of my own regiment died, the
floors of every room in the house were covered over with wounded men.
They were as closely laid on the piazzas, in the barns, sheds and out-build-
ings and on the grass of the door yard. Raw corn meal and bacon were the
only rations which had been furnished. They needed not only surgery and
medicine, but food and washing and clean shirts. The basin and towel
became again the Christian symbol. At length a more decent degree of bod-
ily comfort inspired new hope to some of them and our ambulances came to
carry the survivors across the river to their friends.

Many names occur to me of individual chaplains of whom it would be
pleasant to speak at length, did time permit: such as John Adams of Maine,
Alonzo Quint of Massachusetts, Henry Hopkins, President of Williams College, Henry Clay Trumbull of Connecticut, who served his country in several Confederate prisons, Charles McCabe of Ohio, captured at Winchester
and confined four months in Libby; who, to the end of his earnest life, wore
the popular and honorable title of Chaplain McCabe and we must not forget John Ireland, the great archbishop of Minnesota.

But permit me to take a moment to speak of one who fell on the skirmish line. Arthur Buckminster Fuller, Chaplain of the 16th Massachusetts,

came from a family distinguished in the literary circles of Cambridge and Concord, in which his older sister, Margaret Fuller, had been a brilliant light. He was a scholar as well as a preacher. His courage, enthusiasm, and sympathy for the men of his regiment had greatly endeared him to them.

He was older in years than the most of us, and the exposures of the field brought on a severe sickness which kept him three months at home in the summer of 1862. Twice he rejoined his regiment only to be sent back as an invalid. President Lincoln promised to appoint him chaplain of a hospital and he resigned his place in the regiment[.] Having received his discharge on the 10th of December and carrying the paper on his person he went down to the river where the first attempts to cross over into Fredericksburg were in progress. The sharpshooters were making it impossible to lay a bridge and a call was made for volunteers to cross in the pontoon boats. It came to him as one last chance to serve his country. True, he was no longer in the service. If taken prisoner, he was not liable to exchange; if he fell, his widow could claim no pension. He was unattached, but he was free. He found a rifle and cartridges and stepped into the boat. He passed the river, joined in the rush up the farther bank, and took his place in the skirmish line on the third street from the river. Captain Dunn of the 19th Massachusetts, who was in command of the line says, "He saluted me saying, 'I must do something for my country, what shall I do?' I replied that there was never a better time than the present and assigned him a place on my left. I thought that he could render valuable aid because he was perfectly cool and collected. I have seldom seen a person on the field so calm and mild in his demeanor, evidently not acting from impulse or mortal rage." It was but a few minutes before the bullet found its mark and he fell lifeless. He had borne his testimony. When the line was forced back, his body was left, and when later recovered all his valuables had been stolen. Congress afterward gave a special pension to his widow.

There were chaplains of all denominations, and the spirit of oneness among them would have seemed rather remarkable at home. When there were revivals and men wanted to join the Church they were taken into a Christian Brotherhood, leaving out for the time the ordinance of baptism, but partaking of the Lord's Supper together. I have the register of our Brigade Brotherhood now where I read the roll of seventy-eight men, some of whom fell upon the field within a month after they had in their full vigor signed their names to that agreement. We, who were Protestants, used to think that the Roman Catholic chaplains had some advantage in the firm grip they had upon their men. While I was calling one day on Father O'Hagan of the 4th

Excelsior (my regiment was the 3d), a couple of my men came to his door to
arrange for confession. He made an appointment for the next morning and
dismissed them with this plain message, "Tell your fellows in the 3d regiment
that if they don't come over for their Easter I shall be after them with a
stick." This vigorous way with men was used to good purpose by Father
Corby of the 88th New York at Gettysburg when, just as the Irish brigade,
what was left of them, formed in six companies, was ordered into action, the
good priest appeared before the line, motioned them to their knees and, in
one tense moment of devotion, pronounced absolution and the blessing of
the holy church upon such as should fall. Then they sprang to their feet and
drove home their impetuous charge. Whenever a sick man in the regimental
hospital asked for a priest, any chaplain would do his best to bring him, and
often Catholic and Protestant rode side by side at funerals. During the battle
at Spottsylvania I found in the field hospital a dying man who was anxious to
see a priest. Father O'Hagan was not with us then and I rode two miles
before I found Father Corby and urged him to return with me. "But," said he,
"there are fifty right here whose souls may be passing. I cannot leave them."
"Then what shall we do?" I asked. "Tell him to confess to you," was the
priest's answer, "and tell him that I said so and that whatever you say to him
or do for him is right." With this sacred commission I rode back in haste and
was in time to give the message as I kneeled upon the grass beside the dying
boy, listened to what he had to say, offered such comfort and hope as was
given me, and commended him in prayer into the keeping of our gracious
Lord. He seemed to be satisfied and presently the light faded from his eyes
and he was gone.

One can hardly fail to hear in the memory of such times the echo of
that fine classic of Miles O'Reilly:

> By communion of the banner
> Battle scarred but victor banner
> By the baptism of the banner
> Brothers of one church are we.

Chaplain Twichell tells a story of Father O'Hagan and himself. During
the first battle of Fredericksburg, when the wounded were being brought into
hospital in great numbers, they had been occupied all day and far into the
night in their hard and loving work. After midnight, when exhausted nature
demanded an hour of rest, these two lay down to sleep. It was December and
bitter cold. Presently there came a call out of O'Hagan's blanket, "Joseph,"

and the answer was "Well, Joseph." Their first names were alike. "I'm cold," said one and "I'm cold," said the other. "Then let's put our two blankets together." And so they did, lying close with blankets doubled. Presently there was a movement as of one struggling with suppressed laughter. "What are you laughing at?" demanded Twichell. "At this condition of things," was the reply. "What? at all this horrible distress?" "No! No! but at you and me; a Jesuit priest and a New England Puritan minister—of the worst sort— spooned close together under the same blanket. I wonder what the angels think." And, a moment after, he added, "I think they like it."

On long winter evenings when other topics failed, a favorite point of controversy between these two inseparable Josephs was as to the religious views of their commander of brigade, and of division and of corps, for one man had been all three. This was General Sickles and both the chaplains claimed him. When the general was hurt at Gettysburg the news reached Twichell at the field hospital behind Round Top whither he had just conveyed a wounded man. Springing to the saddle, the chaplain put spurs to his horse and dashed out toward the Trostle house, to get to his commander. Meeting an ambulance on the road, he called out, "Where's the general?" And the driver answered, "Inside."

Instantly checking his horse and turning back as soon as he could, he overtook the ambulance at last and, without ceasing his trot, lifted the curtain. Inside, in fact, lay the prostrate form of the general and another man, a figure in black was also there, kneeling beside him. It was Father O'Hagan in the act of administering the last rites of the Church Within the hour these friends stood side by side at the operating table, each with folded towel and by turns giving chloroform to the general while his leg was being cut away by the surgeons, and it was there that they noted from his lips the word that was thought at the time to be his dying message, that "in such a conflict, one man's life is not very much to give."

One evening, not long after, we were resting from the engrossing labors of the field hospital and to while away the time Twichell, O'Hagan, and I fell to talking over our pipes of the bright days when the war should be over. "I'll tell you," said Twichell, turning to me, "in about ten years from now you and I will step from the railway train, one bright summer afternoon, at a pretty village in central New York. Passing up the shady street we will ask where the Presbyterian minister lives, and will find a handsome cottage with a broad porch covered with vines and flowers and out on the lawn in front, two or three sweet little children will be playing. When we ring at the door there will come to meet us a tidy young woman with bright eyes, just the nicest that you can imagine, and I will say to her, "Good afternoon, Mrs. O'Hagan, is the Father at home?"

And O'Hagan cried out, "Tut, tut, boys, now you are tempting me."

He was a delightful companion and a true man. He held many positions of honor and importance after the war. Like another chaplain in the same brigade, he came to be a college president. He was at Holy Cross in Worcester. He has long since passed to his eternal reward.

But I must not dwell on personal recollections, though they may serve in one way or another to illustrate the lights and shadows of army life.

In one word, the significance of the chaplaincy was this: that the government offered to each regiment one man to be a friend to every man. While other officers might be good friends, this man was to make a business of kindliness. Not a commander, not a fighter, not hemmed in by any rules or any rank; left to himself to reach men by their hearts if he touched them at all, and by their hearts to make them better soldiers; a man to be sought in the hour of need; to stand for truth, purity, and all righteousness; for honorable living and hopeful dying; and having done all to stand by, in the spirit of service, according to the pattern of the Master. Many regiments did not understand and did not care; many commanders found it impossible to secure the man they would gladly have welcomed to such a post; many men who undertook the service fell short, perhaps far short of their opportunities; but many also gained for themselves much love and a good name and a share in the final triumph.

Rosters

UNION CHAPLAINS

Name	Life Dates	Denomination	Association
Abbott, Orrin P.		Methodist	98th New York National Guard
Abbott, Stephen Gano	1819–		1st New Hampshire
Abbott, William W.	1836–1925	Methodist	23rd New Jersey
Acker, Henry Jacob	1832–1874	Presbyterian	86th New York
Adair, Samuel Lyle	1811–1898	Congregational	Hospital
Adams, Alfred S.	1825–1865	Methodist	1st Maine Heavy Artillery
Adams, Charles Coffin	1837–1888	Episcopalian	22nd Connecticut
Adams, George Athearn	1821–1903	Presbyterian	11th Ohio Cavalry
Adams, John Ripley	1802–1866	Congregational	5th Maine; 121st New York
Adams, John Wesley	1832–	Methodist	2nd New Hampshire
Adams, Samuel R.	–1862	Methodist	26th Indiana
Adams, William Richard	1830–1911		133th Illinois
Addington, Thomas	1829–1912	Quaker	84th Indiana
Agnew, Benjamin Lashells	1833–1919	Presbyterian	76th Pennsylvania
Aiken, William	1809–1886	Presbyterian	8th Pennsylvania Reserves
Albright, Joseph R.	1832–1862		87th Indiana
Alderman, John W.	1835–	Methodist	20th & 130th Ohio
Alexander, James Madison	1825–1870	Presbyterian	14th Missouri; 66th Illinois
Allen, Archibald Cameron	1815–1883	Presbyterian	70th Indiana
Allen, Charles L.	1837–	Methodist	12th Ohio
Allen, Cyrus B.	1825–1916	Disciples of Christ	133rd Indiana
Allen, John Wheelock	1813–1885	Congregational	174th New York
Allen, Michael Meir	1830–	Jewish	5th Pennsylvania Cavalry
Allen, Nicholas T.	1815–1900		26th Connecticut
Allen, Truman F.	1840–1903	Methodist	48th Wisconsin
Allender, Richard B.	1816–1898	Methodist	22nd Iowa
Allington, William	1820–		94th Ohio
Altman, Daniel S.	1818–1893	Presbyterian	1st Illinois Cavalry; 151st Illinois
Alvord, Augustus V.	1834–1904		31st U.S. Colored Troops
Alvord, Nelson	1812–	Baptist	43rd Missouri
Ambler, Edward C.	1807–1891		67th Pennsylvania

UNION CHAPLAINS *continued*

Name	Life Dates	Denomination	Association
Ambrose, Mordecai James William	1815–1903	Methodist	7th Kentucky Cavalry; 47th Kentucky Mounted Infantry
Ambrose, Thomas Lyford	1829–1864	Church of Christ	12th New Hampshire
Ames, Almon S.			11th Indiana; Hospital
Ames, George W.	1814–1881		18th Indiana
Ames, Lyman Daniel	1812–1879	Christian	29th Ohio
Ames, William D.			41st Wisconsin
Anderson, Charles			46th Wisconsin
Anderson, Edward	1833–1916	Congregational	37th Illinois
Anderson, John Alexander	1834–1892	Presbyterian	3rd California
Anderson, Joseph			3rd Michigan; Hospital
Andrews, Edwin Norton	1832–1923	Congregational	2nd New Jersey Cavalry
Andrews, John Kennedy	1821–1896	Presbyterian	126th Ohio
Andrus, Elizur	1822–1902		6th Michigan; 1st Michigan Heavy Artillery
Armsby, Lauren	1817–1904	Congregational	8th Minnesota
Armstrong, Chester Solon	1826–1890	Presbyterian	4th Michigan Cavalry
Armstrong, Hallock	1823–1904	Presbyterian	50th Pennsylvania
Armstrong, Morrow P.	1830–	Methodist	36th Indiana
Arnold, Lewis P.	1825–		11th Kentucky
Arthur, John W.			Hospital: Delaware
Aschwander, Joseph	–1864		Hospital: Washington, D.C.
Asher, Jeremiah W.	1812–1865	Baptist	6th U.S. Colored Troops
Ashmore, Hiram H.		Presbyterian	25th Illinois
Atcheson, William			42nd Indiana
Atchison, William Dowling	1832–1917	Methodist	45th Illinois
Atkinson, Thomas		Episcopalian	Hospital: Nashville
Atmore, William C.		Methodist	15th Kentucky
Audis, Thomas		Methodist	2nd Iowa
Ault, John			126th Pennsylvania

UNION CHAPLAINS *continued*

Name	Life Dates	Denomination	Association
Austin, John H.			122nd Illinois
Averill, James	1815–1863		23rd Connecticut
Axline, Andrew		Presbyterian	2nd Iowa
Axline, Daniel W.		Methodist	20th Kentucky
Axtell, Nathan Gibbs	1827–1903	Methodist	30th New York
Ayers, James T.	1805–1865	Methodist	104th U.S. Colored Troops
Ayers, Samuel	1803–1887	Methodist	7th Kansas Cavalry
Babb, Clement Edwin	1821–1906	Presbyterian	22nd Ohio
Babbidge, Charles	1806–1898	Unitarian	6th & 26th Massachusetts
Bacon, Charles L.	1813–1893	Baptist	85th New York
Bacon, Henry Martyn	1827–1894	Presbyterian	63rd Indiana
Badger, Norman	–1876	Congregational	Hospital and Post: Louisville
Bagley, William			35th Iowa
Baird, John F.	1835–1863	Presbyterian	87th Pennsylvania
Baker, Nathan M.	–1922		116th Illinois
Baker, Oscar E.	1827–	Baptist	141st Ohio
Baker, William Asbury	1821–1862	Methodist	46th Ohio
Baker, William Melville	1822–1873	Congregational	97th Illinois
Baldridge, Samuel Coulter	1828–1898	Presbyterian	11th Missouri
Baldwin, Burr	1789–1882	Presbyterian	Hospital: Beverly, W.Va.
Baldwin, Caleb P.		Methodist	114th Illinois
Baldwin, John S.			3rd Wisconsin Cavalry
Balkam, Uriah	1812–1874	Congregational	16th Maine
Ball, Clement E.			13th Missouri
Ball, George S.	1822–1902	Unitarian	21st Massachusetts
Balloch, James			Hospital: Maryland
Bankson, Elijah			130th Illinois
Bantly, John			9th Wisconsin
Barb, James C.	–1900	Lutheran	8th Tennessee
Barbee, John Ray	1828–1902	Baptist	13th Kentucky
Barber, Daniel M.			53rd Pennsylvania

UNION CHAPLAINS *continued*

Name	Life Dates	Denomination	Association
Barber, Lorenzo D.	1821–1882	Methodist	2nd U.S. Sharpshooters
Barbour, Alanson			9th Iowa
Barbour, Emerson			137th Indiana
Barger, John S.		Methodist	73rd Illinois
Barker, Edward	1823–		40th Massachusetts; 91st New York
Barker, Stephen	1829–1893	Unitarian	1st Massachusetts Heavy Artillery
Barlow, Joseph Lansing	1818–	Baptist	125th New York
Barnes, Asa		Methodist	73rd U.S. Colored Troops
Barnes, Charles Montgomery	1833–1907	Congregational	93rd Illinois
Barnes, George Seymour	1829–1913	Methodist	2nd New Hampshire; 29th U.S. Colored Troops
Barnes, Henry Elbert	1832–1910	Congregational	72nd Illinois
Barnes, James S.			48th Illinois
Barnes, John D.	1836–1918	Baptist	13th New York
Barnes, Rezin M.		Methodist	6th Indiana
Barnes, William A.	1823–1897	Baptist	5th New York Heavy Artillery
Barnett, Thomas		Methodist	19th Indiana
Barnhart, Abram C.		Methodist	11th Indiana Cavalry
Barr, Andrew	1820–1864	Presbyterian	141st Pennsylvania
Barr, David Eglinton		Episcopalian	2nd Louisiana; 81st U.S. Colored Troops
Barr, Samuel Emmet			66th Indiana
Barry, Alfred Constantine	1821–1888		4th Wisconsin Cavalry; 19th Wisconsin
Barstow, Charles	1826–		157th New York
Bartlett, Edward Otis	1835–1909	Presbyterian	150th New York
Bartlett, George Washington	1828–1864	Unitarian	14th Maine; 1st Maine Cavalry
Bartlett, Peter Mason	1820–1901	Presbyterian	1st New York Mounted Rifles
Barton, Arthur J.		Baptist	23rd Iowa

UNION CHAPLAINS *continued*

Name	Life Dates	Denomination	Association
Barton, Frederick Augustus	1809–1881	Congregational	10th Massachusetts
Bartow, Henry B.		Episcopalian	12th New York
Bartow, Thomas B.	–1869	Episcopalian	U.S. Navy
Barwick, Joseph S.	1815–1890	Methodist	85th Illinois
Bass, Job G.	1819–1890	Methodist	90th New York
Bassett, James	1834–1906	Presbyterian	56th Illinois
Bast, Ephraim	1814–1886	Evangelical	73rd Pennsylvania
Bates, Alvan Jones	1820–1877	Congregational	2nd & 14th Maine
Bates, Henry H.	1808–1868	Episcopalian	22nd New York
Bates, Samuel D.	1829–		163rd Ohio
Bathurst, Reuben Archibald	1832–1897		148th Illinois
Battelle, Gordon	1814–1862	Methodist	1st West Virginia
Baugh, Marcellus	1812–	Methodist	5th Kentucky Cavalry
Baughman, Jacob G.	1831–		144th Ohio
Baumes, John Ross	1833–1918	Baptist	61st New York
Baxter, Samuel	1816–		82nd New York
Bayless, John S.	–1865	Methodist	16th Kentucky
Bayne, Thomas	1826–1906	Episcopalian	8th Vermont
Beach, Richard M.			49th Wisconsin
Beal, Alfred U.	1828–	Methodist	89th Ohio
Beale, James Hervey	1834–1909	Presbyterian	1st Pennsylvania Cavalry
Bean, James T.			1st Indiana Cavalry
Bear, Richard McAllister		Methodist	Hospital: Pennsylvania
Beardsley, Isaac Haight	1831–1902	Methodist	188th Ohio
Beasley, Allen D.	1809–1863		40th Indiana
Beatty, Archibald		Episcopalian	34th New Jersey
Beatty, Samuel M.		Methodist	Hospital: Ohio
Beck, Charles Augustus	1828–1895	Church of Christ	26th Pennsylvania
Beck, Theodore Romeyn	1830–1896	Dutch Reformed	13th New Jersey
Beckel, Frederick A.		Episcopalian	34th Wisconsin
Becker, August "Red"	1814–1871		7th New York

UNION CHAPLAINS *continued*

Name	Life Dates	Denomination	Association
Beckley, Levi B.	1822–1895	Baptist	48th Pennsylvania
Beckwith, John H.	1811–1877		2nd U.S. Colored Cavalry
Beecher, James Chaplin	1828–1886	Congregational	67th New York
Beecher, Thomas Kinnicut	1824–1900	Congregational	141st New York
Beeks, Greene C.	–1878	Methodist	44th Indiana
Beers, Hiram Wadsworth		Episcopalian	3rd Wisconsin Cavalry
Behlin, Charles	1817–		107th Ohio
Bennett, Russell B.	1829–1898	Methodist	32nd Ohio
Benson, Archibald T.	1816–1894	Disciples of Christ	128th Illinois
Benson, Henry	1812–1883	Presbyterian	49th New York
Benson, Homer Henry	1816–1899	Presbyterian	10th Wisconsin
Benson, William	1820–	Methodist	9th Michigan Cavalry
Bentel, Christian Gotthold			Hospital: Connecticut
Benton, Orlando Newell	1827–1862	Presbyterian	51st New York
Benton, Samuel Austin	1808–1865	Congregational	14th Iowa
Berger, Charles Ernst	1826–1889	Lutheran	65th New York
Berk, John			6th Wisconsin
Berridge, Leeds Kerr			Hospital: Pennsylvania
Bethauser, Charles M.		Methodist	2nd West Virginia Cavalry
Beugless, John D.	1836–1887	Baptist	2nd Rhode Island; U.S. Navy
Bigger, Matthew M.	1820–1872	Presbyterian	50th Illinois
Billings, Liberty	1820–1877	Unitarian	4th New Hampshire
Billingsley, Amos Stevens	1818–1897	Presbyterian	101st Pennsylvania; Hospital
Bingham, Adoniram Judson	1820–1868	Baptist	10th Massachusetts
Bird, Theodore			103rd Pennsylvania
Birge, Lewis Mead	1833–1873		173rd New York
Bischof, Emil			32nd Indiana
Bishop, Horace Smith	–1898		Post: Ft. Fillmore, N.Mex.
Bishop, Pleasant W.			37th Illinois
Bittinger, Edmund Coskery	1819–1889	Presbyterian	U.S. Navy
Black, William H.	1836–1909	Methodist	23rd Kentucky

UNION CHAPLAINS *continued*

Name	Life Dates	Denomination	Association
Blackburn, Joseph	1820–	Methodist	70th Ohio
Blair, Stephen	1827–1863		63rd Illinois
Blaisdell, James Joshua	1827–1896	Congregational	40th Wisconsin
Blake, Charles E.	1818–1892	Baptist	13th Maine
Blake, Charles Morris	1819–1893	Congregational	13th Missouri; 2nd New York Heavy Artillery
Blake, Isaac			75th U.S. Colored Troops
Blake, John	1811–1893	Episcopalian	U.S. Navy
Blanchard, Jonathan	1817–1864	Methodist	26th Michigan
Blankenship, Perry M.	1811–1880	Methodist	59th Indiana
Bliss, Luman A.	1826–1891	Methodist	51st New York
Blodgett, Gains Mill		Presbyterian	Hospital: New York
Blythe, Joseph William	1808–1875		Hospital: Indiana
Bogart, Wiliam E.	1837–	Baptist	1st Vermont Heavy Artillery
Bogen, Frederick William	1813–1885		41st New York
Boggs, John		Presbyterian	118th Ohio
Bokum, Hermann	1807–1878		Hospital: Tennessee
Bolles, Lorenzo, Jr.			21st Iowa
Bolles, Silas	1810–1894	Methodist	6th U.S. Colored Heavy Artillery
Bolton, James W. W.	1834–	Methodist	5th West Virginia Cavalry
Boltwood, Henry Leonidas	1831–1906		67th U.S. Colored Troops
Bond, Emmons Paley	1824–1899	Baptist	14th Connecticut
Bonte, John H. C.	–1896	Episcopalian	43rd Ohio
Boole, William Hilliker	1827–1896	Methodist	74th New York
Bordwell, Daniel Newcomb	1828–1888		27th Iowa
Boudrye, Louis Napoleon	1833–1892	Methodist	5th New York Cavalry
Boughton, Harvey		Unitarian	97th U.S. Colored Troops
Bowdish, Arvine C.	1832–1889	Methodist	149th New York
Bowdish, Charles G.	1834–1873	Methodist	11th Minnesota
Bowen, Benjamin Franklin	1840–1915	Baptist	84th U.S. Colored Troops
Bowen, Charles James	1827–1870	Congregational	Hospital: Baltimore, Md.

UNION CHAPLAINS *continued*

Name	Life Dates	Denomination	Association
Bowen, Ira W.	1809–1864		35th Wisconsin
Bowers, Stephen		Methodist	67th Indiana
Bowker, Samuel	1814–1892	Congregational	26th Maine
Bowker, Seth D.	1827–		124th Ohio
Bowles, John R.	1826–1874	Baptist	55th Massachusetts
Bowman, George R.	1814–1887		129th Ohio
Bowman, John	1816–1903	Methodist	49th New York
Bowman, John A.	1814–1889	Episcopalian	13th New York; Hospital
Bowman, Joseph A.			184th Pennsylvania
Bowman, Martin			22nd & 44th Iowa
Boyakin, Williamson F.			30th Illinois
Boyd, Francis A.	1843–	Church of Christ	109th U.S. Colored Troops
Boyd, John L.			135th Indiana
Boyden, Jesse S.		Baptist	10th Michigan
Boyden, Orville P.		Methodist	75th Indiana
Boyle, Francis Edward	1827–1882	Roman Catholic	Hospital: Washington, D.C.
Bradford, James Henry	1836–1913	Congregational	12th Connecticut
Bradley, George S.	1830–1900		22nd Wisconsin
Bradley, Joseph Henry	1838–1909		10th New York Cavalry
Bradley, William	1821–1909	Unitarian ?	40th Missouri
Bradner, Thomas Scott		Presbyterian	124th New York
Bradrick, Thomas Hudson	1832–1917	Baptist	67th U.S. Colored Troops
Bradshaw, Arthur		Methodist	115th Illinois
Bradshaw, Cornelius G.	–1906	Methodist	79th Illinois
Brady, Ebenezer Walker	1827–1886	Methodist	116th Ohio
Brady, Thomas M.	1826–1865	Roman Catholic	15th Michigan
Brakeman, Nelson L.		Methodist	1st Indiana Heavy Artillery; Hospital
Branch, John			10th West Virginia
Brant, Randolph Crowel	1828–1908	Baptist	2nd Kansas
Brasted, Bethuel H.	1832–1919	Baptist	8th New York Cavalry

UNION CHAPLAINS *continued*

Name	Life Dates	Denomination	Association
Brastow, Lewis Orsmond	1834–1912	Congregational	12th Vermont
Bratton, Thomas B.		Methodist	44th Missouri
Brauns, Frederick William	1830–1895	Roman Catholic	Hospital: Baltimore, Md.
Bray, Horace L.		Methodist	12th Maine
Brayton, Gideon F.		Baptist	9th Illinois Cavalry
Brewster, Cyrus	1807–1888	Congregational	Hospital: Readyville, Mass.
Brewster, Samuel A.	1832–	Methodist	40th Ohio
Brickman, Arthur O.	1825–1886		1st Maryland Cavalry; 3rd Maryland
Briggs, Obil Winsor	1820–1902	Baptist	9th Illinois Cavalry
Bright, Samuel M.			155th Ohio
Brisbane, Benjamine Lawton		Baptist	2nd Wisconsin Cavalry
Brisbane, William Henry	1806–1878	Baptist	2nd Wisconsin Cavalry
Bristol, Chauncey E.	1827–1888	Baptist	30th U.S. Colored Troops
Bristol, Daniel W.	1813–1883	Methodist	26th New York; 2nd New York Heavy Artillery
Bristow, James H.	1813–1870	Methodist	5th Kentucky
Brittain, Alem	1809–1889	Methodist	91st Pennsylvania
Britton, James Budd	1810–1889	Episcopalian	11th Wisconsin
Brockway, William H.	1813–1891	Methodist	16th Michigan
Brookins, Silas W.	1834–	Baptist	5th Tennessee Cavalry
Brooks, George Lorin		Episcopalian	10th New Jersey
Brooks, Joseph	1821–1877	Methodist	Missouri units; 56th U.S. Colored Troops
Brooks, Strange		Methodist	9th Kansas Cavalry
Brouse, John A.		Methodist	100th Indiana
Brown, Andrew R.	1818–		64th Ohio
Brown, Charles Edwin	1813–1901	Baptist	3rd U.S. Colored Heavy Artillery; 88th U.S. Colored Troops
Brown, Edwin T.			2nd Ohio Cavalry
Brown, Frederick Thomas	1822–1893	Presbyterian	7th Ohio; Hospital

UNION CHAPLAINS *continued*

Name	Life Dates	Denomination	Association
Brown, George Washington	1820–1915	Methodist	86th Illinois
Brown, James Allen	1821–1882	Lutheran	87th Pennsylvania; Hospital
Brown, James Caldwell	1815–1862	Presbyterian	48th Indiana
Brown, James Harvey		Methodist	Hospital: Pennsylvania
Brown, James Moore		Presbyterian	181st Ohio
Brown, John N.	1819–1895	Methodist	111th New York
Brown, John R.	1825–		156th Ohio
Brown, Joseph T.	1810–1865	Methodist	6th Maryland
Brown, Josiah I.		Methodist	15th Maine
Brown, Samuel L.		Methodist	7th Wisconsin
Brown, Thomas Gibson	1799–1885	Methodist	21st Connecticut
Brown, William			12th Maine
Brown, William M.	–1863		38th Illinois
Brown, William R.	1828–1871		91st New York
Brown, William Young		Presbyterian	Hospital: Washington, D.C.
Brown, Ziba			5th Iowa Cavalry
Browne, George W.	1834–		11th Missouri
Browne, Robert Audley		Presbyterian	100th Pennsylvania
Bruel, James		Roman Catholic	Hospital: Beaufort, S.C.
Bruner, William R.		Methodist	56th Illinois
Brunson, Alfred	1793–1882	Methodist	31st Wisconsin
Brush, Jesse	1830–1916	Congregational	158th New York
Buck, Daniel Dana	1814–1895	Methodist	27th New York
Buck, Elias M.	1823–1903	Methodist	151st New York
Buckley, Charles Waldron	1835–1906	Presbyterian	47th U.S. Colored Troops
Buessing, George K.	1837–1864		125th Illinois
Bulkley, Charles Henry Augustus	1818–1893	Congregational	70th New York
Bull, John W.	1819–1873	Methodist	5th Maryland
Bull, Richard B.			6th Minnesota
Bullen, George	1833–1916	Baptist	16th Maine

UNION CHAPLAINS *continued*

Name	Life Dates	Denomination	Association
Bundy, Isaac	−1899		48th Illinois
Bunn, David P.	1812–1887	Universalist	56th Illinois
Burdett, Michael			Hospital: Delaware
Burdick, Henry Day	1835–1871	Baptist	61st New York
Burge, Hartwell T.	1805–1876	Methodist	3rd Kentucky Cavalry
Burgeler, Charles	1820–		8th New York
Burgess, John	1821–	Methodist	30th Iowa
Burghardt, Peter Hewins	1809–1886	Presbyterian	65th New York
Burke, John			82nd Ohio
Burke, John	−1867		Post: Ft. Hamilton, N.Y.
Burkett, Michael H. B.		Methodist	21st Kentucky
Burkholder, Abraham H.			179th Ohio
Burnett, John H.	1820–1893	Methodist	186th New York
Burnham, George			17th Connecticut
Burns, Andrew	1819–		65th Ohio
Burridge, Leeds K.		Methodist	Hospital
Burrows, Christopher Columbus	1825–1893	Baptist	22nd U.S. Colored Troops
Bush, Eurotus Hastings	1825–1912	Methodist	49th Ohio
Bushong, James W.	1829–1897	Methodist	88th & 195th Ohio
Butler, Francis Eugene	1825–1863	Presbyterian	25th New Jersey
Butler, John George	1826–1909	Lutheran	Hospital: Washington, D.C.
Butler, Thaddeus J.	1835–1897	Roman Catholic	23rd Illinois
Button, Charles	1821–1899	Baptist ?	20th Illinois
Butts, Joshua	1811–	Baptist	47th New York
Byers, Albert G.		Methodist	33rd Ohio
Cadwalader, Joseph	1823–1904		32nd Iowa
Calahan, Thomas			48th U.S. Colored Troops
Calder, Humphrey L.			7th New York Heavy Artillery
Caldwell, James McHenry		Presbyterian	20th Pennsylvania Cavalry
Caldwell, John P.			85th Pennsylvania

UNION CHAPLAINS *continued*

Name	Life Dates	Denomination	Association
Calkins, James Frederick	1816–1893	Presbyterian	149th Pennsylvania
Callahan, Henry	1812–1888	Presbyterian	114th New York
Callender, Nathaniel	–1876	Methodist	Hospital: Camp Dennison, Ohio
Callihan, Charles S.			119th Illinois
Calvert, Porter H.	1820–		11th Kentucky
Camp, Norman William	–1898	Episcopalian	4th New Jersey; Hospital
Camp, Stephen Henry	1837–1897	Unitarian	82nd U.S. Colored Troops
Campbell, Matthew M.		Methodist	82nd Indiana
Campbell, William Thomas		Episcopalian	107th Pennsylvania
Canfield, Charles Taylor	1823–1913	Unitarian ?	36th Massachusetts
Cargill, John D.	1825–		5th Vermont
Carner, William H.	–1917	Baptist	81st Illinois
Carpenter, John R.	1819–1862	Methodist	1st District of Columbia
Carpenter, Samuel Tonkin	–1864		Hospital: Illinois
Carr, Horace Merwin	1834–1923	Baptist	3rd Illinois Cavalry; Hospital Chaplain
Carr, William H.	1812–	Presbyterian	4th New York Heavy Artillery
Carrell, John James	1812–1877	Presbyterian	9th New Jersey
Carrier, Joseph C.		Roman Catholic	6th Missouri
Carroll, George Ryerson	1831–1895	Presbyterian	24th Iowa
Carruthers, George N.	1933–1906		51st U.S. Colored Troops
Carson, Lewis Evans	1824–1904	Methodist	38th Indiana
Carter, William H.	1829–1907	Episcopalian	60th Indiana
Cartwright, Barton Hall	1810–1895	Methodist	92nd Illinois
Carven, Thomas George	1821–	Episcopalian	17th New York; Hospital
Carver, Robert	1810–1863	Congregational	7th Massachusetts
Case, William Wickham	1839–1915	Baptist	195th Pennsylvania
Castle, Asbury B.		Methodist	115th Ohio
Catlin, Benjamin Rush	1829–1913	Presbyterian	115th U.S. Colored Troops
Cave, Alfred N.			23rd Missouri

UNION CHAPLAINS *continued*

Name	Life Dates	Denomination	Association
Chaffee, James Franklin	1827–	Methodist	5th Minnesota
Chaffin, John W.			59th Ohio
Chalfant, George Wilson	1837–1914	Presbyterian	130th Pennsylvania
Chamberlain, Jacob S.		Episcopalian	Hospital: Illinois
Chambre, Albert St. John	1840–1911	Episcopalian	8th New Jersey; 1st New Jersey Militia
Champion, J. Hiram	1829–	Methodist	179th Pennsylvania
Channing, William Henry		Unitarian	Hospital: Washington, D.C.
Chapin, Harvey E.	1811–1864	Methodist	147th New York
Chapman, Daniel	1806–1890		105th Illinois
Chapman, Edgar Teft	1829–1911	Episcopalian	2nd & 169th New York
Chapman, Henry	–1893	Methodist	1st U.S. Colored Artillery
Chapman, Henry L.	1832–1915	Methodist	123rd Pennsylvania
Chapman, Henry O.		Methodist	42nd Indiana
Chapman, Lucius W.	1820–1895	Presbyterian	110th Ohio
Chapman, William Hinkle			Hospital: District of Columbia
Charlier, Elisee	1830–	Congregational	119th New York
Charlot, Nathaniel Peck	1810–1899	Episcopalian	22nd Indiana
Chase, Benjamin A.		Methodist	4th Maine
Chase, Dudley		Episcopalian	Post: Benton Barracks, Mo.
Chase, Moses Bayley	–1875	Episcopalian	U.S. Navy
Chase, Samuel			14th Illinois Cavalry
Chase, Stephen Freeman	1835–1920	Methodist	3rd Maine
Chase, W. Dempster	1840–1921	Methodist	193rd New York
Chase, William Thomas	1839–1898	Baptist	81st U.S. Colored Troops
Cheney, George Nathan	1829–1863	Episcopalian	33rd New York
Cheney, Laban Clark	1808–1864	Methodist	4th Ohio Cavalry
Cherry, Henry T.	1808–1891	Presbyterian	10th Michigan Cavalry
Cheshire, John E.	1815–	Baptist	2nd New York
Chevers, Mark Lindsay	–1875	Episcopalian	Post: Ft. Monroe, Va.
Chidlaw, Benjamin Williams	1811–1892	Presbyterian	39th Ohio

UNION CHAPLAINS *continued*

Name	Life Dates	Denomination	Association
Childs, Thomas P.	1817–	Baptist	44th Ohio
Chipman, Draper		Methodist	38th Illinois
Chittenden, Lyman Sylvester	1819–1892	Methodist	24th & 67th Indiana
Chittenden, Richard Lewis	1830–1913	Episcopal	43rd Ohio
Chrisler, William B.		Disciples of Christ	5th Kentucky Cavalry
Christy, Richard C.	1827–1878	Roman Catholic	78th Pennsylvania
Chubbuck, Emory F.	1836–1872	Episcopal	31st Massachusetts
Chubbuck, Francis S.	1812–1890	Methodist	95th U.S. Colored Troops
Church, Andrew J.		Methodist	3rd Maine
Church, LaFayette	1816–1907	Baptist	26th Michigan
Cilley, Daniel P.	1806–1888	Baptist	8th New Hampshire; 2nd New York Cavalry
Clapp, Alexander Huntington	1818–1899	Congregational	10th Rhode Island
Clark, Edward Lord	1838–1910	Congregational	12th Masschusetts
Clark, Edward Warren	1820–1905	Presbyterian	47th Masschusetts
Clark, L. Harvey			7th Iowa
Clark, Lucien	1839–1923	Methodist	153th Ohio
Clark, Milton C.	1833–1921	Baptist	6th Kentucky Cavalry
Clark, Orson B.	1810–1885	Universalist	83rd Pennsylvania
Clark, Seth G.	1818–		10th Ohio Cavalry
Clark, Thomas C.	1833–1904		8th Iowa Cavalry; 16th U.S. Colored Troops
Clark, Thomas Winthrop			99th New York; Hospital
Clarke, C. P.	1804–1870		11th Illinois
Clarke, Ethan Ray	1818–1873		25th New York Cavalry; 1st Rhode Island Cavalry
Clarke, Jonas Bowen	1816–1894	Congregational	23rd Massachusetts
Clausen, Claus Lauritz	1820–1892	Lutheran	15th Wisconsin
Claypool, James H.		Methodist	12th Indiana Cavalry
Cleaveland, John Payne	1799–1873		30th Massachusetts
Clemans, Sylvester W.	1818–1887	Methodist	115th New York

UNION CHAPLAINS *continued*

Name	Life Dates	Denomination	Association
Clendenning, Jonathan M.	1840–	Methodist	96th Illinois
Cleveland, Festus P.	1817–1900	Methodist	53rd Illinois
Cleveland, Martin B.	–1901	Methodist	44th New York
Clevenger, George J.			135th Illinois
Cliffe, William	1812–1866	Methodist	98th Illinois
Clifford, Zenas S.		Methodist	29th Illinois
Cline, Enoch Clark	1831–	Presbyterian	11th New Jersey
Clinton, Orson P.	1808–1890		21st Wisconsin
Clothier, Charles W.	1820–1881		88th Pennsylvania
Clutz, Charles	1835–	Baptist	11th Michigan Cavalry
Cobb, Daniel		Methodist	6th Minnesota
Coburn, Milo P.	1832–1870		30th U.S. Colored Troops
Cochran, Warren			6th Wisconsin
Coe, Isaac H.	1818–1911		4th Massachusetts Heavy Artillery
Coffin, James L.		Baptist	10th Wisconsin
Coffin, Lorenzo S.	1823–1915	Congregational	32nd Iowa
Coffin, William P.			13th Indiana Cavalry
Coggeshall, Israel		Methodist	19th Michigan
Coggeshall, John M.	1820–1863	Baptist	1st Iowa Cavalry
Coit, Gurdon Saltonstall	1808–1869	Episcopalian	1st U.S. Sharpshooters
Colby, Joseph	1812–	Methodist	12th Maine
Colby, William P.			17th Massachusetts
Cole, Charles			1st Maryland (Potomac Home Brigade)
Cole, Jacob		Baptist	31st Illinois
Coleman, James Armistead	1831–1879	Methodist	U.S. Navy
Collier, George W.	1825–1905	Methodist	34th & 36th Ohio
Collins, Gamaliel	1816–1891		72nd Pennsylvania
Collins, Nathan G.	1815–1902		57th Illinois
Collins, William Hertzog	1831–1910	Methodist	10th Illinois

UNION CHAPLAINS *continued*

Name	Life Dates	Denomination	Association
Colt, Samuel Fisher	1817–1893	Presbyterian	96th Pennsylvania
Colton, Joseph			13th Indiana
Coltrin, Nathaniel Potter	1820–1877	Presbyterian	33rd Illinois
Compton, George N.	1838–1893	Methodist	63rd Illinois
Conant, Augustus H.	1811–1863		19th Illinois
Condron, George M.			2nd Delaware
Conklin, Henry H.	1828–1883		8th Michigan
Conner, John T.			101st Indiana
Conrad, John M.			29th Iowa
Consor, S. L. M.		Methodist	5th Pennsylvania Reserves
Conway, Thomas W.	1840–1887		9th New York; 79th U.S. Colored Troops
Conwell, Francis A.	1813–1885	Methodist	1st Minnesota
Cook, Elijah T.	–1863		43rd Indiana
Cook, Joseph T.			139th Illinois
Cook, Joshua	1821–	Presbyterian	8th New York Heavy Artillery; 10th New York
Cook, Philip Barnes	1832–1907	Presbyterian	85th Indiana
Cook, Philos Gunikos	1807–1895	Presbyterian	94th New York
Cooley, Ruel			142nd Illinois
Cooley, Rufus, Jr.		Methodist	47th Wisconsin
Coom, Samuel		Presbyterian	21st New Jersey
Cooney, Peter Paul	1822–1905	Roman Catholic	35th Indiana
Cooper, Edward	1815–1889	Presbyterian	8th Ohio Cavalry
Cooper, Jacob	1830–1904	Presbyterian	3rd Kentucky
Cooper, Varnum A.	1835–1916	Methodist	18th Connecticut
Coplin, Alanson	1834–1906		87th U.S. Colored Troops
Corby, William	1833–1897	Roman Catholic	88th New York
Corcoran, Edward P.	1832–	Roman Catholic	61st Ohio
Corkhill, Thomas Edward	1822–1897	Methodist	25th Iowa
Corkhill, William Henry	1821–	Methodist	Benton Barracks, Mo.; Hospital

UNION CHAPLAINS *continued*

Name	Life Dates	Denomination	Association
Cornforth, Columbus	1831–1883	Baptist ?	150th Pennsylvania
Corson, Cornelius	1836–		71st New York National Guard
Cotton, Thomas	1824–1907	Methodist	129th Illinois
Covey, Emory Holden	1830–	Baptist	101st New York
Cowan, John	1818–1902		6th New York Heavy Artillery
Cowan, John Fleming	1801–1862	Presbyterian	Hospital: Missouri
Cowles, John Guiteau Welch	1836–1914	Congregational	55th Ohio
Cox, Francis			154th Indiana
Cox, John H.	1833–1902	Methodist	1st & 21st Missouri
Coxe, Benjamin F.		Methodist	99th U.S. Colored Troops
Coyner, David H.	1807–		88th Ohio
Cozier, Benjamin Frnkln Wilson	1836–1903	Methodist	3rd Ohio Cavalry
Crabbs, John	1822–		67th Ohio
Craft, David	1832–1908	Presbyterian	141st Pennsylvania
Craig, John Liggett	1828–1865	Presbyterian	17th Indiana
Crain, Cyrus S.	1825–1895	Baptist	44th New York
Crane, Edward D.		Methodist	39th New Jersey
Crane, Ezra F.	1810–1896	Baptist	23rd & 107th New York
Crane, James Burnet	1819–	Methodist	Hospital: Pennsylvania
Crane, James L.	–1879	Methodist	21st Illinois
Crary, Benjamin Franklin		Methodist	3rd Minnesota
Cravath, Erastus Milo	1833–1900	Congregational	101st Ohio
Crawford, George C.	1820–1878	Methodist	31st Maine
Crawford, Howison C.			39th Iowa
Crawford, James M.		Methodist	83rd Indiana
Crawford, James M.	1832–1908	Presbyterian	93rd New York
Crawford, John Agnew	1822–	Presbyterian	Hospital: Pennsylvania
Crawford, Levi Parsons	1823–1914	Congregational	105th Illinois
Creed, C. Van Renselaer			31st U.S. Colored Troops
Cresap, William S.			10th Indiana
Cressey, Timothy Robinson	1800–1870	Baptist	2nd Minnesota

UNION CHAPLAINS *continued*

Name	Life Dates	Denomination	Association
Crever, Benjamin Heck	1817–1875	Methodist	Hospital: Frederick, Md.
Crews, Hooper		Methodist	100th Illinois
Crippen, John T.	1831–1912	Methodist	117th New York
Crislip, Abraham R.			13th West Virginia
Crissey, William Stoddart	1811–1882	Methodist	115th Illinois
Critchfield, Norman B.	1838–1919	Methodist	28th & 171st Pennsylvania
Crocker, George Dauchy	1822–1888	Baptist	2nd New York Provisional & 6th New York Cavalry
Cromack, Joseph C.	1812–1900	Methodist	19th & 22nd Massachusetts
Crooks, Josiah F.	1830–1890	Methodist	98th Ohio
Crouch, Christopher James	–1873	Methodist	Hospital: Pennsylvania
Crouch, Darius			8th Missouri
Crouch, Lewis P.			55th Illinois
Crowell, Ezra		Baptist	10th New York Cavalry
Crumb, J. W.	1812–	Baptist	8th New York National Guard
Cudworth, Warren Handel	1825–1883	Unitarian	1st Massachusetts
Cuming, Francis Higgins	1797–1862	Episcopalian	3rd Michigan
Cummings, Ephraim Chamberlain	1825–1897	Congregational	15th Vermont
Cummings, Gilbert, Jr.	1825–1873		51st Massachusetts
Cummings, Silas S.	1814–1903	Methodist	4th Rhode Island
Cunningham, Amos D.			5th Indiana Cavalry; 138th Indiana
Cunningham, William	1827–1879	Presbyterian	56th Pennsylvania
Curry, James W.	1831–1900	Methodist	138th Pennsylvania; 6th West Virginia
Curry, William Wallace	1824–1921		53rd Indiana
Curtis, Burton H.			142nd Indiana
Curtis, David A.		Methodist	18th Michigan
Cushman, Isaac Somes	1823–1870	Methodist	33rd Massachusetts
Cutler, Temple	1828–	Congregational	9th Maine

UNION CHAPLAINS *continued*

Name	Life Dates	Denomination	Association
Daily, William Mitchell	1812–1877	Methodist	Hospital: St. Louis, Mo.
Dale, John	1812–	Presbyterian	75th Indiana
Dale, Lewis	–1895	Methodist	19th Indiana
Dallas, Marion W.	–1896		104th Ohio
Daniels, William V.			Hospital: Indiana
Darr, Daniel C.			6th Indiana
Darrach, William Bradford	1836–1909	Presbyterian	20th New York National Guard
Darrow, George R.	1820–1906	Baptist	3rd New Jersey
Dashiell, Alfred Henry, Jr.	1824–1908	Episcopalian	57th Massachusetts
Davidson, John H.			172nd Pennsylvania
Davis, Charles A.	1802–1867	Methodist	U.S. Navy
Davis, Jesse Perrin	–1882		7th Illinois
Davis, Joshua Butts	1833–1899	Baptist	7th New York Cavalry
Davis, Werter Renick	1815–1893	Methodist	12th Kansas
Davis, William B.	1823–1901		187th Ohio
Day, Alvah	1798–1882	Presbyterian	91st Illinois
Day, Luman P.			174th Pennsylvania
Day, Robert	1806–		10th New York Cavalry; Hospital
Day, Samuel	1808–1881		8th Illinois
Dayton, Durrell W.	1824–1909	Methodist	2nd Vermont
De Bois, James	1817–		23rd New York
De Costa, Benjamin Franklin	1831–1904	Episcopalian	5th & 18th Massachusetts
De La Matyr, George Gilbert	1825–1892	Methodist	8th New York Heavy Artillery
De Walden, Thomas Blaides	1811–1873		25th New York
Dean, Lyman H.	1830–	Methodist	30th Michigan
Dean, Martin G.	1828–		145th New York
Dean, Silas F.	1832–		5th New Hampshire
Dean, William K.			124th Indiana; 57th Ohio
Decker, Michael	1814–1874		34th Illinois
DeFoe, Augustus		Baptist	6th Illinois Cavalry
DeForest, Henry Swift	1833–1896	Congregational	11th Connecticut

UNION CHAPLAINS *continued*

Name	Life Dates	Denomination	Association
DeLaMater, Isaac	1818–1892	Presbyterian	72nd Indiana
Delany, James	1803–1896		18th Wisconsin
DeLay, Jacob	1819–		1st Ohio Heavy Artillery
Delo, John A.		Lutheran	11th Pennsylvania Reserves
Delo, Reuben F.	1827–1897	Lutheran	30th Indiana
Denby, William		Methodist	6th Missouri Cavalry
Denison, Frederic	1819–1901	Baptist	1st Rhode Island Cavalry; 3rd Rhode Island Heavy Artillery
Dennison, Charles Wheeler			Hospital: Massachusetts
Devan, Thomas Thomas	1809–1890		Hospital: New York
Devoe, Stephen T.	1824–	Baptist	9th New York Heavy Artillery
Dewing, Thomas S.		Presbyterian	Hospital: New York
Dibble, Phileo K.	1821–1890		9th Missouri Cavalry Militia
Dickerson, James Stokes	1825–1876	Baptist	5th Delaware
Dickinson, Lucius C.	1826–	Methodist	9th Vermont
Dickinson, Sanford B.	1831–1921	Methodist	148th New York
Dickson, Robert		Presbyterian	100th Pennsylvania
Dill, James Horton	1821–1863	Congregational	89th Illinois
Dilley, Alexander Bainbridge	1823–1893	Congregational	106th New York
Dillon, James M.	1833–1866	Roman Catholic	63rd & 182nd New York
Dillon, John	1815–	Methodist	18th Ohio
Dixon, Charles	1822–1910		16th Connecticut
Dixon, James J. A. T.			146th Illinois
Dixon, William T.			11th Pennsylvania Reserves
Doane, George Hobart	1830–1905	Roman Catholic	New Jersey
Doane, Hiram	1806–1863	Congregational	47th Illinois
Dobson, Augustus F.	1820–		15th New York National Guard
Docher, Rudolph			5th Missouri
Dodd, Stephen Grover	1826–		25th Massachusetts
Dodge, George Webb	1820–1881	Baptist	11th New York

UNION CHAPLAINS *continued*

Name	Life Dates	Denomination	Association
Dodge, John Varick	1815–1907	Presbyterian	Hospital: Indiana
Dodge, Richard Varick	1822–1885	Presbyterian	Hospital: West Virginia
Doehn, John George Rudolph			5th Missouri Reserves; Hospital
Donaldson, John S.	1809–1878?	Methodist	18th Indiana
Dooley, Thomas B.	1813–	Episcopalian	14th Michigan
Doolittle, John Birge	1836–1915	Congregational	15th Connecticut
Dore, John S.	1841–1878		6th New Hampshire
Dorrance, George W.	1811–1888	Baptist	U.S. Navy
Dotson, William A.	1834–1879	Methodist	125th U.S. Colored Troops
Dougherty, George T.		Methodist	10th Indiana
Doughty, Benjamin F.	1825–1879	Methodist	8th Michigan Cavalry
Doughty, George S.			79th New York
Dowell, William T.		Methodist	3rd Tennessee
Dowling, Levi H.		Disciples of Christ	152nd Indiana
Drake, Jeremiah M.		Presbyterian	1st Ohio Cavalry
Drake, Lemuel F.	1822–1875	Methodist	17th, 31st, & 121st Ohio
Drake, Reuben A.		Methodist	7th Pennsylvania Cavalry
Drew, Francis	1811–		2nd Michigan Cavalry
Driver, Joseph Metcalf	1801–1878		Hospital: Massachusetts
Drumm, John Hetherington	1827–1879	Episcopalian	52nd Pennsylvania
Drumm, Thomas	1824–1896	Episcopalian	9th New Jersey; 102nd New York
Drummond, James	1835–1918	Methodist	2nd Iowa Cavalry; Hospital: W. Va.
Drummond, John H.		Methodist	10th Kansas
Drury, Asa	1802–1870	Baptist	18th Kentucky
Dubois, George Washington		Episcopalian	11th Ohio
Dubois, Herbert G.	1806–	Methodist	86th Ohio
Dudley, Adolphus Spring	1835–1909	Presbyterian	146th Ohio
Dunmore, George Washington	1820–1862	Congregational	1st Wisconsin Cavalry
Dunn, Jacob B.	1824–1911		161st Ohio
Dunning, Edward Osborn	1810–1874	Congregational	Hospital: Cumberland, Md.

UNION CHAPLAINS *continued*

Name	Life Dates	Denomination	Association
Duryea, Isaac Groot	1810–1866	Dutch Reformed	81st New York
Duryee, William Rankin	1838–1897	Dutch Reformed	1st Kentucky
Dutcher, David C.	1823–	Methodist	139th New York
Duval, Richard P.		Methodist	6th Kansas Cavalry
Dwight, James Harrison	1830–1872	Presbyterian	66th New York
Dwyer, Ransom O.	1813–1864		2nd New York Cavalry
Eads, John R.	1829–	Methodist	4th Kentucky Mounted
Eagan, Francis D.			8th Pennsylvania Cavalry
Earl, Lewis W.	–1902	Methodist	21st Michigan
Earnshaw, William	1828–1885	Methodist	49th Pennsylvania; Hospital: Tennessee
Eastman, William Reed	1835–1925	Congregational	72nd New York
Eaton, Jacob	1833–1865	Congregational	7th Connecticut
Eaton, Joel W.	1831–1912	Methodist	169th New York
Eaton, John, Jr.	1829–1906	Congregational	27th Ohio
Eaton, Samuel Witt	1820–1905	Congregational	7th Wisconsin
Eaton, William Wentworth	–1889	Church of Christ	12th U.S. Colored Troops
Eberhart, Albert G.	1810–1881	Baptist	12th Iowa
Eberhart, David Christian	1826–1913	Methodist	87th Pennsylvania
Eberhart, Uriah	1821–	Methodist	20th Iowa
Eberhart, Wilford A. P.	1820–1899	Methodist	1st Pennsylvania Light Artillery
Eckles, John Graham	1833–1900	Congregational	4th Iowa
Eddy, Alfred		Methodist	4th Illinois Cavalry
Eddy, Augustus	1798–1870	Methodist	Hospital: Indiana
Eddy, Herman J.		Baptist	33rd Illinois
Eddy, Hiram J.	1813–1893	Presbyterian	2nd Connecticut
Eddy, John Reynolds	1829–1863	Methodist	72nd Indiana
Eddy, Richard	1828–1906	Universalist	60th New York
Edgerton, Christopher H.	1828–1866	Methodist	93rd New York
Edwards, Arthur, Jr.	1834–1901	Methodist	1st Michigan
Edwards, Elijah Evan	1831–1915	Episcopalian	7th Minnesota

UNION CHAPLAINS *continued*

Name	Life Dates	Denomination	Association
Edwards, George G.	1836–1869		49th U.S. Colored Troops
Edwards, Henry		Episcopalian	Hospital: Maryland
Egan, Costney Louis	1823–	Roman Catholic	9th Massachusetts; Hospital
Eggers, Hermann		Lutheran	Hospital: Tennessee
Eldred, Andrew J.	1824–	Methodist	12th Michigan
Eldridge, William V.		Methodist	56th Illinois
Elgin, William	1838–1923	Baptist	14th U.S. Colored Troops
Elliott, Jared Leigh	1807–1881	Presbyterian	Ft. Washington, Md.
Elliott, John Woods	–1868		Hospital: Pennsylvania
Elliott, Julius	1834–1886		10th Illinois Cavalry
Ellis, Caleb Holt	1825–	Methodist	11th Maine
Elrod, John		Methodist	13th Iowa
Ely, Isaac Mills	1819–1880	Congregational	Hospital: Alexandria, Va.
Emerson, Isaac W.		Methodist	13th Kentucky
Emerson, Joseph C.	1819–1877	Methodist	7th New Hampshire
Emerson, W. A. G.	1816–		120th Ohio
Emery, Samuel Hopkins			Hospital: Illinois
Enders, Jacob Henry	1834–1901	Dutch Reformed	153rd New York
Engle, George B.		Episcopalian	14th Wisconsin
Erben, Washington Brown		Episcopalian	6th Pennsylvania Cavalry
Erdman, Albert	1838–1918	Presbyterian	146th New York
Erdman, William Jacob	1834–1923	Presbyterian	2nd New York Cavalry
Erick, Enos W.	1839–1917	Methodist	89th Indiana
Erwin, George			44th Illinois
Eskridge, James A.			136th Indiana
Estabrook, William W.		Episcopalian	15th Iowa
Evans, Francis W.	1823–	Methodist	35th Iowa
Evans, Joseph Spragg	1831–	Baptist	124th Pennsylvania
Evans, Philip Saffery	1828–1913	Baptist	6th & 13th New York Heavy Artillery
Evans, William M.		Methodist	99th Illinois

UNION CHAPLAINS *continued*

Name	Life Dates	Denomination	Association
Everest, Asa Elmore	1820–1899	Congregational	118th U.S. Colored Troops
Everts, William Wallace	1814–1890	Baptist	69th Illinois
Exline, George A.	1822–1891		46th Ohio
Eysenbach, Louis			Hospital: Pennsylvania
Fairchild, Edward B.	1835–1911		34th Massachusetts
Falconer, Enoch G.		Methodist	8th Illinois
Fallows, Samuel	1835–1922	Methodist	32nd Wisconsin
Farr, Alfred B.	1810–1874	Methodist	18th New York
Farr, George W.	1837–	Methodist	109th U.S. Colored Troops
Faull, John	1821–1887	Methodist	27th & 33rd New Jersey
Fay, Barnabas Maynard	1806–1885	Congregational	23rd Michigan
Fehrmann, Herman	1821–		17th Missouri
Feight, John W.			138th Pennsylvania
Feltwell, William V.	1833–	Episcopalian	5th (Veteran) New York
Ferguson, John	1832–1908	Methodist	1st Indiana Cavalry
Ferguson, John Van Epps	1829–1905	Methodist	97th New York
Ferguson, William G.	1832–1898	Methodist	13th Maryland
Ferree, James Inglish			9th Illinois; Hospital
Ferriday, William Calvin	1838–		121st Pennsylvania
Ferril, Thomas Johnson		Methodist	16th Kansas Cavalry
Ferris, Charles G.	1826–1888	Methodist	123rd Ohio
Ferris, Dennis O.	1833–	Methodist	133th New York
Feutschmann, George			3rd Missouri Reserves & 4th Missouri
Fialon, Joseph		Roman Catholic	Ft. Sumner, N.Mex.
Field, Samuel Wheeler	1813–1887	Baptist	12th Rhode Island
Finch, Peter Voorhees	1835–1901	Episcopalian	16th Connecticut
Fischer, Charles A.			32nd Indiana
Fish, John Fletcher	1811–1878	Episcopalian	Jefferson Barracks, Mo.
Fisher, Hugh Dunn	1824–1905	Methodist	5th Kansas Cavalry
Fisk, Phontius Kavasales	–1890	Unitarian	U.S. Navy

UNION CHAPLAINS *continued*

Name	Life Dates	Denomination	Association
Fiske, Asa Severance	1833–1925	Congregational	4th Minnesota
Fitch, Charles		Presbyterian	24th Indiana
Fitch, Chauncey Wheaton	1801–1878	Episcopalian	Hospital: Maryland
Fitzgibbon, James			Hospital: Illinois
Flanders, Alonzo Buck		Episcopalian	4th Rhode Island
Fletcher, Frank	1836–1916	Baptist	134th New York
Fletcher, John			9th Michigan Cavalry
Flower, John W.		Methodist	76th Illinois
Flower, Josiah		Methodist	83rd Pennsylvania
Foersch, John Augustus	1812–1871	Lutheran	7th New York; 15th New York Heavy Artillery
Folsom, Ezekiel		Presbyterian	Hospital: Illinois
Folsom, George Palmer	1826–	Presbyterian	136th New York
Foot, Joseph I.			13th Wisconsin
Foote, Horatio		Congregational	Hospital: Illinois
Foote, Lemuel Thomas	1832–1908	Methodist	151st New York
Ford, Cornelius R.			16th Illinois Cavalry
Ford, John K.	1819–		192nd Ohio
Forman, Jacob G.	1820–1885	Unitarian	1st Missouri Militia; 3rd Missouri
Forsyth, John	1810–1886	Presbyterian	19th New York National Guard
Foskett, Horace B.		Baptist	124th Illinois
Foster, Daniel	1816–1864	Unitarian	33rd Massachusetts
Foster, Robert A.			7th Missouri Cavalry Militia; 27th Missouri Mounted
Fowler, Henry	1824–1872	Presbyterian	19th New York
Fowler, James Hackett	1824–1889	Unitarian	33rd U.S. Colored Troops
Fox, George H.		Baptist	1st Wisconsin Cavalry
Fox, Norman, Jr.	1836–1907	Baptist	77th New York
Francis, Eben	1819–1892	Universalist	127th New York
Frankel, Jacob	1808–		Hospital: Pennsylvania
Frazee, John Hatfield	1829–1907	Dutch Reformed	3rd New Jersey Cavalry

UNION CHAPLAINS *continued*

Name	Life Dates	Denomination	Association
Frazier, John A.	1814–1898	Methodist	73rd Indiana
Frear, George H.	1831–1894	Baptist	3rd Pennsylvania Reserves
Freeman, Lyman N.	1807–	Episcopalian	8th Ohio; Hospital
French, Edward Beecher	1832–1907	Unitarian	39th Massachusetts
French, John William	1810–1871	Episcopalian	U.S. Military Academy
French, Luther P.	1812–	Methodist	20th Maine
French, Mansfield	1810–1876	Methodist	136th U.S. Colored Troops; Hospital Chaplain
French, Russell G.			23rd Ohio
Fries, William H.	1832–1896	Methodist	4th Delaware
Frisbie, Alvah Lillie	1830–1917	Congregational	20th Connecticut
Fritz, Gustav	1830–		20th New York
Frost, Henry Martyn	1835–1866	Episcopalian	7th Vermont
Frost, Nathaniel	–1868	Baptist	U.S. Navy
Fry, Benjamin St. James	1824–1892	Methodist	63rd Ohio
Fry, George V.			36th Ohio
Fry, Henry B.			82nd Ohio
Fuchshuber, Joseph M.		Unified Church of Christ	9th Ohio
Fuller, Americus	1834–	Congregational	106th U.S. Colored Troops
Fuller, Arthur Buckminster	1822–1862	Unitarian	16th Massachusetts
Fuller, Isaac K.		Methodist	1st Iowa
Fuller, Samuel A.		Methodist	1st Maine Cavalry
Fullerton, Alexander H.	1841–1868?	Presbyterian	144th New York
Fullerton, George Humphrey	1838–1918	Presbyterian	1st Ohio
Fullerton, Thomas Artemas	1834–1901	Presbyterian	17th Ohio
Fulton, William	1822–1892	Presbyterian	20th & 68th Pennsylvania
Furbish, Edward Brown	1837–1918	Congregational	25th Maine
Furman, Adoniram Judson	–1918	Baptist	7th Pennsylvania Reserves
Furman, E. S.			140th New York
Fusseder, Francis	1825–1888	Roman Catholic	17th & 24th Wisconsin

UNION CHAPLAINS *continued*

Name	Life Dates	Denomination	Association
Gaddis, Maxwell Pierson	1832–1872	Methodist	2nd Ohio
Gage, Moses D.	1828–1912	Baptist	12th Indiana
Gage, Rodney		Methodist	Hospital: Massachusetts
Gallagher, Mason	1821–1897	Epsicopalian	24th New York
Gallup, Horace M.	–1899	Baptist	17th Michigan
Gamage, Smith P.	1816–1892	Presbyterian	75th U.S. Colored Troops
Gardiner, Robert G.	1806–1888	Methodist	27th Kentucky
Gardner, James Harvey	1833–1904	Methodist	17th Ohio
Gardner, Ozem B.	1829–1864	Methodist	13th Kansas
Gardner, Samuel Spring	1831–1899		73rd, 83rd, & 96th U.S. Colored Troops
Garner, John M.			18th Missouri
Garrison, Samuel F. C.		Methodist	40th Iowa
Gaskins, Elias		Methodist	51st Indiana
Gast, Frederick Augustus	1834–1917	Dutch Reformed	45th Pennsylvania
Gatch, Benjamin F.		Methodist	16th Indiana
Gavit, William H.		Methodist	52nd Pennsylvania
Gaylord, Noah Murray	1823–1873	Universalist	13th Massachusetts; Hospital
Gear, Ezekiel Gilbert	1793–1873	Episcopalian	Ft. Ripley, Kans.
Geer, George Jarvis	1821–1885	Episcopalian	37th New York National Guard
Geer, John James	1833–1867	Methodist	183rd Ohio
George, Benjamin J.	1836–		174th Ohio
Gere, John A.		Methodist	Hospital: Maryland
Gerwig, Adolph	1812–1862	Lutheran	37th Ohio
Geyer, Jacob R.	–1865		140th Indiana
Gibbard, Isaac R.	1833–1911	Methodist	143rd New York
Gibson, James P.	1829–1910		2nd Tennessee Cavalry
Gibson, John Q.	1822–		2nd Ohio Heavy Artillery
Gibson, William J.	1810–1883	Presbyterian	45th Pennsylvania
Gilder, William Henry, Sr.	1812–1864	Methodist	40th New York
Gilham, John D.	–1901	Methodist	117th Illinois

UNION CHAPLAINS *continued*

Name	Life Dates	Denomination	Association
Gillen, Paul E.	1817–1882	Roman Catholic	170th New York
Gilmore, Hiram		Methodist	31st Indiana
Ginal, Henry			98th Pennsylvania
Given, Robert	1809–1895	Methodist	U.S. Navy
Glavis, George O.			Hospital: New Jersey
Gleason, Levi	1833–1910	Methodist	2nd Minnesota
Glenn, John D.			101st Pennsylvania
Godfrey, Alfred C.		Methodist	20th Maine
Goebel, Frederick	1812–		28th Ohio
Goekeritz, Francis			75th Pennsylvania
Golden, Thomas C.	1818–1879	Methodist	25th Wisconsin
Goldschmidt, J. Hieronymus	1832–		29th New York
Golliday, Uri P.	1810–1890		34th Iowa
Gombitelli, James		Roman Catholic	13th Pennsylvania Cavalry
Gonzales, Manuel Joaquin			Hospital: Pennsylvania
Goodfellow, Thomas Miles	1818–1871	Methodist	4th Iowa; 101st U.S. Colored Troops
Goodin, Smith	1819–1896		153rd Indiana
Goodrich, John Ellsworth	1830–1915	Episcopalian	1st Vermont Cavalry
Gordon, Henry	1826–1897		123rd New York
Gordon, Hiram J.	1831–		116th New York
Gorham, George Whitford	1820–1875	Baptist	46th Massachusetts; 1st Massachusetts Cavalry
Goss, George Gideons			Hospital: Washington, D.C.
Goss, Simon Sartwell	1823–1865	Presbyterian	75th New York
Gotthelf, Bernhard Henry	1819–	Jewish	Hospital: Louisville
Gould, John Binney	1824–1908	Methodist	11th Rhode Island
Gozelachowski, Alexander		Roman Catholic	2nd New Mexico
Gracey, Samuel Levis	1835–1911	Methodist	6th Pennsylvania Cavalry; 2nd Pennsylvania Provisional Cavalry

UNION CHAPLAINS *continued*

Name	Life Dates	Denomination	Association
Graeff, Isaac E.		Dutch Reformed	195th Pennsylvania
Graham, Henry Q.			4th Pennsylvania Cavalry
Graham, Richardson		Episcopalian	Hospital: Pennsylvania
Grant, Joel	1816–1873	Congregational	12th Illinois; 113th U.S. Colored Troops
Grassie, Thomas Gordon	1831–1898	Dutch Reformed	108th New York
Graw, Jacob Bentley	1832–1901	Methodist	10th New Jersey
Gray, Albert Zabriskie	1840–1889	Episcopalian	4th Massachusetts Cavalry
Gray, Joseph R. Taylor		Methodist	53rd Pennsylvania
Gray, Richard H.	1837–	Baptist	3rd Kentucky
Grear, Samuel	1808–		11th Tennessee Cavalry
Greeley, Stephen Sewall Norton	1813–1892	Congregational	6th Michigan Cavalry
Green, Asa B.			30th Wisconsin
Green, Jesse C.	1833–		95th Ohio
Green, John M.	–1894	Methodist	81st Indiana
Green, John M.	1832–1915		10th Pennsylvania Reserves
Green, John Murray	–1877		Hospital: Maryland
Green, Louis F.			Missouri Cass County Cavalry
Green, William Alexander	1825–1904		37th U.S. Colored Troops
Greene, Thomas	1818–	Episcopalian	17th Michigan
Greenough, William	1833–1919		147th Ohio
Gregg, Andrew W.	1825–1890	Methodist	7th West Virginia Cavalry
Gregg, James	–1876	Presbyterian	7th U.S. Colored Troops
Gregg, John Chandler	1830–1886	Methodist	127th Pennsylvania; Hospital
Gregg, John Clark	1829–1905	Methodist	62nd & 67th Ohio
Gregg, William B.	1825–1893	Methodist	1st Pennsylvania Reserves
Gregory, Almon	1814–1896		Hospital: Indiana
Gries, William Richards	1826–1872	Episcopalian	104th Pennsylvania
Griffin, Charles			183rd Pennsylvania
Griffing, Leonard B.	1805–1874		100th Ohio

UNION CHAPLAINS *continued*

Name	Life Dates	Denomination	Association
Griffith, Albert F.	1830–		17th New York; Hospital
Griffith, Frederick J.	1821–	Methodist	53rd Ohio
Griffith, Thomas			6th Indiana Cavalry
Grimes, Washington Morris	1822–	Presbyterian	92nd Ohio; Hospital
Griswold, Charles	1832–1906		1st Minnesota Heavy Artillery
Griswold, Francis A.			34th Indiana
Griswold, Salem T.			40th Ohio
Grubbs, William M.		Methodist	26th Kentucky
Gubby, James	1820–1888	Presbyterian	3rd Rhode Island Heavy Artillery; Hospital
Gue, George W.	1840–1901	Methodist	108th Illinois
Gunderman, John, Jr.		Baptist	5th Michigan Cavalry
Gunn, Thomas M.	1840–1917	Presbyterian	21st Kentucky
Gunter, Richard L.			15th Ohio
Gurney, Aaron			9th Indiana
Gushee, Edward Manning	1836–1917	Episcopalian	9th New Hampshire
Guthrie, Robert E.	–1892	Methodist	94th Illinois
Guthrie, Thomas Sander	1830–1920	Universalist	152nd Ohio
Guyon, George		Methodist	73rd Indiana
Hafner, Philip	1826–		45th New York
Hagar, Charles Luther	1819–1893	Methodist	118th New York
Hagerty, Thomas Harvey	1828–1917	Methodist	93rd Illinois
Haigh, William Morehead		Baptist	36th Illinois
Haines, Alanson Austin	1830–1891	Presbyterian	15th New Jersey
Haining, Ira Z.	1825–		140th Ohio
Hale, Charles Reuben	1836–1900	Episcopalian	U.S. Navy
Hale, Charles S.	1835–	Episcopalian	5th Vermont
Haley, William D'Arcy	1818–1890	Unitarian	17th Massachusetts
Hall, Edward Henry	1831–1912	Unitarian	44th Massachusetts
Hall, Francis Bloodgood	1827–1903	Presbyterian	16th New York
Hall, Henry Lewis	1835–1869	Congregational	10th Connecticut

UNION CHAPLAINS *continued*

Name	Life Dates	Denomination	Association
Hall, Perry T.	–1862	Disciples of Christ	79th Indiana
Hall, Thomas A.			35th U.S. Colored Troops
Hall, William Kittredge	1836–1906	Congregational	17th Connecticut
Halteman, David E.	1834–1895	Baptist	15th Illinois
Hamilton, Benjamin B.	–1894	Baptist	61st Illinois
Hamilton, Edward John	1834–1918	Presbyterian	7th New Jersey
Hamilton, James B.	1820–1899	Methodist	31st Indiana
Hamilton, John			155th Illinois
Hamilton, John Alexander	1829–1922	Congregational	6th New Hampshire
Hamilton, John R.		Presbyterian	111th Pennsylvania
Hamilton, Lewis	1810–1881	Presbyterian	2nd Colorado Cavalry
Hammer, George H.	1828–1879	Presbyterian	12th Pennsylvania Cavalry
Hammond, Brant Coryell		Methodist	5th Wisconsin; Hospital
Hammond, Jonathan Pinkney	–1884	Episcopalian	19th Pennsylvania; Hospital
Hammond, Philip Delano	1827–1884	Methodist	35th Illinois
Hammond, William	1837–	Methodist	49th Pennsylvania
Hancock, Lemuel M.	–1883	Methodist	49th Indiana
Haney, Milton L.	1825–1922	Methodist	55th Illinois
Haney, Richard	–1900	Methodist	16th Illinois
Hanna, John C.			145th Illinois
Hannon, Patrick	1829–		99th New York National Guard
Hanson, John Wesley	1823–1901	Universalist	6th Massachusetts
Harden, Benjamin Franklin			106th Indiana Minute Men
Hardenbrook, John A.			6th New York National Guard
Hardy, Anthony Colby	1827–1902		18th New Hampshire
Hare, Michael Huston	1818–1868	Methodist	36th Iowa
Harker, William S.		Methodist	86th Indiana
Harkey, Sidney Levi	1827–	Lutheran	54th Illinois
Harkey, Simeon Walcher	1811–1889	Lutheran	Hospital: Illinois
Harmon, Asa			3rd Michigan Cavalry

UNION CHAPLAINS *continued*

Name	Life Dates	Denomination	Association
Harmstead, Martin E.	–1865	Baptist	4th New Jersey Militia; 5th Pennsylvania Cavalry
Harned, William T.		Disciples of Christ	24th Indiana
Harper, William W.	–1894		13th West Virginia
Harris, Matthias	–1871	Episcopalian	Ft. Washington, Md.
Harris, Ralph	1812–1895		84th Illinois
Harris, Rice E.			35th Illinois
Harris, William C.			106th Pennsylvania
Harrison, Samuel	1818–1900	Congregational	54th Massachusetts
Harrison, T. Spencer	1820–	Baptist	126th New York
Hart, William	1833–1895	Presbyterian	3rd New York Light Artillery
Hartman, Daniel			158th Pennsylvania
Hartranft, Charles R.	1838–1879	Methodist	38th New Jersey
Hartsock, Andrew Jackson	1832–1907?	Brethren	110th & 133rd Pennsylvania
Hartt, Lionel B.	1832–1904		95th New York
Hartwell, Foster	1806–1868	Baptist	120th New York
Hartzell, Abraham			66th Illinois
Harvey, James	1817–1889	Presbyterian	110th Ohio
Harvey, John	1799–		62nd New York
Harwood, Thomas			25th Wisconsin
Haskell, Augustus Mellen	1832–1893	Congregational	40th Massachusetts
Haskell, William M.		Methodist	136th Pennsylvania
Haskins, Benjamin Franklin	1822–	Congregational	138th Illinois
Hassall, Robert	1820–1900	Unitarian	50th Massachusetts
Hassler, John Waldschmidt	1826–1905	Lutheran	2nd Pennsylvania Heavy Artillery
Hastings, William	1827–	Methodist	143rd Ohio
Hathaway, George Whitefield	1807–1891	Congregational	19th Maine
Hatton, William Henry Deacon	1822–	Episcopalian	13th Pennsylvania Reserves
Haven, Gilbert	1821–1880	Methodist	8th Massachusetts
Hawes, Lewis M.			37th Wisconsin
Hawk, Philip J.		Methodist	188th Pennsylvania

UNION CHAPLAINS *continued*

Name	Life Dates	Denomination	Association
Hawker, John	1828–	Baptist	29th Michigan
Hawkins, Gaylord Bela	1816–1862	Methodist	2nd Ohio Cavalry
Hawkins, John W.		German Reformed	83rd U.S. Colored Troops
Hawkins, Joseph	1838–		57th Ohio
Hawley, Chester Warner	1834–1902	Presbyterian	185th New York
Hawley, James Augustus	1813–1868	Congregational	63rd U.S. Colored Troops
Hawley, Zerah Kent	1806–1869	Congregational	59th U.S. Colored Troops; Hospital
Hayden, Gilbert B.		Episcopalian	43rd New York
Hayden, Jeremiah		Baptist	17th Maine
Haynes, Dudley Cammet	1809–1888	Baptist	13th New York Coastal Artillery
Haynes, Edwin Mortimer	1836–1910		10th Vermont
Hayward, Joseph A.	1824–		102nd New York National Guard
Hayward, William W.	1834–	Congregational	13th Maine
Hazen, Jeremiah H.	1824–1890		47th Illinois
Hazen, L. L.			49th Indiana
Heacock, Grosvenor Williams	1822–1877	Presbyterian	74th New York National Guard
Heagle, David A.	1836–1922	Baptist	1st Michigan Sharpshooters
Heath, Nathaniel P.	–1862		43rd Indiana
Heckard, Martin D.		Methodist	16th Illinois
Hedges, Thornton K.			106th Illinois
Heermance, Harrison	1813–1883	Dutch Reformed	128th New York
Heisley, Charles Wesley	1826–1916	Methodist	28th Pennsylvania; Hospital
Hempstead, Henry E.	1820–1862	Methodist	29th Massachusetts
Hempstead, William C. F.			104th Illinois
Henderson, Abner W.	–1872		13th Illinois Cavalry
Henderson, George Donald	1832–1875	Episcopalian	Ft. Riley, Kans.; U.S. Navy
Henderson, Ira		Baptist ?	37th Kentucky Mounted
Henderson, Roswell N.	1822–	Methodist	112th Illinois
Hendrick, James Paul	1828–1898	Presbyterian	10th Kentucky Cavalry
Hendricks, Abram T.	–1866	Methodist	4th Indiana Cavalry

UNION CHAPLAINS *continued*

Name	Life Dates	Denomination	Association
Hendrickson, William			31st Missouri
Henries, Henry Clay	1820–1865		8th Maine; Hospital
Henry, Caleb Sprague	1804–1884	Episcopalian	98th New York
Henson, Joseph	1813–1892	Methodist	84th New York
Hepworth, George Hughes	1833–1902	Unitarian	47th Massachusetts
Hera, Edwin R.			4th Maryland
Herrick, Henry Nathan	1832–1886	Baptist	5th Minnesota
Herrick, John I.			29th Wisconsin
Herrick, Osgood Eaton		Episcopalian	Key West, Fla.
Herron, Robert B.		Presbyterian	14th Kentucky
Hersey, Harvey	1831–	Universalist	17th Maine
Herzberger, Francis	1810–		58th New York
Hestwood, Samuel	1822–1892	Methodist	40th Iowa
Heuring, Frederick A.	1827–1907	Methodist	25th Indiana
Hewes, Charles E.	1814–1887?	Universalist	14th New York
Hibbard, Oliver Davidson	1809–1892	Presbyterian	64th New York
Hibben, Henry B.	1829–1890	Methodist	11th Indiana U.S. Navy
Hibben, Samuel	1834–1862	Presbyterian	4th Illinois Cavalry
Hickman, Martin			35th Missouri
Hicks, John Augustus	–1869	Episcopalian	Hospital: New York
Higgins, Adam C.		Methodist	83rd Illinois
Higgins, Josiah B.	1829–1878		12th New Hampshire
Higgins, Phineas C.		Methodist	21st Maine
Higgins, Simeon C.	1833–1897	Congregational	30th Maine
Higginson, Samuel Storrow	1842–1907		9th U.S. Colored Troops
High, John C.		Methodist	206th Pennsylvania
Hight, John J.	1834–1886	Methodist	58th Indiana
Hill, Charles E.	1824–1908	Methodist	118th Pennsylvania
Hill, Henry	1819–1884	Methodist	3rd New Hampshire; Hospital
Hill, James	1822–1899	Baptist	21st Iowa
Hill, Jesse		Methodist	72nd Indiana

UNION CHAPLAINS *continued*

Name	Life Dates	Denomination	Association
Hill, Joseph J.		Methodist	73rd Ohio
Hill, Thomas	1824–		114th Ohio
Himes, Timothy	1828–		111th Ohio
Hirschman, Carl H.			74th Pennsylvania
Hitchcock, Henry V.	1838–1920		177th Ohio
Hitchcock, Robert Stevens	1818–1891	Presbyterian	2nd Maryland
Hitchock, William Augustus	1934–1898	Episcopalian	U.S. Navy
Hoagland, Ezekiel S.	1815–		9th Ohio Cavalry
Hoback, William K.		Methodist	57th Indiana
Hobart, Ellen Elvira (Gibson)	1821–1901	Religio Philosophical Society	1st Wisconsin Heavy Artillery
Hobart, John	1812–		8th Wisconsin
Hobbs, Alvin L.		Disciples of Christ	69th Indiana
Hobbs, Lewis Merwin	1824–1901	Methodist	3rd U.S. Colored Troops
Hobbs, Marmaduke M. C.		Methodist	80th Indiana
Hobert, Chauncey	1811–1904	Methodist	3rd Minnesota
Hoblet, Joshua C.			35th Ohio
Hodgeman, Stephen Alexander	1808–1887	Presbyterian	74th U.S. Colored Troops
Hodsdon, Frederick A.			24th Maine
Hodson, David		Disciples of Christ	89th Indiana
Hoffman, Enoch			47th Iowa
Hoffman, Henry O.	1836–1908	Methodist	17th Indiana
Holding, Richard	1808–1868	Methodist	115th Illinois
Holland, Elihu Goodwin	1817–1878	Unitarian	156th New York
Hollems, Abraham		German Reformed	25th Iowa
Holliday, James Templin	1810–1881	Methodist	77th Ohio
Holliday, William C.	1838–1921	Methodist	90th Ohio
Hollington, Ambrose	1832–	Methodist	111th Ohio
Hollister, Philander Hatch	1836–1876	Congregational	29th (Colored) Connecticut
Holman, Samuel Augustus	1831–1907	Methodist	48th Pennsylvania

UNION CHAPLAINS *continued*

Name	Life Dates	Denomination	Association
Holman, William			Hospital: Kentucky
Holmes, Theodore James	1833–1906	Congregational	1st Connecticut Cavalry
Holtsinger, John P.	1813–1875	Presbyterian	1st Tennessee Cavalry
Homer, Charles Whitfield	1828–1905	Episcopalian	16th Massachusetts
Honey, George W.		Methodist	4th Wisconsin Cavalry
Honnell, William Harrison	1829–1895	Presbyterian	1st Kentucky Cavalry
Hoover, John Wesley		Methodist	Hospitals: Pennsylvania & Washington, D.C.
Hopkins, Henry H.	1837–1908	Congregational	120th New York; Hospital
Hopkins, John W.			1st Missouri Cavalry Militia
Hopkins, Joseph H.		Methodist	5th Missouri Cavalry Militia
Hopkins, William C.	1834–1910	Episcopalian	7th Vermont
Horn, Adam L.	1824–		4th Pennsylvania Reserves
Horton, George Whitefield	1837–1919	Methodist	70th New York
Houck, William A.		Methodist	205th Pennsylvania
Houghton, Amasa H.			38th Iowa
Houston, Jesse E.			102nd Illinois
Houts, Thomas Franklin		Methodist	22nd Illinois
Hovey, Jonathan Parsons	1810–1863	Presbyterian	71st New York National Guard
Howard, Harris	1824–		7th Rhode Island
Howard, Hiram Lowell	1827–1901	Congregational	59th Massachusetts
Howard, Richard L.		Methodist	124th Illinois
Howard, Thomas Dwight	1826–1910	Unitarian	78th & 88th U.S. Colored Troops
Howbert, Abraham R.	1825–1895	Lutheran	84th Ohio
Howe, Thomas D.	1824–		168th Ohio
Howe, William R.		Methodist	1st West Virginia
Howe, Z. H.			5th Wisconsin
Howell, Horatio Stockton	1820–1863	Presbyterian	90th Pennsylvania
Hoyt, Anson B.	1823–		162nd & 174th New York
Hubbard, George Allen	1831–1904	Baptist	103rd Ohio
Hubbard, William Claudius	1826–	Baptist	98th New York; Hospital

UNION CHAPLAINS *continued*

Name	Life Dates	Denomination	Association
Hudson, Henry Norman	1814–1886	Epsicopalian	1st New York Engineers
Hudson, Jonathan			1st Michigan Cavalry
Hudson, Thomas Boyd	1826–1912	Presbyterian	75th New York
Huffman, Samuel	1806–1900	Methodist	6th Missouri
Humphrey, Frederick		Episcopalian	12th Iowa
Humphreys, Charles Alfred	1838–1921	Unitarian	2nd Massachusetts Cavalry
Hungerford, Benjamin F.	1825–	Baptist	9th Kentucky Cavalry
Hungerford, Bradley		Methodist	28th Illinois
Hunt, Eli L.			Bissell's (Missouri) Engineers
Hunt, Thomas Poage	1794–1876	Presbyterian	7th Pennsylvania Reserves; 2nd Pennsylvania Heavy Artillery
Hunter, Hiram Abiff	1800–1883	Presbyterian	28th Kentucky; Hospital
Hunter, Moses Hoge	1814–1899	Episcopalian	3rd Pennsylvania Cavalry
Hunter, William H.	1831–	African Methodist	4th U.S. Colored Troops
Hunting, Sylvanus Stanley	1825–	Unitarian	27th Michigan
Huntington, Cyrus	1820–1883	Presbyterian	1st Maryland
Huntington, Jonathan	1804–		10th Tennessee
Hurlbert, Russel H.		Methodist	29th Ohio
Hurlbut, Joseph	1799–1875		Ft. Trumbull, Conn.
Hurlbut, Lewis		Methodist	Hospital: Indiana
Huston, Archibald	1823–		122nd Ohio
Hutcherson, Francis A.		Methodist	81st Indiana
Hutchins, Charles Josiah	1825–1887	Presbyterian	39th Wisconsin
Hutchinson, George W.	1823–1911	Methodist	79th U.S. Colored Troops
Hyde, Benjamin F.	–1902		3rd Missouri Cavalry
Hyde, Thomas W.			30th Iowa
Hyde, William Lyman	1819–1896	Congregational	112nd New York
Hyden, Jesse Albert			Hospital: Tennessee
Hyndshaw, James Bailey		Dutch Reformed	Hospital: New Jersey
Ingalls, Pearl P.	1823–1887	Methodist	3rd Iowa Cavalry

UNION CHAPLAINS *continued*

Name	Life Dates	Denomination	Association
Inggram, Ebenezer			49th Kentucky
Inman, Thomas E.	1812–1882	Baptist	1st Minnesota Cavalry
Inskip, John Swanel	1816–1884	Methodist	84th New York
Ireland, John Benjamin	1838–1918	Roman Catholic	5th Minnesota
Irvin, George A.	1820–1896	Presbyterian	88th Indiana
Irwin, John L.		Methodist	14th West Virginia
Irwin, Joseph L.			33rd Indiana
Irwin, Robert			46th Indiana
Isaminger, George W.		Methodist	173rd Ohio
Ives, Simeon Parmelee			68th Illinois; Hospital
Jackson, Eliphalet Woodman			Hospital: Maine
Jackson, James	1826–		45th Ohio
Jackson, James B.			153rd Illinois
Jackson, William	1818–	Baptist	55th Massachusetts
Jackson, William H.			50th Indiana
Jacob, Prosper Hubbard	1808–1886	Presbyterian	3rd Iowa
Jacobi, John Christian	1801–1874	Episcopalian	4th New York Cavalry; Hospital
Jacobs, John W.	–1862		4th Kentucky Mounted Infantry
Jacokes, Daniel C.	1813–1894	Methodist	5th Michigan
James, Horace	1818–1875	Presbyterian	25th Massachusetts
James, Joseph H.		Methodist	3rd New Jersey
Jameson, Love H.		Disciples of Christ	79th Indiana
Jameson, Thorndike Cleaves	1812–1891	Baptist	2nd Rhode Island
Janes, Leigh Richmond	1833–1908	Presbyterian	99th Pennsylvania
Janeway, John Livingston	1815–1906	Presbyterian	3rd New Jersey Militia; 30th New Jersey
Janeway, Joshua B. Howell		Presbyterian	199th Pennsylvania
Jaquess, Isaac Newton	1811–1896	Methodist	73rd Illinois
Jaquess, James Frazier	1819–1898	Methodist	6th Illinois Cavalry
Jarvis, Samuel Farmer		Episcopalian	1st Connecticut Heavy Artillery
Jennison, Joseph Fowler		Presbyterian	203rd Pennsylvania

UNION CHAPLAINS *continued*

Name	Life Dates	Denomination	Association
Jerome, John Adams	–1901	Episcopalian	Hospital: Pennsylvania
Jessup, Samuel	1833–1912	Presbyterian	6th Pennsylvania Reserves
Jewell, William R.		Disciples of Christ	7th Indiana
Johnson, George W.	1832–1903		12th Kentucky; 13th U.S. Colored Troops Heavy Artillery
Johnson, John H.		Methodist	15th Wisconsin
Johnson, John W.		Methodist	42nd Wisconsin
Johnson, Thomas Scott	1839–	Presbyterian	36th & 127th U.S. Colored Troops
Johnson, William D. H.		Baptist	130th Illinois
Johnson, William Tefft	1834–1898		135th Pennsylvania; Hospital
Johnston, James J.	1826–	Methodist	6th Kentucky
Johnston, William Curtis	1839–1862	Presbyterian	13th Kentucky
Jones, Alvah Ridway	1820–1897	Methodist	10th U.S. Colored Troops
Jones, Amos	1821–1903		40th Indiana
Jones, David		Episcopalian	102nd Pennsylvania
Jones, David O.			Hospital: Wisconsin
Jones, Edward			16th Indiana
Jones, Enoch	1832–1898	Methodist	4th U.S. Colored Troops Cavalry
Jones, Erasmus W.	1818–1909	Methodist	21st U.S. Colored Troops
Jones, Evan			1st Kansas; Indian Home Guard
Jones, George	1800–1870	Episcopalian	U.S. Navy
Jones, George Gardner	1822–1891	Episcopalian	13th New Hampshire
Jones, Jefferson Harrison		Disciples of Christ	42nd Ohio
Jones, John Buttrick	1824–1876	Baptist	2nd Kansas; Indian Home Guard
Jones, John D.	–1884	Presbyterian	117th New York
Jones, Joseph	1830–	Methodist	20th Michigan
Jones, Norman	1832–1904	Methodist	176th Ohio
Jones, Peter Franklin	1825–1887	Baptist	1st New York; 21st New York Cavalry

UNION CHAPLAINS *continued*

Name	Life Dates	Denomination	Association
Jones, Thomas W.		Methodist	1st Missouri Cavalry
Jones, William Evan	1827–1913	Presbyterian	161st New York
Jones, William M.			54th Illinois
Jordan, William Harvey	1832–1909	Methodist	150th Illinois
Judd, Henderson		Episcopalian	6th U.S. Colored Troops Cavalry
Judson, Philo	1807–1876	Methodist	8th Illinois Cavalry
Julian, John W.			53rd Indiana
Junkin, David Xavier	1808–1880	Presbyterian	U.S. Navy
Kabus, Robert F.	1818–		107th Ohio
Kalb, George Lewis	1829–1912	Presbyterian	90th Ohio
Karcher, John K.		Unitarian	114th Pennsylvania
Karsner, Charles			Hospital: Pennsylvania
Keagle, Jacob S.	1832–1894	Methodist	52nd Ohio
Keagle, Levi S.	1835–	Methodist ?	162nd Ohio
Keely, Josiah	1805–1864	Baptist	13th Maine
Keeton, Zachariah	1816–1908	Baptist	2nd Arkansas
Kehler, John H.			1st Colorado Cavalry
Keith, William K.		Methodist	7th Maryland
Kellen, Robert W.	1820–1894	Methodist	71st Pennsylvania
Keller, Edward			15th Missouri
Kelley, James M.			5th West Virginia
Kelley, Moses Jones	1817–1898	Baptist	6th Maine
Kelly, Charles Vernon	–1867		Hospital: Wisconsin
Kelly, Mordecai B.			18th Illinois
Kelly, Thomas F.		Roman Catholic	90th Illinois
Kempsey, Matthew Chapman	1832–1895	Baptist	176th New York
Kempton, Daniel		Disciples of Christ	86th Indiana
Kendig, Amos B.	1830–1909	Methodist	9th Iowa
Kendig, Daniel		Episcopalian	Post: Presidio, Calif.
Kendrick, Tunis T.	1835–	Methodist	1st Ohio Heavy Artillery
Kennedy, Crammond	1842–1918	Congregational	79th New York

UNION CHAPLAINS *continued*

Name	Life Dates	Denomination	Association
Kennedy, Joel	1816–1902	Presbyterian	3rd Michigan Cavalry
Kennedy, Oliver H.	1825–1889	Methodist	101st Ohio
Kent, Frederick			65th Illinois
Kephart, Benjamin F.	1838–1908	Methodist	59th U.S. Colored Troops
Kephart, Isaiah LaFayette	1832–1908	Brethren	21st Pennsylvania Cavalry
Kephart, William G.		Presbyterian	10th Iowa
Kerfoot, Richard Thomas		Episcopalian	3rd New York; 3rd Pennsylvania Heavy Artillery
Kerr, Aaron Hervey	1819–1890	Presbyterian	9th Minnesota
Ketcham, Charles Wesley	1830–1889	Methodist	96th Ohio
Ketchum, Isaac Sutherland	–1863	Dutch Reformed	Hospital: Missouri
Keyes, Charles Bright	1801–	Baptist	9th New York Cavalry
Keyes, Edwin R.	–1886	Methodist	6th New York Heavy Artillery
Keyes, J. J.	1837–	Baptist	58th New York National Guard
Keys, Orlando	1824–1866	Methodist	12th Michigan
Kiger, John	1806–1890	Methodist	7th Indiana
Kilian, John			26th Wisconsin
Kimball, John	1831–1897		Hospital: Washington, D.C.
Kimball, John Calvin	1832–1910	Unitarian	8th Massachusetts
Kimball, John Marshall	1828–1887	Congregational	25th New York National Guard
Kimball, Samuel S.			141st Illinois
Kimber, Emmor		Quaker	26th Ohio
Kindred, James W.			8th Kentucky
Kiner, Frederick F.	1833–1901	German Reformed	14th & 27th Iowa
King, Ensign H.		Methodist	15th Iowa
King, Marcus L.		Methodist	39th Kentucky
King, Richard			20th Iowa
King, William	1820–1881	Methodist	110th U.S. Colored Troops
Kingsbery, Sanford Agry	1809–1895	Baptist	17th Illinois
Kingston, Samuel M.		Methodist	1st (U.S.) Louisiana
Kinsolving, George W.		Presbyterian	17th Kentucky

UNION CHAPLAINS *continued*

Name	Life Dates	Denomination	Association
Kip, Isaac Livingston	1835–1901	Dutch Reformed	159th New York
Kirke, Elam			122nd Pennsylvania
Kirkpatrick, Andrew J.		Methodist	4th Iowa Cavalry
Kirkpatrick, John A.	–1889		26th Pennsylvania Militia
Kirkpatrick, Thomas			Hospital: Pennsylvania
Kline, James S.		Methodist	11th Kansas Cavalry
Knapp, James	1812–		20th Ohio
Knapp, William			19th Wisconsin
Knerr, Josiah K.	1840–1917		176th Pennsylvania
Knighton, Frederick	1812–1888	Presbyterian	11th New Jersey
Knowlden, William Henry		Episcopalian	24th Ohio
Knox, George	1816–1864	Baptist	1st, 10th, & 29th Maine
Koehler, Robert			108th Ohio
Kost, Jacob Kellar	1823–1897	Presbyterian	45th Ohio
Kountz, William P.			128th Indiana
Kramer, John W.			1st Maryland
Krauss, Albert	–1912		12th & 41st Missouri
Krebs, Hugo		Lutheran	2nd Missouri Light Artillery
Krebs, W. Diedrich			1st Missouri (U.S.) Reserve Corps
Kroh, Philip H.			109th Illinois
Kruger, Theodore	1827–1906		39th New York; 4th Missouri Cavalry
Lackey, Alexander H.		Presbyterian	Hospital: Illinois
Lacy, William C.	1837–1916		70th Illinois
Ladd, Francis Dudley	1820–1862		Hospital: Pennsylvania
Lakin, Arad S.		Congregational	8th Indiana Cavalry
LaMaster, George W.	1826–1897		110th Illinois
Lamb, Thomas G.	1811–1883	Baptist	29th Ohio
Lambert, Louis A.	1835–1910	Roman Catholic	18th Illinois
Lame, Joseph S.	1832–	Methodist	93rd Pennsylvania

UNION CHAPLAINS *continued*

Name	Life Dates	Denomination	Association
Lanahan, John			Hospital: Virginia
Lancey, S. Herbert			2nd Connecticut (3–month)
Landis, Robert W.		Presbyterian	2nd Missouri Cavalry
Lane, Andrew J.	1828–	Methodist	62nd Ohio
Lane, Gilbert	1828–1896	Dutch Reformed	9th New Jersey; Hospital
Lane, Henry Fayette	1825–1897	Baptist	3rd Massachusetts Cavalry
Lane, John W.	1832–1917	Methodist	80th Illinois
Lane, Joshua D.	1812–1873	Presbyterian	131st New York
Langley, Robert		Methodist	5th Wisconsin
Larimore, James Wilson	1824–1894	Presbyterian	9th Iowa Cavalry; Hospital
Lasher, George William	1831–1920	Baptist	5th Connecticut
Lasley, Mathew N.		Methodist	4th Kentucky Cavalry
Latham, James W.	1830–1872	Methodist	1st & 3rd Iowa Cavalry; 138th U.S. Colored Troops
Lathrop, Ezra R.		Methodist	10th Minnesota
La Tourrette, James Armour Moore	–1891	Episcopalian	Ft. Columbus, N.Y.
Lawrence, John	–1889		15th U.S. Colored Troops
Lawson, Elijah			42nd Missouri
Layton, Safety	1831–	Methodist	17th Indiana
Le Vere, George W.	1820–	Congregational	20th U.S. Colored Troops
Leach, Joseph Allen	1836–1906	Congregational	19th U.S. Colored Troops
Leake, William H.		Methodist	3rd Pennsylvania Reserves
Leakin, George Armistead	1818–1912		Hospital: Maryland
Leard, John M.		Methodist	1st Arkansas
Lee, David J.	–1874	Episcopalian	166th Pennsylvania
Lee, Henry M.	1827–		13th New York National Guard Coastal Artillery
Leek, John Wickliffe	1829–1877	Methodist	27th Connecticut
Lemagie, Charles L.		Roman Catholic	2nd Louisiana Cavalry
Lemmon, John Stephens		Methodist	209th Pennsylvania

UNION CHAPLAINS *continued*

Name	Life Dates	Denomination	Association
Lemon, Orange V.	1812–1889	Methodist	36th Indiana
Lenhart, John L.	1805–1862	Methodist	U.S. Navy
Leonard, Chauncey A.		Baptist	Hospital: Washington, D.C.
Leonard, Henry Codman	1818–1880	Unitarian	3rd Maine; 1st Maine Heavy Artillery
Leonard, James			57th Indiana
Leonard, Joseph Helmer	–1877		Hospital: Illinois
Leonard, William Glidden		Methodist	Hospital: Massachusetts
Lester, James	1812–1896		3rd Missouri Cavalry; 32nd Missouri
Lewis, Charles Davis	1830–1908	Baptist	1st New York Veteran Cavalry
Lewis, Hezekiah R.	1826–		46th Illinois
Lewis, John A.			10th Indiana Cavalry
Lewis, John W.	1832–1911	Methodist	45th & 125th Ohio
Lewis, Rodman	–1869	Episcopalian	U.S. Navy
Lewis, Valentine A.		Presbyterian	2nd New York
Lewis, William G.			24th Ohio
Light, Ezekiel			173rd Pennsylvania
Light, Oliver P.	–1904	Methodist	7th Minnesota
Linan, John	1822–1900	Methodist	49th Missouri
Lincoln, John K.		Congregational	22nd Maine
Linden, James			22nd Missouri
Linell, William B.			10th Illinois
Linn, John Blair	1830–1901	Episcopalian	100th New York
Lipe, Wiley A.	–1909	Lutheran	140th Illinois
Little, Arthur	1837–1915	Congregational	1st Vermont Heavy Artillery
Little, Joseph	1828–1882	Presbyterian	1st (Veteran) West Virginia; 5th West Virginia
Littler, Robert		Methodist	53rd (Reorganized) New York
Livermore, Lark Southgate	1819–1894	Baptist	16th Wisconsin; 5th U.S. Colored Troops Heavy Artillery

UNION CHAPLAINS *continued*

Name	Life Dates	Denomination	Association
Lloyd, Hinton Summerfield	1833–1918	Baptist	16th New York Cavalry
Locke, James R.	–1898	Methodist	2nd Illinois Cavalry
Locke, William Henry	1828–1905	Methodist	11th Pennsylvania
Lockwood, Ezekiel	1803–1877	Baptist	2nd District of Columbia
Lockwood, John H.	1837–1916	Methodist	49th Illinois
Logan, James	1830–		116th Ohio
Logan, Samuel Crothers	1823–1907	Presbyterian	34th Indiana
Long, John	1815–1905		Hospital: Pennsylvania
Long, Leander H.	1824–	Presbyterian	26th & 34th Ohio
Longhead, Samuel			8th Missouri
Longson, Alexander F.			38th & 55th New York
Lord, Edward	1821–	Presbyterian	110th New York
Lovejoy, Charles Hazeltine	1811–1904	Methodist	7th Kansas Cavalry
Lovering, Joseph Foster	1835–1915	Unitarian	17th Maine
Lowery, William P.			2nd & 3rd (U.S.) Tennessee
Lowring, Henry D.		Congregational	154th New York
Lowry, Robert	1826–1899	Episcopalian	Hospital: New York
Lozier, John Hogarth	1830–1907	Methodist	37th Indiana; Hospital
Lucas, Daniel R.	1840–1907	Disciples of Christ	99th Indiana
Luce, Andrew			24th Missouri
Lung, Augustus Henry	1826–1886	Baptist	33rd New York
Luther, Carl A.	1819–1871	Lutheran	29th New York
Lyda, Andrew J.		Methodist	6th West Virginia Cavalry
Lyford, Edward Tuck	1837–1903	Baptist	11th New Hampshire
Lyle, William W.	1825–1893	Presbyterian	11th Ohio
Lyman, Charles Northrop	1835–1905	Congregational	20th Connecticut
Lyman, Osman A.	1817–		41st & 93rd Ohio
Lynch, James			54th Massachusetts
Lyon, Aaron J.		Methodist	11th West Virginia
Lyon, George G.		Methodist	36th Illinois
Lytle, John S.	1820–1879	Methodist	58th Pennsylvania

UNION CHAPLAINS *continued*

Name	Life Dates	Denomination	Association
Machin, Charles	1810–1894	Presbyterian	140th New York
Mack, Daniel Augustus	1825–1883	Methodist	3rd Vermont
Mack, John B.			Hospital: Pennsylvania
MacLaren, John Finlay	1803–1883	Presbyterian	10th Pennsylvania Reserves
Madden, Samuel W.	–1896	Baptist	Hospital: District of Columbia
Mahon, Joseph			1st Maryland
Mahon, William	–1879	Methodist	8th Michigan
Mallory, Daniel Gilbert	1824–1868	Presbyterian	51st Pennsylvania
Manier, Robert H.			48th Illinois
Manly, Ralza Morse	1822–1897	Methodist	16th New Hampshire; 1st U.S. Colored Troops Cavalry
Mann, Jonathan L.	1839–1893	Methodist	9th Tennessee Cavalry
Manning, Jacob Merrill	1824–1882	Congregational	43rd Massachusetts
Mansfield, Francis	1834–1911	Episcopalian	132nd New York
Manville, Nicholas E.			87th Indiana
Maple, William			49th Indiana
Marble, William Horace	1822–1903	Baptist	20th Wisconsin
March, William Gilmore	1826–1895	Presbyterian	115th Ohio
Marks, Edward S.			4th Pennsylvania Reserves
Marks, Junius James	1809–1899	Presbyterian	12th & 63rd Pennsylvania
Marquis, James			7th Indiana Cavalry
Mars, John N.	1803–1884	Methodist	35th U.S. Colored Troops
Marsh, Jeremiah W.			28th Maine
Marshall, Charles H.	1823–1872		132nd Indiana
Marshall, James	1831–1896	Episcopalian	Hospital: Ft. Monroe, Va.
Marshall, Lorenzo		Methodist	192nd New York
Marshall, Samuel	1795–		74th Ohio
Martin, Gideon		Methodist	15th West Virginia
Martin, Michael F.	1818–	Roman Catholic	69th Pennsylvania
Martin, Samuel H.			107th Illinois

UNION CHAPLAINS *continued*

Name	Life Dates	Denomination	Association
Martin, William			53rd Indiana
Mason, Elihu	–1893	Congregational	10th Indiana
Mason, Lemuel Bickford		Universalist	12th Wisconsin
Mason, William C.	–1873		71st Illinois
Massey, Richard H.	1831–1911	Methodist	40th Illinois
Matchett, William Bramwell	1829–1903	Baptist	10th New York
Mateer, Joseph	1823–1883	Presbyterian	155th Pennsylvania
Mather, Asher E.	1823–	Baptist	22nd Michigan
Mather, William Loomis	1806–1868		3rd Wisconsin; Hospital
Mathers, Ebenezer			6th West Virginia
Matlack, Lucius C.	1817–1883	Methodist	8th Illinois Cavalry
Matlock, Joseph		Methodist	16th Ohio
Matthews, James		Methodist	19th Kentucky
Maxson, Darwin Eldridge	1822–1895	Baptist	85th New York
May, Franklin W.	1825–1880	Methodist	2nd Michigan
McAdam, William Taggart	1823–1892	Presbyterian	57th Pennsylvania
McAfee, Josiah Breckbill	1830–1908	Lutheran	83rd U.S. Colored Troops
McAtee, Francis	1823–	Roman Catholic	31st New York
McAyeal, Robert A.	1825–1894		33rd Iowa
McCabe, Charles Cardwell	1836–1906	Methodist	122nd Ohio
McCall, Bovell	–1864	Methodist	13th Tennessee Cavalry
McCarter, James Mayland	1823–1900	Methodist	14th Pennsylvania
McCarthy, Patrick Francis	1824–1882	Roman Catholic	Hospital: Washington, D.C.
McCarty, John	1798–1881		Post: Ft. Vancouver, Wash.
McCarty, John S.		Methodist	89th Indiana
McCarty, John Winspeare	1832–1867	Episcopalian	76th Ohio
McCasslin, Robert		Presbyterian	154th Ohio
McCay, David	1816–1862	Presbyterian	103rd Pennsylvania
McClary, Thomas W.			3rd Delaware
McCleary, Thomas	1821–	Methodist	19th Ohio
McClure, Thomas F.	1817–	Methodist	151st Pennsylvania

UNION CHAPLAINS *continued*

Name	Life Dates	Denomination	Association
McCollum, Bernard		Roman Catholic	116th Pennsylvania
McCook, Henry Christopher	1837–1911	Presbyterian	41st Illinois
McCormick, William			150th Pennsylvania
McCormick, William H.	1832–1908	Methodist	1st New Jersey
McCosker, John	1829–1862	Roman Catholic	55th Pennsylvania
McCoy, John R.			120th Indiana
McCoy, Reuben K.			3rd Missouri Cavalry
McCrae, John H.	1820–1890	Presbyterian	3rd Kentucky Cavalry
McCrea, John			33rd Indiana
McCrossin, Bernard		Roman Catholic	69th New York National Guard
McCulloch, John Scouller	1829–1910	Presbyterian	77th Illinois
McCune, Robert		Congregational	128th Ohio; Hospital
McDaniels, T. W.			4th Pennsylvania (3–month)
McDermond, C. H.			194th Pennsylvania
McDonald, A. C.		Methodist	68th U.S. Colored Troops
McFalls, Thaddeus Banks	–1873	Presbyterian	Hospital: washington, D.C.
McFarland, Allen			98th Illinois
McFarland, David	1810–1898	Baptist	81st New York
McFarland, James Hunter	–1863	Methodist	Hospital: Pennsylvania
McFarland, James Wilson	1830–1902	Presbyterian	74th Ohio; 9th Pennsylvania Reserves
McFarland, William Henderson	1832–1910	Presbyterian	97th Ohio
McGinley, John A.	1832–1914	Presbyterian	1st Pennsylvania Reserves
McGlynn, Edward	1837–1900	Roman Catholic	Hospital: New York City
McGrane, Peter	1820–	Roman Catholic	Hospital: Philadelphia
McGrath, Matthew F.	1833–	Roman Catholic	Hospital: Georgetown, D.C.
McGuire, Latshaw	1831–	Methodist	10th Pennsylvania Reserves
McIlvaine, Isaac			Hospital: New Jersey
McIntyre, James Johnson	1827–1902	Baptist	49th Wisconsin
McIntyre, Thomas K.	1826–	Methodist	53rd Ohio
McKee, David D.	–1884		Hospital: Indiana

UNION CHAPLAINS *continued*

Name	Life Dates	Denomination	Association
McKee, Edward	1830–1891	Roman Catholic	116th Pennsylvania
McKim, Philip	–1897		Hospital: Missouri
McKinley, William	1834–1918	Methodist	8th Wisconsin
McKinney, Arthur Layton	1819–	Disciples of Christ	71st Ohio
McKinney, Edmund	1815–1878	Presbyterian	9th Pennsylvania Cavalry
McLaren, Donald	1834–1920	Presbyterian	U.S. Navy
McLeish, John, Jr.			26th Iowa
McLeod, Alexander	1799–1877	Protestant	84th Pennsylvania; Hospital
McLeod, John Niel	1806–1874	Presbyterian	84th New York National Guard
McLeod, Norman			Post: Camp Douglas, Utah
McMahon, Laurence Stephen	1835–1893	Roman Catholic	28th Massachusetts
McMasters, Sterling Yancey	1813–1875	Methodist	27th Illinois; Hospital
McMillan, Andrew J.	–1878	Presbyterian	14th Kentucky
McMillan, Edward	1804–1864		32nd Illinois
McMillan, John	–1882		109th Pennsylvania
McMonagle, John Hamilton			Hospital: New York
McMurdy, Robert		Episcopalian	Post: Alexandria, Va.
McNair, John	1806–1867	Presbyterian	31st New Jersey
McNair, William Wynkoop	1825–	Presbyterian	1st New York Cavalry
McNamara, John C.	1821–1885	Episcopalian	1st Wisconsin
McNaughton, Samuel W.		Methodist	82nd Indiana
McNeiley, Levi T.		Methodist	3rd Missouri Cavalry Militia
McNeill, Francis Asbury	–1872	Methodist	Hospital: Illinois
McPherson, Robert	1818–1893	Presbyterian	139th Pennsylvania
McRae, Thaddeus	1831–1882	Presbyterian	74th & 91st U.S. Colored Troops
McReading, Charles S.		Methodist	39th Illinois
McReynolds, William M.			60th Ohio
McVickar, John	1787–1868	Episcopalian	Post: Fts. Wood & Columbus, N.Y.
McWhinney, Thomas Martin	1823–1909		57th Indiana

UNION CHAPLAINS *continued*

Name	Life Dates	Denomination	Association
Meachem, Thomas Goldesbrough	1819–1903	Episcopalian	141st New York; 14th New York Heavy Artillery
Means, James	1813–1863	Baptist	Hospital: New Bern, N.C.
Medeira, Addison B.			5th Iowa
Meech, William Witter	1825–1902	Baptist	12th U.S. Colored Troops Heavy Artillery
Meek, John B.			Hospital: Pennsylvania
Meittenger, Gustavus		Roman Catholic	2nd New York
Melick, Philip W.	1824–1902	Presbyterian	153rd Pennsylvania
Mellen, William R. G.	1822–		24th Massachusetts
Meredith, John F.	1827–1900	Methodist	50th Pennsylvania
Meredith, Thomas			5th Indiana Cavalry
Merrell, Samuel Lewis	1822–1900	Presbyterian	35th New York
Merrill, Samuel Hill	1805–1874	Congregational	1st Maine Cavalry; 1st District of Columbia Cavalry
Merrill, Selah	1837–1909	Congregational	49th U.S. Colored Troops
Merrill, Sherman Morton	1829–		177th New York
Merrill, Thomas	1817–1899	Presbyterian	5th Iowa
Merritt, William C.			2nd Illinois Light Artillery
Merwin, James Burtis	1829–1917		Hospital: Illinois
Messenger, Henry H.	1829–		136th Ohio
Messmore, Samuel W.		Methodist	1st (U.S.) North Carolina
Meyer, Edward	1815–	Episcopalian	1st Michigan
Meyers, David L.			14th Missouri Cavalry Militia
Michel, Anton J.			5th Missouri Cavalry
Michell, Tobias Harpur		Episcopalian	Post: Ft. Chadbourne, Tex.
Mickly, Jeremiah Marion	1836–1909	Dutch Reformed	177th Pennsylvania; 43rd U.S. Colored Troops
Middleton, William N.	1812–1888	Methodist	77th U.S. Colored Troops
Mignault, Napoleon		Roman Catholic	17th Wisconsin

UNION CHAPLAINS *continued*

Name	Life Dates	Denomination	Association
Milburn, William	1808–	Methodist	8th Tennessee Cavalry
Miles, Daniel Augustus	1835–1895	Congregational	4th New Jersey
Millar, Andrew M.	1819–1896	Presbyterian	16th New York
Millard, Corydon			4th U.S. Colored Troops Heavy Artillery
Miller, Alexander	1814–1872		8th Ohio
Miller, Alexander R.			202nd Pennsylvania
Miller, Benjamin R.	–1903	Methodist	119th Pennsylvania
Miller, Daniel Henry	1824–1896	Baptist	15th Connecticut
Miller, Enoch K.	1840–1903	Episcopalian	25th U.S. Colored Troops
Miller, Ferdinand			73rd Pennsylvania
Miller, Henry F. H.	1831–		35th Massachusetts
Miller, Ichabod T.		Methodist	94th Illinois
Miller, Joseph C.	–1880	Baptist	13th Illinois
Miller, Levi P.	1808–1872	Methodist	100th U.S. Colored Troops
Miller, Milton J.	1831–1919	Unitarian	110th Ohio
Miller, Obadiah Haymaker		Presbyterian	12th Pennsylvania Reserves
Miller, Rufus L.	1829–		3rd Iowa Cavalry
Milligan, J. Lynn			140th Pennsylvania
Mills, Robert F.		Baptist	13th Kentucky Cavalry
Millsaps, Joseph S.	–1886	Methodist	86th Illinois
Minear, Philip N.		Methodist	25th Illinois
Miner, Simon Gordon	1808–1893	Baptist	7th Illinois Cavalry
Mines, John Flavel	1835–1891	Episcopalian	2nd Maine
Mitchell, David H.	1831–	Methodist	6th Iowa Cavalry
Mitchell, George			52nd Kentucky Mounted Infantry
Mitchell, James	1818–1903	Methodist	133rd & 178th Ohio
Mitchell, John		Methodist	16th Maine
Modisette, Welton Morgan	1815–1902	Congregational	116th New York
Monfort, David			68th Indiana
Monfort, Isaac Watts	–1902	Presbyterian	52nd Indiana

UNION CHAPLAINS *continued*

Name	Life Dates	Denomination	Association
Monroe, Allen W.			139th Indiana
Monroe, Thomas H.	–1888	Methodist	Hospital: West Virginia
Monser, John Waterhouse	1840–1912	Disciples of Christ	76th Illinois
Montgomery, John K.	1836–1920	Presbyterian	16th U.S. Colored Troops
Mooney, Thomas F.		Roman Catholic	69th New York National Guard
Moore, David W.	1830–1899	Presbyterian	97th Pennsylvania
Moore, Henry D.		Congregational	13th Maine
Moore, Homer H.	1820–1913	Methodist	34th U.S. Colored Troops
Moore, John Henry	1823–1880	Presbyterian	154th Illinois
Moore, Joseph G.	1831–1864		159th Ohio
Moore, Samuel T.	1830–1902	Methodist	6th & 8th New Jersey
Moore, William D.		Presbyterian	6th Pennsylvania Heavy Artillery
Moore, William Porter		Presbyterian	142nd Pennsylvania
Moors, John Farwell	1819–1895	Unitarian	52nd Massachusetts
More, James H.	–1922		95th Illinois
Morrill, David Tilton	1825–1893	Baptist	26th New Jersey
Morrill, Stephen Sargeant	1831–1878		Hospital: Illinois
Morris, Edward			50th Wisconsin
Morris, John Moses	1837–1873		8th Connecticut
Morris, Joseph	1812–1888	Methodist	54th & 114th Ohio
Morris, William	1828–		149th Ohio
Morrison, Andrew Brown	1831–1916	Methodist	26th Illinois
Morrison, Marion	1821–1900	Presbyterian	9th Illinois
Morrison, William L.			21st Kentucky
Morrow, James M.	1818–1864	Methodist	99th Ohio
Morse, Frank C.	1836–1871	Methodist	37th Massachusetts
Morton, Aaron Delos	1823–1905	Methodist	105th Ohio
Morton, Robert Slemmons		Presbyterian	17th Pennsylvania Cavalry
Moss, Jasper J.	–1895	Disciples of Christ	1st Indiana Heavy Artillery
Moulton, Tyler C.	1825–		3rd Massachusetts Cavalry
Mudge, Warham	1822–1891	Baptist	9th New York Heavy Artillery

UNION CHAPLAINS *continued*

Name	Life Dates	Denomination	Association
Mullen, Daniel	1837–1878	Roman Catholic	9th Connecticut
Munger, Enos	1825–1873	Baptist	62nd U.S. Colored Troops
Munhall, Thomas			Post: Ft. Kearney, Neb.
Munn, Charles Anderson	1828–1910	Presbyterian	100th Indiana
Murdock, Alexander Vernon	1828–1886	Presbyterian	38th New York
Murdock, Daniel A.	–1863	Presbyterian ?	13th Kansas
Murphey, Thomas Grier	1817–1878	Presbyterian	1st Delaware
Murphy, Dennis	1833–1895	Methodist	19th Iowa; 98th U.S. Colored Troops
Murphy, Patrick Joseph R.	1823–	Roman Catholic	58th Illinois; Hospital
Mussehl, William	1818–		68th New York
Myers, Peter J. H.			23rd New York National Guard
Nash, Charles Pitman	1831–1913	Universalist	7th Michigan Cavalry
Nash, Michael	1825–1895	Roman Catholic	6th New York
Nash, Richard C.	1810–1865		10th Kentucky
Nason, Charles	1822–1885	Methodist	8th Maine; 2nd Maine Cavalry
Nave, Orville James			Post: Ohio
Neal, Moses	1833–		110th Illinois
Nebeker, Lucas		Methodist	17th Indiana
Needham, Arnold T.	1838–	Methodist	13th Illinois
Neill, Edward Duffield	1823–1893	Presbyterian	1st Minnesota; Hospital
Nelson, William Francis	1808–1875	Baptist	Hospital: Illinois
Nevin, Alfred	1816–1890	Presbyterian	Hospital: Philadelphia, Pa.
Newell, Chester	1803–1892	Episcopalian	U.S. Navy
Newell, Frederick R.	–1864		1st Missouri Militia
Newman, Wyngate J.	–1893	Methodist	101st Illinois
Newton, Joel Worthington	1799–1865	Congregational	U.S. Navy
Niccolls, Samuel Jack	1838–1915	Presbyterian	126th Pennsylvania
Nichols, James	1811–1864		108th New York
Nichols, Joseph Hulbert	1805–1862	Episcopalian	19th Wisconsin
Nichols, William A.	1814–1904	Methodist	94th New York

UNION CHAPLAINS *continued*

Name	Life Dates	Denomination	Association
Nickerson, Linus M.	–1888		122nd New York
Nickerson, William H.	1814–	Methodist	32nd Ohio
Noble, Mason	1809–1881	Presbyterian	U.S. Navy
Noble, Thomas K.	1832–1913	Congregational	128th U.S. Colored Troops
Noble, William Francis Pringle	1827–1882		Hospital: Pennsylvania
North, Reuben	1801–1883	Methodist	1st Arkansas Cavalry
Northrop, Henry Horatio	1814–	Presbyterian	13th Michigan
Northrup, Gilbert S.			9th Kansas Cavalry
Northrup, Nehemiah B.			Hospital: Washington, D.C.
Norton, Levi Warren	1819–1900	Episcopalian	72nd New York
Norton, Samuel H.		Episcopalian	68th New York National Guard
Norton, William W.	1822–1890	Congregational	154th New York
Noyes, Charles H.			Hospital: New York & Mass.
Noyes, McWalter Bernard	1837–1885	Episcopalian	5th Rhode Island Heavy Artillery
Nugent, Andrew J.		United Brethen	116th Indiana
Nute, Ephraim, Jr.	1820–	Unitarian	1st Kansas
Nye, Joel W.	1835–1913	Baptist	18th Illinois
Oakely, Thomas H.	1815–1890		1st Ohio Light Artillery
O'Brien, Edward	1827–	Roman Catholic	17th Illinois Cavalry
O'Brien, Nicholas O.		Roman Catholic	28th Massachusetts
O'Callaghan, Joseph	1823–	Roman Catholic	69th New York National Guard
O'Hagan, Joseph B.	1826–1878	Roman Catholic	73rd New York
O'Higgins, William T.	1819–	Roman Catholic	10th Ohio
Olds, Abner D.	1815–1897	Congregational	59th U.S. Colored Troops
Oliver, Robert William		Episcopalian	82nd Pennsylvania
Olmstead, Lemuel Gregory	1808–1880	Presbyterian	Hospital: Alexandria, Va.
Olmsted, Edward B.		Presbyterian	Hospital: Illinois
Olmsted, Franklin White	1810–1898		Hospital: Vermont
O'Neill, William J.	1831–1887	Methodist	118th Pennsylvania
O'Reilly, Bernard	1820–	Roman Catholic	69th New York National Guard
Ormond, Marcus	–1881		140th Pennsylvania

UNION CHAPLAINS *continued*

Name	Life Dates	Denomination	Association
Ormsby, Duke Camp	1836–	Episcopalian	132nd New York; Hospital
Osborn, Andrew G.			14th Pennsylvania Cavalry
Osborne, Corra	–1884		43rd New York
Otis, Norman Leonard	1834–1916	Methodist	8th Michigan Cavalry
Otis, William B.		Episcopalian	12th New Jersey
Ouellet, Thomas	1820–	Roman Catholic	69th New York; Hospital
Overton, Alfred A.		Baptist	33rd Wisconsin
Oviatt, George Alexander	1811–1887	Congregational	25th Connecticut Militia
Oviatt, George D.	1821–		87th Ohio
Oyler, James M.	–1863	Methodist	23rd Missouri
Pace, Lewis Clark	1835–1925	Methodist	25th Missouri
Paddock, William Hemans Perry	1817–1872		Hospital: Pennsylvania
Page, Charles E.	1838–		17th New York National Guard
Page, Charles Henry	1801–1876	Episcopalian	Post: Newport Barracks, Ky.
Page, Christian J.			28th New Jersey
Paige, James Alexander		Presbyterian	Hospital: Missouri
Paine, Albert	1819–1901		Post Hospital: Ft. Monroe, Va.
Paine, Samuel S.	1831–		2nd Minnesota Cavalry
Palen, Vincent	–1884	Baptist	Hospital: Virginia
Palmer, Anthony	1815–	Methodist	12th New York Cavalry
Palmer, Edwin Beaman	1833–1904	Congregational	19th Maine
Palmer, George R.		Methodist	10th Missouri
Palmer, John A.		Methodist	54th Illinois
Palmer, Lucius L.	1825–1895	Methodist	142nd New York
Parker, Henry Elijah	1821–1896	Congregational	2nd New Hampshire
Parker, John		Methodist	128th New York
Parker, Lemuel D.	1834–	Methodist	18th Kentucky
Parker, Lewis			12th Kentucky
Parkinson, Royal	1815–1882	Congregational	23rd U.S. Colored Troops
Parks, James Henry			Hospital: New York

UNION CHAPLAINS *continued*

Name	Life Dates	Denomination	Association
Parmalee, Moses Payson	1834–1902	Congregational	3rd Vermont
Parrish, Hugh L.	1813–	Methodist	102nd Ohio
Parsons, Eben Burt	1835–1913	Presbyterian	116th U.S. Colored Troops
Parsons, Wilson R.			66th Ohio
Patten, William Aaron	1815–1905	Congregational	32nd Maine
Patterson, David B.	–1870		78th U.S. Colored Troops
Patterson, Nicholas M.		Methodist	42nd Indiana
Patterson, Reuben F.	1832–1908	Presbyterian	68th Indiana
Patterson, Thomas	1835–1909	Methodist	22nd & 3rd Prov. Pennsylvania Cavalry
Patterson, William C.	1811–		1st Massachusetts Cavalry
Pattison, Holmes A.	1830–1892	Methodist	11th Michigan
Patton, James L.	1830–1890	Congregational	5th U.S. Colored Troops
Paul, Timothy S.			7th & 8th Kentucky
Paulson, John	1822–	Methodist	8th Kansas
Payson, Albert L.	1805–1893		25th Michigan
Payson, Edward Phillips	1840–1913	Congregational	146th New York
Peake, Ebenezer Steele	1830–1905	Episcopalian	28th Wisconsin
Pearce, Isaac A.	1840–1912		139th Pennsylvania
Pearce, Liston H.			132nd Illinois
Pearce, William	1803–1897	Baptist	77th Ohio
Pearson, Benjamin Hanaford	–1873		11th Illinois
Pease, Loomis Hoyt	1811–1887	Presbyterian	44th New York
Peate, John	1820–1903	Methodist	164th Ohio
Peet, James	1828–1866	Methodist	50th U.S. Colored Troops
Pelan, William			2nd Indiana Cavalry
Pell, John P.		Methodist	12th Kentucky Cavalry
Pendell, David L.	1817–		158th New York
Penniman, Jesse A.	1818–1878	Episcopalian	67th New York
Pentecost, George Frederick	1842–1920	Baptist	8th Kentucky Cavalry
Pepper, George Whitfield	1833–1899	Methodist	80th Ohio

UNION CHAPLAINS *continued*

Name	Life Dates	Denomination	Association
Percival, Chester Smith	1822–1892	Episcopalian	12th New York
Perkey, Martin	1816–	Methodist	68th Ohio
Perkins, Francis Brown	1833–1906	Congregational	10th Massachusetts
Perkins, Horace			9th Maine
Perkins, William			7th Illinois
Perry, Cyrus Murdock	1839–1919	Presbyterian	24th New York Cavalry
Perry, John A.			1st Rhode Island Light Artillery
Perry, John Bulkley	1825–1872	Congregational	10th Vermont
Peterson, William S.		Methodist	103rd Illinois
Pettibone, Ira Fayette	1824–1897		74th Illinois
Pettigrew, Samuel			Hospital: Missouri
Petty, Asbury L.	1831–	Methodist	52nd Ohio
Pfeiffer, Alexander			3rd Missouri
Phelps, Henry M.	–1875	Presbyterian	87th Illinois
Phelps, John M.	–1884		9th West Virginia
Phelps, Winthrop Henry	1818–1885	Congregational	2nd Connecticut Heavy Artillery
Philbrook, Hiram Alfred	1834–	Methodist	8th Maine
Philips, William	–1892		Hospital: Pennsylvania
Phillips, Benjamin Thomas	1820–1892	Presbyterian	83rd New York; Hospital
Phillips, Enos M.			1st Wisconsin Cavalry
Phillips, George S.	1818–1865	Methodist	49th Ohio
Phillips, John W.			136th Illinois
Pierard, Aristide Edmond	1820–		53rd New York
Pierce, Edward R.	1833–1890	Methodist	55th U.S. Colored Troops
Pierce, John M.		Methodist	85th Pennsylvania
Pierce, Mial R.	1815–	Methodist	92nd New York
Pierce, Richard R.	1832–	Methodist	5th Ohio Cavalry; 91st Indiana
Pierce, Samuel Everett	1827–	Presbyterian	4th Massachusetts
Pierce, William Gifford	1816–1887	Congregational	77th Illinois
Pierpont, John	1785–1866	Unitarian	22nd Massachusetts
Pierson, Nathaniel Edwards	1814–1872		89th New York

UNION CHAPLAINS *continued*

Name	Life Dates	Denomination	Association
Pilcher, George W.			11th Illinois Cavalry
Pile, Graft Martin	1824–1912		54th Pennsylvania
Pile, James H.			60th U.S. Colored Troops
Pile, William A.	1829–1889	Methodist	1st Missouri Light Artillery
Pillsbury, Caleb D.	1817–1897	Methodist	22nd Wisconsin
Pillsbury, Theodore L.	1812–		21st Michigan
Plannett, John W.			211th Pennsylvania
Platt, Abraham	1805–		57th New York
Platt, Charles Henry	1822–1869	Episcopalian	28th New York
Plimpton, Salem Marsh	1820–1866	Congregational	4th Vermont
Plum, Francis			151st Ohio
Poague, James S.	1821–1898	Presbyterian	17th Illinois
Poe, Abraham B.		Methodist	72nd Ohio
Poinier, Samuel Thane	1837–1909	Baptist	15th Kentucky
Pollock, James T.	1834–1917	Presbyterian	91st Indiana
Polster, Toby			2nd Missouri
Pomeroy, John Jay	1834–1889	Presbyterian	3rd Pennsylvania Reserves; 198th Pennsylvania
Pope, Richard E.	1811–1894	Methodist	52nd U.S. Colored Troops
Porter, Elbert S.	1820–1888	Dutch Reformed	47th New York National Guard
Porter, James Franklin	1838–	Methodist	138th Pennsylvania
Porter, Jeremiah	1804–1893		1st Illinois Light Artillery
Porter, Joseph			61st U.S. Colored Troops
Porter, William C.	1834–1911	Presbyterian	20th Indiana
Portman, James Gilson	1830–	Baptist	9th Michigan
Post, George Edward	1838–1909	Presbyterian	15th New York Engineers
Post, Jacob	1821–		184th New York
Post, William S.			81st Illinois
Poston, William		Methodist	8th Iowa
Potter, Samuel Sandford	1814–1899	Presbyterian	Hospital: New Albany, Ind.
Potter, William James	1830–1893	Baptist	Hospital: Massachusetts

UNION CHAPLAINS *continued*

Name	Life Dates	Denomination	Association
Potts, Nixon			6th West Virginia
Poucher, John	1823–1891	Methodist	38th Ohio; 40th U.S. Colored Troops
Poulson, Thomas L.	1831–1913	Methodist	1st (U.S.) Maryland
Powell, Alfred H.		Methodist	24th Missouri
Powell, Cuthbert H.	–1897		Hospital: Washington, D.C.
Powell, Thomas	1836–		65th Ohio
Prescott, Oliver Sherman		Episcopalian	Hospital: Rhode Island
Preshaw, John M.	1820–1889	Methodist	152nd Illinois
Price, William			2nd Kentucky
Pritchard, Benjamin F.		Methodist	5th Michigan
Pritchett, Edward Corrie	1812–1892	Presbyterian	50th New York Engineers
Proudfit, Alexander	1839–1897	Presbyterian	Hospital: New Jersey
Proudfit, John Williams	1803–1870	Dutch Reformed	Hospitals: New Jersey & Pennsylvania
Proudfit, Robert Ralston	1836–1897	Presbyterian	2nd & 10th New Jersey
Purdy, Edward James		Episcopalian	Hospital: New Albany, Ind.
Purrington, Collamore		Baptist	1st & 7th Maine
Putnam, Simeon	–1864		3rd Minnesota
Putnam, William	1823–1913	Baptist	160th New York
Pyatt, James B.	1813–1891		9th Pennsylvania Reserves
Pye, George			6th Indiana
Pyne, Henry Rogers	1834–1892	Episcopalian	1st New Jersey Cavalry
Quimby, John	1811–1862		93rd Pennsylvania
Quinn, Thomas		Roman Catholic	1st Rhode Island Light Artillery
Quint, Alonzo Hall	1828–1896	Congregational	2nd Massachusetts
Raffensperger, Edwin Bowman	1824–	Presbyterian	14th Ohio
Ragan, Zacariah	1804–1875		25th Ohio; Hospital
Railsback, Lycurgus	1834–1897	Presbyterian	44th U.S. Colored Troops
Rakestraw, George G.		Methodist	201st Pennsylvania

UNION CHAPLAINS *continued*

Name	Life Dates	Denomination	Association
Rammel, Joel G.			3rd Pennsylvania Cavalry; 114th Pennsylvania
Rand, James S.			1st Iowa Cavalry
Randall, Asa B.			54th U.S. Colored Troops
Randall, Edward Herbert	1837–	Episcopalian	13th Vermont
Randle, Irwin B.	1811–1893		144th Illinois
Randolph, Benjamin F.	1837–1875?	Presbyterian	26th U.S. Colored Troops
Rankin, Adam L.	–1895		113th Illinois
Ransom, Albert		Methodist	87th Illinois
Ransom, Elijah	1820–1893	Methodist	30th Illinois
Ransom, Milo M.	–1866	Methodist	5th New Hampshire
Rawson, Silas		Congregational	38th Indiana
Rawson, Thomas Read	1803–1876		Hospital: New York
Raybold, Henry B.			8th New Jersey
Raymond, Charles Atwater			Hospital: Virginia
Raymond, Lewis	1807–1887		51st Illinois
Raymond, William Gould	1819–1893	Baptist	Hospital: New York
Rayner, James Orlando	1825–1888		Post: Ft. Steilacoom, Wash.
Read, Benjamin L.		Baptist	15th Kansas Cavalry
Read, Philander	1830–1904	Presbyterian	76th U.S. Colored Troops
Reasoner, John Rogers	1835–1925	Methodist	55th Kentucky Mounted; 119th U.S. Colored Troops
Record, Lewis Leonard	1816–1871		23rd Massachusetts
Reed, Benjamin N.	1813–1894	Methodist	66th Pennsylvania
Reed, George H.			50th Ohio
Reed, George Joseph	1822–	Presbyterian	2nd Kentucky Cavalry
Reed, Jacob E.			38th Illinois
Reed, James F.			62nd Pennsylvania
Reed, Joseph C.		Methodist	29th Indiana
Reese, Aquila Asbury		Methodist	Post: Maryland
Reese, Armenius T.		Methodist	129th Indiana

UNION CHAPLAINS *continued*

Name	Life Dates	Denomination	Association
Reese, William Waters		Presbyterian	Hospital: Washington, D.C.
Reger, John W.	1815–1893	Methodist	7th West Virginia; Hospital
Reichhelm, Emanuel Julius	1811–	Disciples of Christ	82nd Illinois
Reid, Hiram Alvin	1834–1906		5th Wisconsin
Reidy, Owen	1829–	Presbyterian	86th U.S. Colored Troops
Remington, Chauncey H.	1827–1904	Baptist	11th Iowa
Reubolt, John A.			27th & 46th Pennsylvania
Reynolds, Charles	1834–1912	Methodist	86th Ohio
Reynolds, Charles	–1885	Episcopalian	2nd Kansas. Cavalry; Post: Ft. Riley, Kans.
Reynolds, William Morton	1812–1876	Episcopalian	2nd Illinois Light Artillery
Rice, William Henry	1840–1911	Moravian	129th Pennsylvania
Richards, Samuel			20th Illinois
Richardson, Charles Herbert	1833–1903	Baptist	92nd & 98th New York
Richardson, Ezekiel	1836–1900		5th New York Heavy Artillery
Richardson, George W.		Methodist	11th U.S. Colored Troops
Richardson, Hiram Stone	1828–	Methodist	76th New York
Richardson, Nathaniel Smith	1806–1883	Episcopalian	36th Massachusetts
Richardson, Willard	1815–1897	Presbyterian	89th New York
Richmann, Frederick W.	1820–1885	Lutheran	58th Ohio
Richmond, James Cook	1808–1866	Episcopalian	2nd Wisconsin
Ricks, John W.		Methodist	48th Kentucky Mounted
Riddle, Matthew Brown	1836–1916	Dutch Reformed	2nd New Jersey Militia
Righly, Charles	1808–	Episcopalian	1st New York Cavalry
Riley, Girrard P.	1821–		50th Ohio
Rinker, Henry	1825–	Presbyterian	86th New York
Riordan, George T.			17th Wisconsin
Rittenhouse, Charles A.		Dutch Reformed	7th Pennsylvania Cavalry
Rizer, Peter	1812–1886		79th New York
Rizzo da Saracena, Leo	1832–1897	Roman Catholic	9th Connecticut
Roach, James P.			47th Iowa

UNION CHAPLAINS *continued*

Name	Life Dates	Denomination	Association
Robb, Hamilton	–1881	Baptist	46th Indiana
Robb, Wilson		Methodist	18th Iowa
Roberts, Eli F.	1827–1882	Methodist	137th New York
Roberts, George C. M.			Post: Ft. McHenry, Md.
Roberts, Hiram P.			84th & 137th Illinois
Roberts, Isaac F.	–1901	Episcopalian	44th Indiana
Roberts, John L.	1818–	Methodist	4th Vermont
Roberts, Thomas	1833–		12th Ohio Cavalry
Robie, John E.	1811–1872	Methodist	21st New York
Robinson, James Andrew	1827–1897	Episcopalian	32nd New York
Robinson, John Hiram	1822–1900	Methodist	25th New Jersey
Robinson, Mark	1808–1885		52nd Indiana
Robinson, Rodman H.	1820–1886	Methodist	32nd New York
Robinson, William Moore	1827–1912	Presbyterian	114th New York
Rockwood, George Arden	1832–1899	Congregational	8th U.S. Colored Troops
Rodgers, Jesse G.			30th Missouri
Rodgers, John D.	1814–1879	Methodist	23rd Indiana
Rodgers, William H.	1808–1886	Presbyterian	69th Ohio
Rodrock, William D. C.		German Reformed	47th Pennsylvania
Roe, Alfred Cox	1823–1901	Presbyterian	83rd & 104th New York
Roe, Charles Hill	1800–1872	Baptist	65th Illinois
Roe, Edward Payson	1838–1888	Presbyterian	2nd New York Cavalry; Hospital
Roe, John P.	1833–		97th New York
Roe, John Phipps	1825–1905	Methodist	24th Wisconsin
Rogers, Barton F.	1831–1897		15th Illinois
Rogers, James B.	–1864	Baptist	14th Wisconsin
Rogers, Lester Courtland	1829–1900	Dutch Reformed	29th New Jersey
Rogers, William H.	1834–	Methodist	189th New York
Rollinson, William		Baptist	Post: Ft. Schuyler, N.Y.
Root, Nathaniel William Taylor	1829–1872	Episcopalian	9th Rhode Island
Root, Stephen Eastman	1834–	Baptist	9th Michigan

UNION CHAPLAINS *continued*

Name	Life Dates	Denomination	Association
Rose, Frank Bramwell	1836–1910	Methodist	14th New Jersey
Rose, Julius David	1825–1890	Episcopalian	7th New Jersey
Roseboro, Samuel Reed	1823–1895	Presbyterian	126th Illinois
Rosenberg, Jacob A.	–1886		Hospital: New York
Ross, Randal	1818–1877	Presbyterian	15th Ohio
Rossiter, Frank Z.			39th Ohio
Rouse, John Hill	1807–1870	Episcopalian	Hospital: Massachusetts
Rowden, Philip	1827–		1st Michigan
Rowe, Aaron			122nd U.S. Colored Troops
Rowe, Charles Henry	1834–1890		Hospital: Maine
Rowe, Elihu Thayer	1813–1867		14th New Hampshire
Rowland, Adoniram Judson	1840–1920	Baptist	175th Pennsylvania
Rowling, John H.		Episcopalian	103 Pennsylvania
Royce, L. R.	1831–		135th Ohio
Rush, James C.		Quaker ?	9th Kentucky
Russell, Byron P.		Methodist	105th New York
Russell, Daniel	1824–		104th New York
Russell, James Watson	1828–1904	Congregational	13th U.S. Colored Troops
Russell, Jesse Barber	1833–1900	Methodist	23rd Michigan
Russell, Otis F.		Methodist	27th Maine
Russell, Peter T.			39th Iowa
Rutledge, Edward		Episcopalian	61st Illinois
Rutledge, William J.	1820–1900	Methodist	14th Illinois
Ryder, William Henry	1822–1888	Universalist	67th Illinois
Ryerson, Abraham George	1817–1887	Dutch Reformed	22nd New Jersey
Sabin, Elias H.	1824–		14th Indiana
Sage, James R.	1833–		121st New York
Sage, Orin N.	–1884		Hospital: Ohio
Salter, Charles Cotton	1832–1897	Congregational	13th Connecticut
Salter, Thomas C.	1870–1872	Episcopalian	U.S. Navy
Sanders, Charles Walton	1805–1912		131st & 208th Pennsylvania

UNION CHAPLAINS *continued*

Name	Life Dates	Denomination	Association
Sanders, Levi W.	1816–1863		125th Illinois
Sandford, Arthur W.			36th Indiana
Sandoe, George		German Reformed	123rd Illinois
Sands, Charles		German Reformed	59th Indiana
Sands, John D.	1815–1909		19th Iowa
Sanford, Amos W.			8th Indiana
Sanford, David Platt	1819–1883	Episcopalian	20th Connecticut
Sanford, Miles	1816–	Baptist	27th Massachusetts
Sanger, George J.	1826–1914	Universalist	42nd Massachusetts
Sargeant, Horatio L.	1833–1866	Baptist	14th Ohio
Sargeant, James	1814–		59th Ohio
Sargeant, Joseph	1817–1863		13th Vermont
Sargent, John C.		Methodist	91st Illinois
Sarner, Ferdinand Leopold	1820–1874	Jewish	54th New York
Satterfield, Thomas R.	1828–1909	Methodist	95th Illinois
Saunders, William T.	1836–1871	Methodist	83rd Indiana
Savage, John R.	1830–	Methodist	12th Michigan
Savidge, Charles H.	1823–		4th Minnesota
Sawyer, Samuel C.	1823–1902		47th Indiana
Scandlin, William G.	1828–1871	Unitarian	15th Massachusetts
Schilling, Joseph G.			1st Maryland
Schindel, Jeremiah		Lutheran	110th Pennsylvania
Schloegel, Charles A.	1823–		5th New York National Guard
Schmidt, Henry D.		Methodist	43rd Illinois
Schmitz, Fred H. Wilhelm	–1895		32nd Indiana
Schneider, James Henry	1839–1864		2nd U.S. Colored Troops
Schnellendreussler, Herman Frederick Francis	1819–1898	Dutch Reformed	16th New York Heavy Artillery
Schofield, James	1801–1888		35th Missouri; Hospital
Schoonmaker, Anthony H.	–1889	Methodist	132nd Pennsylvania

UNION CHAPLAINS *continued*

Name	Life Dates	Denomination	Association
Schoonmaker, Sylvester Franklin	1836–1887		7th Michigan; 34th New York
Schreiner, Louis	1824–		27th Pennsylvania
Schultz, James P.	1834–		175th Ohio
Schuyler, Montgomery	1814–1896	Episcopalian	Hospital: Missouri
Scofield, William C.	1826–1909	Congregational	104th Illinois
Scott, Abel H.			129th Illinois
Scott, Ferris	1830–1879	Baptist	148th New York
Scott, George McCulloch	1820–1908	Methodist	96th Ohio
Scudder, Joseph	1826–1911	Dutch Reformed	59th New York; Ft. Columbus, N.Y.
Scully, Thomas	1833–1902	Roman Catholic	9th Massachusetts
Seage, Johnne B.	1809–1883	Baptist	4th Michigan
Searle, Jeremiah	1836–	Dutch Reformed	143rd New York
Sears, Clinton William	1820–1863	Methodist	95th Ohio
Seibke, Charles H.			28th New York National Guard
Sellers, William		Methodist	12th Kansas
Severance, John Franklin	1817–1898	Presbyterian	21st Massachusetts
Sewall, John Smith	1830–1911	Congregational	8th Massachusetts
Sewell, Benjamin F.	1807–1885		29th Pennsylvania
Seymour, Charles		Episcopalian	Hospital: Pennsylvania
Seymour, James B.			101st Illinois
Seymour, Ova Hoyt	1826–1889	Presbyterian	157th New York
Shaffer, Stephen D.	1822–		47th Ohio
Sharron, John C.	1815–1875		5th Iowa
Shaw, Addison C.		Methodist	23rd Michigan
Shaw, George Stetson	1837–1909	Unitarian	135th U.S. Colored Troops
Shaw, Horatio Watson		Congregational	29th Indiana
Shelling, Charles	1826–1887	Methodist	56th New York
Shelton, Orville Clarkson		Methodist	Hospital: Virginia
Shepard, Benjamin H.	1821–1876	Baptist	17th U.S. Colored Troops

UNION CHAPLAINS *continued*

Name	Life Dates	Denomination	Association
Shinn, James G.	1822–1903		23rd Pennsylvania; Hospital
Shinn, John	1824–	Methodist	89th Ohio
Shiras, Alexander	1813–1894	Episcopalian	Hospital: Pennsylvania
Shortridge, Lemuel		Disciples of Christ	130th Indiana
Shrigley, James		Universalist	Hospital: Pennsylvania
Shuey, John P.	1816–1880		123rd Illinois
Shumate, Nathan	1821–1895	Methodist	59th Illinois; 9th Missouri
Simmons, John T.		Methodist	28th Iowa
Simons, Ezra DeFreest	1840–1888	Baptist	125th New York
Simons, Volney M.		Methodist	5th Vermont
Simpson, Benjamin F.	1835–1871	Methodist	40th New York
Simpson, Jeremiah L.			4th West Virginia Cavalry; 17th West Virginia
Simpson, Lewis J.	–1880	Presbyterian	120th Illinois
Simpson, Theodore William	1807–1890		Hospital: Maryland
Sittler, Robert	1818–1863	Protestant	74th New York
Skaggs, Greenberay E.	1820–1899	Baptist	46th U.S. Colored Troops
Skidmore, Albert F.	1827–1867	Baptist	139th New York
Skinner, Anson			45th Iowa
Skinner, Clark			Hospital: Maryland
Skinner, Elias			24th Iowa
Skinner, Henry C.	1831–1867	Baptist	21st Ohio; 8th Indiana
Slaughter, William			3rd West Virginia Cavalry
Slaysman, George Major	1822–1904	Baptist	130th Pennsylvania
Sloan, Isaac Oliver	1821–1899		Hospital: Philadelphia
Sloan, Samuel P.			21st Iowa
Slusser, Francis M.		Methodist	33rd Iowa
Smart, James Shirley	1825–1892	Methodist	23rd Michigan
Smart, William Stevenson	1833–1912	Congregational	14th Vermont
Smith, Anthony W.			13th Ohio
Smith, Benjamin R.	1838–1873	Methodist	56th Pennsylvania

UNION CHAPLAINS *continued*

Name	Life Dates	Denomination	Association
Smith, Charles Lewis	1837–1921	Methodist	9th Indiana
Smith, Claudius Buchanan	1818–1904	Baptist	2nd Vermont
Smith, David N.		Methodist	18th Iowa
Smith, George Williamson	1836–1925	Episcopalian	U.S. Navy
Smith, Harry	1833–1888		9th Indiana
Smith, Ira P.	1814–1900		26th New York
Smith, James J.	1822–		6th (U.S.) Tennessee Cavalry
Smith, James Tuttle		Episcopalian	Hospital: New York
Smith, John Buck	1836–1910	Presbyterian	19th Ohio
Smith, John Carpenter	1809–1893	Episcopalian	Hospital: D.C.
Smith, John W.		Methodist	48th Indiana
Smith, Levi Ward	1819–1863	Episcopalian	Hospital: Pennsylvania
Smith, Matthew Hale	1816–1879	Congregational	12th New York National Guard
Smith, Moses	1830–1904	Congregational	8th Connecticut
Smith, Moss Ingersoll	1826–1880	Methodist	3rd Michigan
Smith, Stephen H.			200th Pennsylvania
Smith, Thomas	1824–1895	Presbyterian	53rd U.S. Colored Troops
Smith, Thomas Franklin	1833–1916	Baptist	8th New York National Guard
Smith, Vaughan		Methodist	Purnell Legion, Md.
Smith, William Augustus	1833–1914	Methodist	79th Illinois
Smith, William Copley	1820–1897		Hospital: Pennsylvania
Smith, William Hutchinson	1829–1909	Methodist	75th Illinois
Smith, William O.	–1896		35th Kentucky Mounted Infantry
Smuller, Henry W.	1808–		6th New York Heavy Artillery; 18th New York National Guard
Snead, James A.	1806–1866		40th Kentucky Mounted
Snow, Charles Andrew	1829–1903	Baptist	3rd Massachusetts
Snow, Joseph Crocker	–1901	Universalist	23rd Maine
Snow, William Franklin	1838–1871	Unitarian	5th Massachusetts
Snyder, Henry	–1875		Hospital: Washington, D.C.
Snyder, William W.		Methodist	9th Indiana Cavalry

UNION CHAPLAINS *continued*

Name	Life Dates	Denomination	Association
Soule, George	1823–1867	Congregational	11th Connecticut
Sovereign, Thomas	1801–1888	Methodist	5th New Jersey
Sowle, Abram M.			74th Indiana
Spackman, Henry Spencer	–1875	Episcopalian	Hospital: Pennsylvania
Sparks, Reuben H.		Methodist	124th Indiana
Spaulding, Samuel Jones	1820–1892	Congregational	48th Massachusetts
Spear, Charles	1801–1863		Hospital: Massachusetts
Spears, John			6th Tennessee
Speer, Joshua K.			123rd Illinois
Spellman, Richard D.			101st Indiana
Spence, John Fletcher	1828–1912	Methodist	48th Ohio; 2nd Ohio Heavy Artillery
Spencer, Travis O.	1830–	Methodist	89th Illinois
Spencer, William A.	1840–1901	Methodist	8th Illinois Cavalry
Spicer, Wayne	1824–		188th New York
Spillman, Jerome			5th Iowa Cavalry
Spooner, John Alden	–1890	Episcopalian	Hospital: Maryland
Sprague, Ezra	1819–1881	Universalist	119th New York
Springer, Francis	1810–1892	Lutheran	10th Illinois Cavalry; 1st (U.S.) Arkansas
Springer, Isaac E.	1839–1922	Methodist	3rd Wisconsin
Springer, John M.	1837–1864	Methodist	3rd Wisconsin
Squire, Albert C.			147th Illinois
St Clair, James F.		Methodist	65th Indiana
St Clair, Peter			81st Indiana
Staengel, Wilhelm	1824–		9th Ohio
Stafford, George W.	1817–1902	Methodist	40th Indiana
Staples, Carlton Albert	1827–1904	Unitarian	Bissell's Missouri Engineers
Staples, John Long	1814–1898	Methodist	168th Pennsylvania; 2nd District of Columbia
Staples, Nahor Augustus	1831–1864	Unitarian	6th Wisconsin

UNION CHAPLAINS *continued*			
Name	Life Dates	Denomination	Association
Starr, Daniel S.	1820–		31st Iowa
Start, William A.		Universalist	58th Massachusetts
Steadman, Darius S.		Methodist	105th Pennsylvania
Steck, Charles F.		Presbyterian	79th Pennsylvania
Steele, John	1832–1862	Presbyterian	13th Iowa
Steele, Samuel	1822–1886	Methodist	7th West Virginia
Steever, David M.	1819–	Methodist	9th New York Cavalry
Steffen, Peter Friedrich	1823–1911	Lutheran	52nd New York
Stephan, Joseph Andrew	1822–	Roman Catholic	Hospital: Nashville
Stephenson, Evan			15th Indiana
Stevens, David	1805?–	African Methodist	36th U.S. Colored Troops
Stevens, Elias W.			44th Wisconsin
Stevens, Henry	–1869		Hospital: West Virginia
Stevens, Henry S.	1832–1913	Baptist	14th Connecticut
Stevens, Moody Adoniram	1828–1909	Congregational	82nd New York
Stevens, William Henry	1831–1901	Methodist	148th Pennsylvania
Stevenson, Thomas	1818–1867		6th Pennsylvania Reserves; 49th Pennsylvania, 114th U S Colored Troops
Stevenson, Thomas M.	1825–1898	Presbyterian	78th Ohio
Stewart, Alexander Morrison	1814–1875	Presbyterian	13th & 102nd Pennsylvania
Stewart, Charles Samuel	1798–1870	Presbyterian	U.S. Navy
Stewart, Charles W.			117th & 148th Indiana
Stewart, Isaac Ingersoll	–1864	Methodist ?	Hospital: Iowa
Stewart, John D.	1824–1902		125th Pennsylvania
Stewart, William H.	1831–1913	Baptist	U.S. Navy
Stewart, William Henry Nassau	1822–	Episcopalian	11th Pennsylvania Cavalry
Stickney, Washington	1811–1833	Presbyterian	2nd New York Mounted Rifles
Stillwell, James R.	1832–1887	Methodist	79th Ohio
Stimson, Edward P.	1806–		14th New York Cavalry; 25th New York National Guard

UNION CHAPLAINS *continued*

Name	Life Dates	Denomination	Association
Stimson, Hiram K.	1804–	Baptist	9th New York Cavalry
Stinson, Robert	1814–1863		6th New Hampshire
Stockbridge, Joseph	1811–1894	Baptist	U.S. Navy
Stockton, William C.	1820–1902	Methodist	24th New Jersey
Stockton, William R.	–1896	Episcopalian	61st Pennsylvania
Stokes, George			18th Wisconsin
Stone, Andrew Leete	1815–1892	Congregational	45th Massachusetts
Stone, Benjamin Washington	1813–1884	Episcopalian	2nd New York Cavalry
Stone, Edward Payson	1830–1920	Congregational	6th Vermont
Stone, Hiram	1824–	Episcopalian	Post: Ft. Leavenworth, Kans.
Stone, Levi Huntoon	1806–1892	Presbyterian	1st Vermont
Storer, Thomas			134th Pennsylvania
Stoughton, Jonathan C.	1819–1900	Methodist	127th Illinois
Stout, Silas T.		Methodist	84th Indiana
Stowe, Theodore		Presbyterian	114th Ohio
Stowe, William P.	–1896	Methodist	27th Wisconsin
Stratton, Frank K.	1834–1927	Methodist	11th New Hampshire
Stratton, Royal B.	1827–1875	Methodist	16th New York
Street, Thomas W.	1829–		80th New York
Strickland, William E.	1833–	Methodist	4th New York Cavalry
Strickland, Willam Peter	1809–1884	Methodist	48th New York
Strong, Addison Kellogg	1823–1895	Presbyterian	7th Michigan
Strong, Charles			46th Pennsylvania
Strong, Daniel G.	1836–	Methodist	4th Ohio
Strong, Erastus Albert	1809–1866	Episcopalian	3rd Ohio
Strong, Henry N.	1826–1886	Episcopalian	4th Michigan
Strout, Silas Franklin		Methodist	9th Maine
Stuart, John	1821–	Presbyterian	5th Ohio Cavalry
Stubbs, Aaron J.			132nd Ohio
Stuckenberg, John Henry Wilbrandt	1835–1903	Lutheran	145th Pennsylvania

UNION CHAPLAINS *continued*

Name	Life Dates	Denomination	Association
Stuff, George L. S.	1822–1893	Methodist	42nd Illinois
Sullivan, John M.		Methodist	70th Ohio
Suman, John J.	1818–1884	Lutheran	8th Maryland
Summerbell, Nicholas	1816–1889	Disciples of Christ	115th Indiana
Sumner, Samuel S.	–1884		22nd Kentucky
Sutton, Joseph Ford	1827–1912	Presbyterian	102nd New York
Swallow, Benjamin			Hospital: Washington, D.C.
Swan, Benjamin Chestnut	1823–1908	Presbyterian	131st Illinois
Swaney, Alexander	1813–	Presbyterian	98th Ohio
Swartz, Benjamin C.	–1905	Methodist	41st Illinois
Swartz, Taylor D.	1836–1865	Methodist	210th Pennsylvania
Sweet, Joshua			Post: Ft. Ridgley, Minn.
Sweetland, Lucius	1832–	Episcopalian	4th New York National Guard; 13th New York Cavalry
Symmes, John H.			2nd Maryland (Potomac Home Brigade)
Taffe, John		Disciples of Christ	11th Kentucky Cavalry
Taft, Edwin Augustus	1837–1877	Baptist	179th New York
Taladrid, Damasio		Roman Catholic	1st New Mexico; 1st New Mexico Cavalry
Talbot, Hiram V.	1834–1886	Methodist	152nd New York
Talbot, Mortimer R.	–1863	Episcopalian	U.S. Navy
Talbot, William K.	–1880		Hospital: Beaufort, S.C.
Talbott, Jeremiah J.			15th Kentucky
Tansey, Oliver H.			143rd Indiana
Tarr, Charles W.			109th U.S. Colored Troops
Tawney, Daniel A.	1833–		179th Ohio
Taylor, Alfred H.	1812–1866	Baptist	137th Pennsylvania
Taylor, Chauncey P.			3rd U.S. Colored Troops Heavy Artillery
Taylor, Fitch Waterman	1803–1865	Episcopalian	U.S. Navy

UNION CHAPLAINS *continued*

Name	Life Dates	Denomination	Association
Taylor, George	1810–1897	Methodist	8th Michigan
Taylor, J. Rice	1818–1900	Episcopalian	123rd U.S. Colored Troops
Taylor, Oliver	1818–1891	Episcopalian	5th Michigan Cavalry
Taylor, Robert	1838–		2nd Michigan Cavalry
Taylor, Robert F.	1838?–1866	Presbyterian	78th Illinois
Taylor, Thomas J.	1829–	Episcopalian	39th Iowa
Taylor, Timothy B.			74th Illinois
Taylor, William Howell	1834–1914	Presbyterian	48th New York
Taylor, William S.	1821–		36th Ohio
Teed, David		Methodist	46th Illinois
Tefft, Benjamin Franklin	1813–1885	Methodist	1st Maine Cavalry
Terry, George W.	1825–1913	Methodist	97th Indiana
Teter, Isaac P.	1829–1900	Methodist	7th Iowa; Hospital
Thacher, Seth Tracy			93rd U.S. Colored Troops
Thacker, Elisha	1828–1910	Baptist	45th Kentucky Mounted Infantry
Thayer, Joseph Henry	1828–1901	Congregational	40th Massachusetts
Thomas, Abel Charles	1807–1880	Universalist	6th Massachusetts Militia
Thomas, Arthur G.	–1886	Baptist	Hospital: Pennsylvania
Thomas, Benjamin Franklin			52nd Illinois
Thomas, Chauncey Boardman	1834–1881	Congregational	Hospital: Alexandria, Va.
Thomas, John	1821–1908	Presbyterian	84th & 110th Pennsylvania
Thomas, John M.	–1894	Methodist	77th & 155th Pennsylvania
Thomas, Jonathan E.			56th Ohio
Thomas, Joseph Conable			88th Illinois
Thomas, Porter	1804–1876	Episcopalian	51st New York
Thomas, Robert Y.			17th Kentucky Cavalry
Thomas, Thomas Snowden		Methodist	Hospital: Maryland
Thomas, William H.	1840–	Methodist	4th New Hampshire
Thompson, Charles James	1830–1913	Baptist	15th New York Engineers
Thompson, George W.		Disciples of Christ	147th Indiana
Thompson, Robert G.	1816–1895	Presbyterian	64th Ohio

UNION CHAPLAINS *continued*

Name	Life Dates	Denomination	Association
Thompson, Robert R.	1825–		5th New York Cavalry
Thompson, Zenas	1804–1882		6th Maine
Thorburn, Alexander McA	1836–1894		91st New York
Thorpe, Wallace W.		Presbyterian	3rd New York
Thrush, John			Hospital: Washington, D.C.
Tiffany, Charles Comfort	1829–1907	Episcopalian	6th Connecticut
Tilden, Alanson	1828–1918	Baptist	59th New York
Tilton, Hezekiah C.		Methodist	13th Wisconsin
Tipton, Lorenzo D.		Baptist	5th Tennessee Mounted
Tipton, Thomas Weston	1817–1899	Congregational	1st Nebraska Cavalry
Tissot, Peter	1823–1875	Roman Catholic	37th New York
Todd, John			46th Iowa
Todd, Miles G.			23rd Wisconsin
Todd, Ohiphant Monroe		Presbyterian	78th Ohio
Tolford, David Wilson	–1875		10th Iowa; Hospital
Topliffe, Oliver A.			99th Illinois
Torrence, Adam			11th Pennsylvania Reserves
Townsend, Ebenezer Grant	1819–1895	Methodist	3rd New York Cavalry
Tracy, David Burnham	1829–	Methodist	1st Michigan Engineers
Trainer, Thomas H.	1820–1891	Methodist	12th West Virginia
Trapp, William R.			4th Missouri Cavalry Militia
Trask, Eben G.	–1887	Universalist	4th Illinois Cavalry
Trimble, Hiram Milton	1808–1881		62nd Illinois
Trimble, William J.	1839–1920		142nd Ohio
Truckenmiller, D. S.		Lutheran	16th Pennsylvania Cavalry
Truesdale, James Clark	1833–1904	Presbyterian	105th Pennsylvania
Truesdell, Charles G.	1827–	Methodist	2nd Iowa Cavalry
Truman, David			1st West Virginia Cavalry
Trumbull, Henry Clay	1830–1903	Congregational	10th Connecticut
Tucker, A. H.			5th Missouri Cavalry
Tucker, Ezra		Methodist	108th U.S. Colored Troops

UNION CHAPLAINS *continued*

Name	Life Dates	Denomination	Association
Tull, William T.		Methodist	4th Delaware
Tullis, Amos K.		Methodist	102nd & 134th Illinois
Tully, David	1819–	Presbyterian	77th New York
Turner, Henry McNeal	1832–1915	African Methodist	1st U.S. Colored Troops
Turner, J. D.			6th Pennsylvania Cavalry
Turner, James B.			4th Pennsylvania Cavalry
Turnt, Ferdinand	1803–		103rd New York
Tuttle, Edmund Bostwick	1815–1881	Episcopalian	Hospital: Chicago
Tuttle, Isaac Henry	–1896	Episcopalian	176th Pennsylvania
Twichell, Joseph Hopkins	1838–1918	Congregational	71st New York
Twitchell, Justin Edwards	1835–1900	Congregational	131st Ohio
Tyler, Charles Mellen	1831–1918	Congregational	22nd Massachusetts
Tyng, Stephen Higginson, Jr.	1839–1898	Episcopalian	12th New York National Guard
Ufford, John C.		Episcopalian	6th Iowa
Underdue, James	1828–	Baptist	39th U.S. Colored Troops
Underwood, William	1832–1906	Methodist	118th Illinois
Upham, Nathaniel Lord	1833–1917	Congregational	35th New Jersey
Upson, Henry	1831–1911	Congregational	13th Connecticut
Utter, Russell D.			150th Indiana
Vahey, John		Roman Catholic	Hospital: Alton, Ill.
Van Antwerp, David Davis	–1887	Episcopalian	Hospital: North Carolina
Van Antwerp, John			26th Iowa
Van Burkalow, James Turley	–1909	Methodist	Hospital: Delaware
Van Buskirk, David Rife	1831–1908		134th Indiana
Van De Mark, William Nelson	1843–1928		92nd U.S. Colored Troops
Van Deusen, Russell Dudley	1832–1887		12th Ohio
Van Doren, William Theodore	1819–1885	Dutch Reformed	7th Missouri Cavalry
Van Horne, Thomas Budd	1821–1895	Baptist	13th Ohio; Post: Chattanooga
Van Ingen, John Visger	1806–1877	Episcopalian	8th New York Cavalry
Van Nest, Peter S.	1814–1893	Presbyterian	36th Wisconsin
Van Nostrand, Aaron	1830–1863	Epsicopalian	105th Ohio

UNION CHAPLAINS *continued*

Name	Life Dates	Denomination	Association
Van Petten, John Bullock	1827–1908	Methodist	34th New York
Van Santvoord, Cornelius	1816–1901	Dutch Reformed	80th New York; Hospital
Van Wyck, George Peter	1821–1899	Dutch Reformed	56th New York
Vanderveer, Cyrus G.	1835–1868	Dutch Reformed	8th Iowa
Vandewater, Asaph C.		Methodist	32nd Illinois
Vansyckle, Reuben			Hospital: New Jersey
Varney, James Alvan	1825–1894		7th Maine
Vassar, Thomas Edwin	1834–	Baptist	150th New York
Vaux, William	–1882	Episcopalian	Hospital: Washington, D.C.
Vertican, F. W.		Methodist	1st West Virginia Cavalry
Vette, William			26th Wisconsin
Vetter, John			5th U.S. Colored Troops Cavalry
Vinson, Felix W.		Methodist	24th Iowa
Vinton, Robert Spencer		Methodist	Hospital: Baltimore
Vogel, Henry Carrier	1806–1887	Baptist	61st New York
Wade, Joseph F.	1818–		2nd New York Mounted Rifles
Waggoner, William Henry	1812–1893	Universalist	106th New York
Wainwright, George W.			52nd Illinois
Wainwright, Jonathan Mayhew		Episcopalian	2nd Connecticut Heavy Artillery
Wald, Paul			Hospital: Pennsylvania
Waldron, Samuel Wallis, Jr.			31st New York
Walker, Charles W.	1820–1889		1st New Hampshire Heavy Artillery
Walker, Edward Ashley	1834–1866		1st Connecticut Heavy Artillery
Walker, Henry C.			12th Wisconsin
Walker, Jesse L.	1831–	Methodist	25th Indiana
Walker, Joseph M.		Methodist	38th Wisconsin
Walker, Levi S.		Methodist	60th Illinois
Walker, Simeon			15th Illinois Cavalry
Walker, Thomas M.	–1888	Presbyterian	118th Illinois; 50th U.S. Colored Troops

UNION CHAPLAINS *continued*

Name	Life Dates	Denomination	Association
Walker, William Carey	1818–1886	Baptist	18th Connecticut
Wall, Edward	1825–1915	Presbyterian	3rd New York Cavalry
Wallace, John Stinger	1831–1906	Episcopalian	U.S. Navy
Wallace, Richard M.	1817–1893	Methodist	12th West Virginia
Wallace, Robert Howard, Jr.	1828–	Presbyterian	168th New York
Walter, Alfred H.		Methodist	20th Wisconsin
Walther, John L.	–1862	Lutheran	43rd Illinois
Walton, William B.		Methodist	2nd Maryland
Walworth, John	1804–1895		43rd Wisconsin
Ward, Ferdinand de Wilton	1812–1891	Presbyterian	104th New York
Wardner, Nathan	1833–1898	Methodist	96th New York
Wardwell, Irving B.	–1863	Methodist	28th Maine
Waring, William	1833–	Baptist	102nd U.S. Colored Troops
Warner, Abraham Joseph	1821–	Episcopalian	12th Illinois Cavalry
Warner, Edward Y.	1833–	Methodist	3rd Ohio Cavalry
Warner, Lorenzo		Methodist	4th Ohio
Warren, Joseph		Presbyterian	26th Missouri & 64th U.S. Colored Troops
Warriner, Edwin	1839–1898	Methodist	1st Connecticut Cavalry
Washburn, Israel	1796–1864		12th Massachusetts
Washburn, Ransom A.	1814–1902	Baptist	109th New York
Watson, Elisha Freeman	1814–1900	Episcopalian	11th Massachusetts
Watson, John Lee	1797–1884	Episcopalian	U.S. Navy
Watson, Joseph J.			2nd Iowa Cavalry
Watson, Josiah P.			12th Indiana
Watts, Jonathan	1816–	Methodist	86th New York
Way, Ebon J.	–1886		Post: Ft. Delaware, Del.
Way, William Chittenden	1824–1896	Methodist	24th Michigan
Wayland, Heman Lincoln	1830–1898	Baptist	7th Connecticut
Wayman, Manasseh B.	–1864	Methodist	3rd Iowa Cavalry
Weakly, John W.		Methodist	75th Ohio

UNION CHAPLAINS *continued*

Name	Life Dates	Denomination	Association
Weaver, William W.	1829–1911		2nd Tennessee Cavalry
Webb, John	1825–1896	Methodist	38th Iowa
Webb, Thomas E.	1831–1913	Methodist	14th Indiana
Webber, George Nelson	1826–1907	Presbyterian	1st Connecticut (3–month)
Webster, Alonzo	1818–1887	Methodist	6th & 16th Vermont; Hospital
Webster, Charles B.	1837–	Unitarian	89th U.S. Colored Troops
Webster, Charles H.			29th Maine
Webster, Harvey	1826–1901	Methodist	6th Vermont
Webster, John Gott	1824–1887	Episcopalian	27th New York
Weirich, Christian E.	–1863	Methodist	23rd Wisconsin
Weiss, Solomon W.	1831–1916	Methodist	143rd Pennsylvania
Welch, Joseph		Methodist	91st Pennsylvania
Welch, Moses Cook	1827–1913	Congregational	5th Connecticut
Weller, Henry			87th Indiana
Wellman, Lysander Luroy	–1894	Baptist ?	52nd Wisconsin
Wells, Eli Mather Porter		Episcopalian	22nd Indiana
Wells, George W.			11th Wisconsin
Wells, James	1815–1892	Congregational	11th Maine
Wells, Martin L.			145th Indiana
Wenholz, William E.			149th Illinois
Werth, John Edabduel	1835–1910	Presbyterian	75th New York; 13th Missouri Cavalry
West, Nathaniel	–1864		Hospital: Pennsylvania
Weston, Sullivan Hardy	1816–1887	Episcopalian	7th New York National Guard
Wetherbee, Seba F.	1815–1890	Methodist	15th Maine
Whallon, Thomas	1812–1891	Presbyterian	101st Indiana
Wheatley, Richard	1831–	Methodist	28th Connecticut
Wheeler, Alfred	1824–	Methodist	55th Ohio
Wheeler, Edwin Seabury	1836–1918	Baptist	80th U.S. Colored Troops
Wheeler, George	1819–		93rd New York National Guard
Wheeler, Henry A.	–1925	Methodist	17th Pennsylvania Cavalry

UNION CHAPLAINS *continued*

Name	Life Dates	Denomination	Association
Wheelock, Edwin Miller	1829–1901	Unitarian	15th New Hampshire
Whitaker, J. Addison	1828–	Presbyterian	11th Pennsylvania Cavalry
Whitcomb, Lewis J.	–1903	Methodist	13th Michigan
Whitcomb, William Chalmers	–1864		Hospital: Massachusetts
White, David	1818–1901		107th Illinois
White, Erskine Norman	1833–1911	Presbyterian	22nd New York National Guard
White, Garland H.	1831–	African Methodist	28th U.S. Colored Troops
White, Henry Sumner	1829–1915	Methodist	5th Rhode Island Heavy Artillery
White, James	–1873	Methodist	Hospital: New Jersey
White, James			160th Ohio
White, James H.	1814–1873	Methodist	37th Iowa
White, John Brown	1810–1887	Baptist	117th Illinois
White, Myron	1815–1887	Methodist	123rd New York
White, Oren D. W.			92nd Illinois
Whitehead, John Milton	1823–1909	Baptist	15th Indiana
Whitehead, William Manlove	1823–1874	Baptist	97th Pennsylvania
Whiting, Edward P.	1830–1877		166th Ohio
Whitney, Buel	1823–		104th Ohio
Whitney, Leonard	–1862		11th Illinois Cavalry
Whitney, Walter R.			191st Pennsylvania
Whittaker, Jonathan G.	1819–		172nd Ohio
Whitted, Thomas A.	1811–1871	Methodist	27th Indiana
Whittemore, Benjamin Franklin	1824–1894	Methodist	30th & 53rd Massachusetts
Whittlesey, Eliphalet	1821–1909	Congregational	1st & 19th Maine
Whittlesey, John Smalley	1812–1862	Congregational	11th Iowa
Wiget, Bernardin F.	1842–1843	Roman Catholic	Hospital: Washington, D.C.
Wightman, Joseph Colver	1828–1882	Baptist	24th Connecticut
Wilford, Anthony			3rd Minnesota
Wilhelm, John Calhoun	1835–	Presbyterian	45th U.S. Colored Troops
Wilkin, Elias D.	1830–1895	Methodist	21st Illinois
Wilkin, William			5th Missouri

UNION CHAPLAINS *continued*

Name	Life Dates	Denomination	Association
Wilkins, Elijah R.	1822–	Methodist	5th New Hampshire
Will, John			2nd (U.S.) Missouri Reserve Corps
Willey, Junius Marshall	1821–1866	Episcopalian	3rd Connecticut (3–month)
Williams, Albert G.		Methodist	62nd Pennsylvania
Williams, Charles Ashley			Hospital: Iowa & New York
Williams, Charles Henry	1819–	Methodist	138th Ohio
Williams, Francis Charles	1821–	Unitarian	8th Vermont
Williams, John			43rd Indiana
Williams, John W.	1825–1863		131st New York
Williams, Lorenzo D.		Methodist	111th Pennsylvania
Williams, Samuel M.	1826–1904		1st Tennessee
Williams, Thomas J.		Methodist	39th Missouri
Williams, William George	1822–1902	Methodist	145th Ohio
Williams, William Graves	1806–1874	Presbyterian	Hospital: Memphis
Williams, William Henry	1823–	Episcopalian	87th New York
Williamson, Claiborne S.			119th Illinois
Willis, Martin Wyman	1821–	Unitarian ?	4th New Hampshire
Willis, Samuel B.	1808–1898	Presbyterian	127th New York
Willson, Edmund Burke	1820–1895	Unitarian ?	24th Massachusetts
Willson, William		Presbyterian	6th Kansas Cavalry
Wilmer, Lemuel			Post: Port Tobacco, Md.
Wilson, Amos		Methodist	23rd Ohio
Wilson, David A.			8th Missouri Cavalry Militia
Wilson, James A.		German Reformed	2nd Iowa
Wilson, James E.			99th Pennsylvania
Wilson, James T.		Methodist	207th Pennsylvania
Wilson, Joseph S.	1818–		6th Kansas Cavalry
Wilson, Moses Eaton	1822–1909	Episcopalian	10th New York Heavy Artillery
Wilson, Stacey	–1875	Methodist	81st Pennsylvania
Wilson, Walter			117th U.S. Colored Troops

UNION CHAPLAINS *continued*

Name	Life Dates	Denomination	Association
Wilson, William	1800–1870		Hospital: Pennsylvania
Wilson, William Hamilton	1822–1893	Presbyterian	17th Iowa
Wilson, William S.			88th Indiana
Winchester, Warren Weaver	1824–1889		Hospital: Massachusetts
Windsor, Anthony H.	1837–1912	Methodist	91st Ohio
Windsor, John M.			11th New York Cavalry
Wines, Frederick Howard	1838–1912	Presbyterian	Hospital: Missouri
Winslow, Ezra Dyer	1839–1892	Methodist	36th New York; 10th Massachusetts; U.S. Navy
Winslow, Gordon	1803–1864	Episcopalian	5th New York
Winslow, Horace	1814–1905	Presbyterian	5th Connecticut
Winslow, Jedediah	1819–1893	Episcopalian	20th New York Cavalry
Winters, Wilhelm	1826–1881	Presbyterian	46th New York
Wise, John G.	1825–		191st Ohio
Witted, James G.		Methodist	58th U.S. Colored Troops
Wittig, E. Louis			74th Pennsylvania
Woart, John	–1893	Episcopalian	Hospital: Hilton Head, S.C.
Wolf, Franklin Benjamin	1834–1865		94th Illinois
Wolfe, Francis S.	1830–1910	Methodist	95th New York
Wolff, Frederick			8th New York
Wood, Henry	1806–1873	Presbyterian	U.S. Navy
Wood, John E.			21st Connecticut
Wood, Miles		Methodist	93rd Indiana
Wood, Norman Nelson	1808–1874	Baptist	2nd Missouri Cavalry Militia
Wood, Preston	1825–1904	Methodist	38th Illinois
Wood, William Francis	1826–1890		1st Indiana Cavalry
Woodbury, Augustus	1825–1895	Unitarian	1st Rhode Island
Wooden, Thomas J. O.	1818–		161st New York
Woodhull, George Spafford	1829–1912	Presbyterian	4th West Virginia
Woodruff, Curtiss Trowbridge	1817–1887	Episcopalian	6th Connecticut
Woods, John	1838–1918	Presbyterian	35th Ohio

UNION CHAPLAINS *continued*

Name	Life Dates	Denomination	Association
Woods, John W.			5th Illinois Cavalry
Woods, John Washington	–1864		Hospital: Virginia
Woodward, George Wheelock	1810–1887	Unitarian	45th Illinois
Woodward, John H.	1809–	Congregational	1st Vermont Cavalry
Woodworth, Charles Louis	1820–1898	Congregational	27th Massachusetts
Woodworth, Horace G.		Baptist	96th Illinois
Woodworth, Nathan			31st Wisconsin
Woolard, James B.		Methodist	111th Illinois
Woolley, Joseph J.	1837–	Congregational	8th Connecticut
Worcester, David			29th Iowa
Worden, Horace	1812–1895		18th U.S. Colored Troops
Workman, Thomas Culley		Methodist	10th Indiana
Worthington, Nicholas C.		Methodist	51st Ohio
Wrage, Hermann Dietrich	1831–		68th New York
Wright, Alpha	1813–1889	Methodist	6th Missouri Cavalry Militia; 25th Missouri
Wright, Cornelius M.			102nd Illinois
Wright, Dean C.			7th Ohio
Wright, John E. M.	1822–1895	Congregational	8th Maine
Wright, John Flavel	1795–1879	Methodist	1st Kentucky; Hospital: Cincinnati, Ohio
Wright, Newton Perry	–1864		39th Iowa
Wright, Sela Goodrich	1816–1906		70th U.S. Colored Troops
Wright, William Janes	1831–1903	Presbyterian	76th Pennsylvania; Hospital
Wyatt, Albert Harmon	1839–1909	Methodist	109th New York
Wyatt, James C., Jr.	–1863	Presbyterian	79th New York
Wyatt, William W.	1812–1879	Methodist	109th New York
Wyckoff, Alfonso D.	1830–1919		64th Illinois
Yancey, Walter T.	1818–1903	Methodist	66th U.S. Colored Troops
Yard, Robert Boyce	1828–1875	Methodist	1st New Jersey
Yelton, Charles		Disciples of Christ	143rd Illinois

UNION CHAPLAINS *continued*

Name	Life Dates	Denomination	Association
York, Coleman W.	−1872	Baptist	7th Kentucky Cavalry
Young, James	1826–1897	Presbyterian	81st Ohio
Yourtee, Samuel L.	−1880	Methodist	5th & 83rd Ohio
Zundt, Hermann	1805–	German Evangelical	54th New York
Zyla, Anthony P.	−1865		39th & 58th New York

CONFEDERATE CHAPLAINS

Name	Life Dates	Denomination	Association
Acton, James C.	1820?–1878	Methodist	Hospital: Georgia
Adams, George F.			J. B. Magruder's Virginial Division
Adams, Shockley D.	1829–1894	Methodist	North Carolina Militia
Adams, Smith	1839–1888	Methodist	11th Mississippi; 22nd Texas Cavalry
Addison, Oscar M.	1820–1898	Methodist	13th Texas
Adwood, Francis			Hospital: South Carolina
Alrich, Nicodemus		Lutheran	1st South Carolina Artillery
Aldrich, William Augustus	1836–1903	Episcopalian	1st Virginia
Alexander, James Harvey	1826–1906	Presbyterian	27th Mississippi
Alford, James B.	1813–1883	Methodist	51st North Carolina
Allen, A. C.	1818–1880	Methodist	41st Mississippi
Allen, Edward	1799–		7th Missouri Cavalry
Allen, G. H.			Post: Richmond, Va.
Allen, Littleberry Woodson		Baptist	J. B. Magruder's Virginia Staff
Allison, Joseph Basley	1828–1883	Methodist	Forrest's Tennessee Cavalry
Allston, Robert B.		Methodist	6th South Carolina
Ambler, Thomas Marshall	1829–1907	Episcopalian	Chimborazo Hospital, Richmond, Va.
Ammons, Allen			39th North Carolina
Amons, John			16th North Carolina
Anderson, James Madison	1837–1906	Methodist	40th Virginia
Anderson, John Monroe	1821–1879	Presbyterian	12th South Carolina Regiment
Anderson, Robert Burton	1833–1889	Presbyterian	4th North Carolina
Andrews, Allen S.	1822–1898	Methodist	32nd Alabama
Andrews, John N.		Methodist	13th North Carolina
Andrews, Mark Samuel	1826–1898	Methodist	12th Alabama
Angere, Augustus		Lutheran	Hospital: Mississippi
Anthony, M. R.			1st Missouri
Anthony, O. P.			Georgia State Troops
Anthony, William H.	1819–1884	Methodist	1st Turney's Tennessee

CONFEDERATE CHAPLAINS *continued*

Name	Life Dates	Denomination	Association
Archer, G. W.			41st Mississippi
Archer, Henry S.		Baptist	41st Mississippi
Ard, Joseph W.	–1878	Methodist	6th Mississippi
Armstrong, R. C.			9th Texas Cavalry
Armstrong, William H.		Methodist	7th Tennessee
Arrington, Marcus	1820–1894	Methodist	Missouri State Guards
Ash, Vincent			2nd Kentucky Cavalry
Ashmore, Joseph Slocum		Methodist	25th Georgia
Atkinson, William D.			6th Regiment Georgia State Troops
Atwood, Charles H.		Presbyterian	5th Missouri
August, Peter Francis	1821–1887	Methodist	15th & 58th Virginia
Auld, Frederick	1834–1902	Methodist	24th South Carolina
Avirett, James Battle	1835–1912	Episcopalian	7th Virginia Cavalry
Awalt, Solomon			11th Texas
Axson, Samuel Edward	1836–1884	Presbyterian	1st Georgia
Bachman, Jonathan Waverly	1837–1924	Presbyterian	60th Tennessee
Bagby, George Franklin	1836–1902	Baptist	40th Virginia
Bailey, E. A.			13th Texas
Bailey, William Matthew		Methodist	8th Tennessee
Baird, Alexander J.		Presbyterian	Georgial T. Anderson's Brigade
Baker, A. A.			1st Tennessee Cavalry
Baker, G. E.			3rd Arkansas
Baker, Robert M.	1834–1884	Episcopalian	17th Virginia Cavalry
Bakewell, Alexander Gordon	1822–	Episcopalian	38th Mississippi
Baldwin, Benjamin J.		Methodist	31st Georgia
Baldwin, Livias H.	1831–		5th Louisiana
Ball, Dabney	1820–1878	Methodist	1st & 5th Virginia Cavalry
Balthis, Mayberry Goheen	1837–1895	Methodist	10th Virginia
Banks, William	1814–1875	Presbyterian	4th South Carolina
Bannon, John B.	1829–1913	Roman Catholic	1st Missouri Brigade

CONFEDERATE CHAPLAINS *continued*

Name	Life Dates	Denomination	Association
Barbee, James D.	1832–1905	Methodist	6th Alabama
Barber, Samuel B.		Baptist	47th Virginia
Barker, Josiah P.	1817–1894	Methodist	40th Alabama
Barley, Martin			8th South Carolina
Barnes, M. J.			12th Arkansas
Barnett, James J.			16th Tennessee
Barnwell, Robert W., Jr.	–1863	Episcopalian	Hospital: Warren Springs, Va.
Barr, John Calvin		Presbyterian	22nd Virginia
Barrett, Edward Benjamin		Baptist	45th Georgia
Barrett, Mills B.			16th Virginia
Barrett, Robert Graham	1830–1910	Methodist	49th North Carolina
Bartlett, Joseph S.			7th Missouri Cavalry
Bartlett, Wm. Frederick Vincent	1831–1903	Presbyterian	Post: Port Hudson, La.
Barton, Jefferson			34th Georgia
Bayless, J. S.			Marshall's Kentucky Infantry
Beadles, Robert Blackwell	1832–1907	Methodist	55th Virginia
Beale, Edward W.			48th North Carolina Militia
Beck, Thomas J.			44th Georgia
Beckwith, John Watrus	1831–1890	Episcopalian	Post: Demopolis, Ala.
Bell, Van A.			6th Georgia Cavalry Battalion
Bennett, John R.	1812–1884	Methodist	1st Missouri State Guard
Bennett, W. Thomas		Baptist	12th Tennessee
Bennett, William Wallace	1821–1887	Methodist	Post: Richmond, Va.
Bennick, Augustus R.		Methodist	34th North Carolina
Berry, L. M.			23rd North Carolina
Berry, William W.	1833–1905	Methodist	2nd Virginia Cavalry
Best, Elvey A.		Baptist	7th North Carolina
Betts, Alexander Davis	1832–1918	Methodist	30th North Carolina
Betts, Charles Bowen	1828–1903	Presbyterian	6th South Carolina
Bibb, Martin		Baptist	60th Virginia

CONFEDERATE CHAPLAINS *continued*

Name	Life Dates	Denomination	Association
Bidgood, George Langhorne	1835–1905	Methodist	General Hospital No. 9: Richmond, Va.
Bidgood, Richard West	1815–1871	Methodist	32nd Virginia
Biggs, J. B.			33rd Tennessee
Bikle, Louis Albert		Lutheran	20th North Carolina
Billups, Dozier Gayle	1833–1911	Methodist	Ft. Morgan, Ala.
Binet, William		Episcopalian	Hospital: Alabama
Birdwell, George			10th Virginia Cavalry
Black, B. B.			4th Arkansas
Black, William Samuel	1836–1897	Methodist	26th South Carolina
Blackwell, John Davenport	1822–1887	Methodist	18th Virginia
Blackwell, Thomas M.			11th Mississippi Cavalry
Blair, Brice Benton	1839–1871	Presbyterian	37th Virginia Cavalry Battalion
Blanton, Lindsay Hughes	1832–1914	Presbyterian	54th Virginia
Bledsoe, Adam Clarke	1839–1896	Methodist	15th Virginia Cavalry
Bliemel, P. Emmeran	1831–1864	Roman Catholic	10th Tennessee
Blount, William C.		Methodist	Hospital: Petersburg, Va.
Blue, Oliver R.	1822–1893	Methodist	45th Alabama
Bocock, John Holmes	1813–1872	Presbyterian	7th Virginia
Boggs, Charles Henry	1830–1920	Methodist	9th Virginia Cavalry
Boggs, David Chalmers		Presbyterian	2nd Missouri Cavalry
Boggs, Francis Johnston	1821–1894	Methodist	1st Virginia
Boggs, George Washington		Presbyterian	8th South Carolina
Boggs, William Ellison	1838–1920	Presbyterian	6th South Carolina
Bolthis, L. M. Y.			10th Virginia
Bolton, James			53rd North Carolina
Bolton, John G.	1841–1892	Methodist	50th Tennessee
Bond, G. J.			Arkansas Battalion, Army of the West
Booker, George Edward	–1899	Methodist	48th Virginia
Boothe, A. H.			26th Mississippi

CONFEDERATE CHAPLAINS *continued*

Name	Life Dates	Denomination	Association
Borah, J. T.		Cumberland Presbyterian	1st Mississippi
Bore, M.			7th (C.S.A.) Georgial Cavalry
Bosley, J. P.			3rd Kentucky Mounted
Bostick, William M.			61st North Carolina Militia
Bouchelle, J. N.			13th South Carolina
Boude, Henry Buckner	1833–1912	Presbyterian	11th Tennessee Cavalry
Bounds, E. McKenzie		Methodist	3rd Missouri
Bowles, Jefferson T.	–1864	Lutheran	53rd Georgia
Bowman, W. C.		Methodist	58th North Carolina
Bowman, Walter Spencer		Lutheran	50th Virginia
Boyce, James Pettigrew	1827–1888	Baptist	16th South Carolina
Boyls, George W.	1832–1895	Methodist	11th Mississippi Cavalry
Brady, John W.	1832?–1864	Methodist	39th Georgia
Bray, Bannister R.		Methodist	40th Georgia
Brearley, Henry Martyn	1834–1908	Presbyterian	8th South Carolina
Breck, W. C.			42nd Alabama
Breeman, Thomas H.			2nd Texas
Brent, Oscar J.	1829–1883	Methodist	28th North Carolina
Brewer, A. G.		Baptist	5th Alabama
Brewer, George E.			25th Alabama
Brewer, R. H.			1st Alabama Cavalry
Brigance, J. N.			7th Arkansas
Bright, George	1812–1874	Methodist	23rd Georgia
Brillhart, Jacob	1808–1874	Methodist	36th Virginia
Bristow, James Benjamin		Baptist	55th Virginia
Brittain, Jabez Mercer		Baptist	38th Georgia
Broadus, Andrew		Baptist	J.B. Gordon's Georgia Brigade
Broaddus, William Francis Ferguson	1801–1876	Baptist	Post: Charlottesville, Va.
Broadus, J. N.		Baptist	23rd South Carolina

CONFEDERATE CHAPLAINS *continued*

Name	Life Dates	Denomination	Association
Brooke, George Gibson	1808–1878	Methodist	Imboden's Virginia Cavalry Brigade
Brooks, A. T.			43rd Tennessee
Brooks, Calvin Herlock	1827–1916	Methodist	20th Texas
Brooks, E. H.		Baptist	60th Georgia
Brooks, H. C.			51st North Carolina
Brooks, Henry Erasmus		Baptist	44th Georgia & 2nd North Carolina Battalion
Brooks, S. E.			Georgia State Troops
Brown, Alexander Blaine	–1863	Baptist	Braxton's Virginia Artillery Battalion
Brown, Henry	1804–1881	Presbyterian	Post: Camp Lee, Va.
Brown, J. S.			11th Georgia Artillery Battalion
Brown, John Calvin	1831–1912	Presbyterian	60th Virginia
Brown, John M.		Presbyterian	37th Arkansas
Brown, Joseph	1809–1880	Presbyterian	19th Alabama
Brown, Manning	1827–1892	Methodist	2nd South Carolina Cavalry
Brown, Thomas F.	1832–1882	Methodist	Hospital: Georgia
Brown, William S.			75th North Carolina Militia
Browne, Henry Vincent		Roman Catholic	4th & 10th Tennessee
Browning, William H.	1819–1907	Methodist	154th Tennessee
Bryan, Daniel H.			15th Florida Cavalry
Bryson, John Henry	1831–1897	Presbyterian	9th Kentucky Mounted Infantry
Buchanan, S. H.		Cumberland Presbyterian	Monroe's 1st Arkansas Cavalry
Buck, Charles W.			42nd Alabama
Buckels, William N.		Baptist	Virginia–Tennessee Rail Road Hospital: Bristol, Va.
Buie, John Duncan	1837–1919	Methodist	7th (C.S.A.) Georgia Cavalry; 10th Georgia Cavalry
Buist, J. F.		Presbyterian	17th South Carolina

CONFEDERATE CHAPLAINS *continued*

Name	Life Dates	Denomination	Association
Buller, Daniel			12th Alabama
Bunting, Robert Franklin	1828–1891	Presbyterian	8th Texas Cavalry
Burgess, Wyley	1809–1878	Presbyterian	22nd Alabama
Burleson, R. C.		Baptist	15th Texas
Burnham, Joel C.			9th Georgia
Burns, R. H.		Methodist	12th Tennessee Cavalry
Burroughs, Anthony		Cumberland Presbyterian	14th Mississippi
Burrow, Albert		Cumberland Presbyterian	12th Tennessee Cavalry
Burton, Robert O.	1811–1892	Methodist	Camp: Garysburg, N.C.
Butler, George E.		Methodist	3rd Arkansas
Butt, Shannon Fletcher		Methodist	42nd Virginia
Buxton, Jarvis		Episcopalian	Hospital: Asheville, N.C.
Bynum, Bart Pace			55th Alabama
Byrd, Samuel M.		Episcopalian	41st North Carolina
Caker, W. L.			10th South Carolina
Caldwell, Oliver Benjamin	1838–1905	Presbyterian	43rd Tennessee Cavalry
Callahan, Humphrey Edwards			16th Texas Cavalry
Cameron, Josiah P.			24th Alabama
Cameron, Stephen Frick		Episcopalian	1st Maryland
Cameron, William E.			26th Alabama
Camp, J. C.		Baptist	10th Georgia
Camp, W. F.		Methodist	10th Mississippi
Campbell, Abner B.		Baptist	9th Georgia
Campbell, Alex			29th Texas Cavalry
Campbell, Charles D.		Baptist	4th Georgia Cavalry
Campbell, James Boykin	1837–1907	Methodist	6th South Carolina Cavalry
Campbell, James McDonald	1830–1864	Methodist	1st Georgia
Campbell, John P.			Post: Marion, Ala.
Campbell, T. H.			3rd Georgia Cavalry Battalion

CONFEDERATE CHAPLAINS *continued*

Name	Life Dates	Denomination	Association
Campbell, Thomas S.	1810–1889	Methodist	Post: Chesterfield, S.C.
Capers, T. H.			18th Alabama
Capers, William Tertius	1825–1894	Methodist	10th South Carolina
Caperton, Alexander Cotton		Baptist	9th Mississippi
Caples, William P.	–1886	Methodist	Missouri State Guard
Carius, Anthony		Roman Catholic	1st Louisiana
Carlisle, John Mason	1827–1905	Methodist	7th South Carolina
Carmichael, James D.	1835–1911	Episcopalian	30th Virginia
Carpenter, John T.	1834–1897	Baptist	Post: Richmond
Carr, John F.	1834–1906	Methodist	9th Arkansas
Carrington, Alexander Broadnax	1834–1910	Presbyterian	37th Virginia
Carroll, William H.		Baptist	4th Alabama
Carson, Theodore Myers	1834–1902	Episcopalian	7th Virginia Cavalry
Carson, W. B.		Baptist	14th South Carolina
Carter, George W.	1830–1913	Methodist	19th Mississippi
Carter, Levi M.			5th Georgia
Carter, William Arthur	1836–1922	Presbyterian	31st Alabama Hospital
Caruthers, Eli Washington	1793–1865	Presbyterian	17th South Carolina
Casey, A. M.			13th Arkansas
Caskey, Thomas W.		Disciples of Christ	16th Mississippi Cavalry
Cason, Jeremiah H.	1816–1896		11th Mississippi
Cass, William			Chickasaw Georgia Mounted Rifles
Cassidy, Hugh E.		Baptist	47th Georgia
Castleton, Thomas		Presbyterian	Post: Houston, Tex.
Cauley, Sam			2nd Arkansas
Chaddick, Stokely		Cumberland Presbyterian	7th Texas
Chadwick, William Davidson		Cumberland Presbyterian	4th Alabama

CONFEDERATE CHAPLAINS *continued*

Name	Life Dates	Denomination	Association
Camberlain, Corydon			1st Mississippi Minutemen
Chamberlain, Hiram		Presbyterian	3rd Texas Infantry
Chamberlain, William A.		Methodist	20th Arkansas
Chambers, J. D.			Hospital: Emory & Henry College, Va.
Chambliss, J. E.			Davis's Mississippi Brigade
Chaplin, Charles Crawford		Baptist	Post: Danville, Va.
Chapman, John Bond	1830–1880	Presbyterian	32nd Tennessee
Chapman, Marcus Boatner	1846–1910	Methodist	Louisiana's Washington Artillery; 26th Mississippi
Chastain, Albert		Baptist	29th North Carolina
Cheatham, Henry Clay			8th North Carolina
Cherry, Sterling McAlister	1835–1914	Methodist	37th Georgia
Cherry, William Dow	1837–1905	Methodist	29th North Carolina
Churchill, Orren			31st North Carolina
Clampitt, George N.	–1896		12th Louisiana
Clawson, Samuel R.			Chimborazo Hospital: Richmond
Cleghorn, Elisha Burnham	1812–1881	Presbyterian	17th Louisiana
Clemmens, A. E.			3rd Texas Cavalry
Cleveland, Thomas Parmelee	1837–1928	Presbyterian	13th Georgia
Clifton, W. L.	1836–1911	Methodist	29th Alabama
Cline, James Madison	1832–1913	Methodist	52nd North Carolina
Clopton, J. C.		Baptist	25th Alabama
Cobb, Needham Bryan		Baptist	14th North Carolina
Cochran, D. M.		Methodist	19th Arkansas
Coffin, Claiborne		Presbyterian	27th Alabama
Cohen, Abraham David	1822–	Missionary Baptist	46th North Carolina
Cole, John		Episcopalian	6th Virginia Cavalry
Collis, S. M.		Baptist	29th North Carolina
Collum, J. W.			24th Tennessee
Colton, Cornelius			36th Alabama

CONFEDERATE CHAPLAINS *continued*

Name	Life Dates	Denomination	Association
Colton, James Hooper	1834–1893	Presbyterian	53rd North Carolina
Compere, E. L.			2nd Arkansas Cherokee Mounted Volunteers
Cone, William H. C.	1825?–1862	Methodist	19th Georgia
Connalay, Isaac G.			55th North Carolina
Conner, G. C.			56th Georgia
Connerly, David C. B.		Methodist	51st Alabama
Conners, D. C.			15th Alabama
Conrad, Thomas Nelson	1837–1905	Methodist	3rd Virginia Cavalry
Cook, James Osgood Andrew	1838–1919	Methodist	2nd Georgia Battalion
Cooper, Robert English	1833–1887	Presbyterian	Cobb's Georgia Legion
Cooper, Silas H.			6th Florida
Corbett, W. B.			4th South Carolina
Cosby, James Smith	1837–1894	Episcopalian	38th Virginia
Cousar, James A.	1829–1882	Presbyterian	8th South Carolina
Cowgill, James A.			114th Virginia Militia
Cox, Ara Bishop		Methodist	22nd North Carolina
Cox, Jacob H.	1819–1896	Methodist	8th Texas
Cox, Samuel Keener	1823–1909	Methodist	23rd Alabama
Coyle, Patrick F.		Roman Catholic	Florida Brigade
Craig, John Newton	1831–1900	Presbyterian	5th South Carolina
Crawford, William H.			61st Tennessee
Crews, Hiram George	1830–1917	Baptist	56th Virginia
Crichlow, W. B.			18th Tennessee
Cridlin, Ransdell White	1840–1913	Baptist	38th Virginia
Crisman, William B.		Cumberland Presbyterian	17th Tennessee
Crocker, William Andrew	1825–1901	Methodist	14th Virginia
Croghan, Charles J.	1826–	Roman Catholic	17th Tennessee
Crooks, Charles Fenton	1822–1904	Methodist	14th Virginia Cavalry
Crooks, Robert Nelson	1830–1916	Methodist	Chimborazo Hospital: Richmond, Va.

CONFEDERATE CHAPLAINS *continued*

Name	Life Dates	Denomination	Association
Cross, Joseph		Methodist	2nd Tennessee
Crouch, Benjamin T.	−1862	Methodist	1st Tennessee Cavalry
Crowson, Richard M.	1814–1885	Methodist	28th Louisiana
Crumley, William Monroe	1816–1887	Methodist	Georgia Hospital: Richmond, Va.
Cullen, Dabney Phillips	1833–1916	Methodist	27th Louisiana
Cullom, Jeremiah Walker	1828–1916	Methodist	24th Tennessee
Cummings, Jesse H.	−1862	Methodist	36th Texas Cavalry
Cunningham, James Thompson	−1912	Roman Catholic	Armstrong's Mississippi Brigade
Cunningham, William Madison	1812–1870	Presbyterian	4th Georgia
Curry, W. G.		Baptist	5th Alabama
Curry, William L.		Baptist	50th Georgia
Cushman, George F.			29th Alabama
Dabney, Robert Louis	1820–1898	Presbyterian	18th Virginia; T. J. Jackson's Staff
Dame, George Washington	1812–1895		Hospital: Danville, Va.
Damus, Fred W.		Episcopalian	17th Alabama; Hospital
Daniel, David G.		Baptist	29th Georgia
Daniel, Francis Marion			33rd Alabama; Hospital
Davenport, Silas D.			Hospital: Texas
Davenport, Thomas H.	1835–1888	Methodist	3rd Tennessee
Davidson, Edward Chaffin	1832–1883	Presbyterian	11th Mississippi
Davies, William	1829–1885	Methodist	1st Florida
Davis, James Allen		Baptist	Hospital: Liberty, Va.
Davis, Lewis F.			19th Arkansas
Davis, Nicholas A.	1824–1894	Presbyterian	4th Texas
Davis, Richard Robert	1830–1892	Episcopalian	6th Virginia Cavalry
Davis, W. M.		Baptist	11th Georgia Artillery Battalion
Davis, William J.	1838–1919	Methodist	1st Arkansas
De Chaignon, Antoine		Roman Catholic	18th Louisiana
Deans, John Franklin	1839–1903	Baptist	61st Virginia
Deckey, D. S.			Hospital: Rome, Ga.

CONFEDERATE CHAPLAINS *continued*

Name	Life Dates	Denomination	Association
Denniston, E. C.			26th Louisiana
Denny, George Hutcheon	1834–1893	Presbyterian	50th Virginia
DePass, James Perryman	1839–1907	Methodist	16th South Carolina
Devotie, J. H.		Baptist	2nd Georgia
Dewitt, M. B.	–1901	Presbyterian	8th Tennessee
Dicharry, Pierre Felix		Roman Catholic	3rd Louisiana
Dockson, Andrew Flint	1825–1879	Presbyterian	25th South Carolina
Dickson, Henry R.			12th South Carolina
Dill, Edward D.		Baptist	22nd South Carolina
Dobbs, Charles Holt, Sr.	1835–1920	Presbyterian	12th Mississippi
Dodd, Jacob E.		Methodist	5th Georgia
Dodge, William Ashbury	1844–1904	Methodist	23rd Georgia
Dodson, Charles Carrell	1832–1884	Methodist	46th North Carolina
Dodson, William M.	–1886	Methodist	2nd Missouri
Doll, Penfield		Methodist	18th Georgia
Donnelly, T. J.			Post: Demopolis, Ala.
Dowd, Patrick W.			39th North Carolina Militia Regiment
Dowe, Gales		Episcopalian	9th Louisiana
Downing, Lewis			1st Arkansas Cherokee Mounted Rifles
Drewry, T. C. C.		Methodist	Winder Hospital: Richmond, Va.
Dryden, Constantine Francis	1809–1882	Methodist	12th Missouri
DuBose, John Elias	1819–1895	Episcopalian	2nd Florida Cavalry
Dubose, William Porcher	–1918	Episcopalian	Kershaw's South Carolina Brigade
Duckett, N. A.			3rd Texas Cavalry
Duke, Thomas L.		Methodist	19th Mississippi
Dumas, W. F.		Methodist	10th Mississippi Cavalry
Duncan, James Armstrong	1830–1877	Methodist	Hospital: Richmond
Duncan, William Wallace	1839–1908	Methodist	13th South Carolina

CONFEDERATE CHAPLAINS *continued*

Name	Life Dates	Denomination	Association
Dunlap, William Carnes	1838–1896	Methodist	12th South Carolina
Dunlap, William Carnes	1838–1896	Methodist	8th Georgia
Dunlop, James E.	1833–1904	Presbyterian	21st South Carolina
Dunn, Ballard S.		Episcopalian	1st Louisiana
Dunwoody, James Bulloch	1816–1902	Presbyterian	2nd Georgia
Durant, Henry Hill	–1861	Methodist	5th South Carolina
Duval, William J.			3rd Florida
Eagleton, George Ewing	1831–1899	Presbyterian	44th Tennessee
Earle, F. W.			3rd Arkansas Cavalry
Easter, George W.		Episcopalian	9th Virginia
Easter, John D.	1830–1912	Presbyterian	Post: Rome, Ga.
Eatman, Thomas J.		Methodist	33rd North Carolina
Edmondson, John A.		Methodist	20th Tennessee
Edwards, George R.			23rd Georgia
Edwards, William Emory	1842–1903	Methodist	Drewry's Bluff, Va.
Eichelbarger, Webster		Lutheran	20th South Carolina
Ellington, John F.			117th North Carolina Militia
Elliott, Collins D.		Methodist	1st Tennessee
Elliott, Stephen, Sr.	–1866	Episcopalian	9th South Carolina
Ellis, Charles C.		Methodist	4th Alabama
Ellis, John Alexander	1830–1893	Methodist	20th Tennessee
Ellis, Lewis B.	1826–1883	Methodist	11th Missouri
Ellison, Benjamin F.	–1864	Presbyterian	Madison's Arizona Brigade Cavalry
Ely, Foster	1836–1916	Methodist	18th Mississippi
Embry, George T.			27th Georgia
Engle, Joseph Jackson	1833–1911	Methodist	42nd Virginia
Erwin, James S.	1829–1881	Methodist	34th North Carolina
Erwin, Thomas Washington	1827–1911	Presbyterian	Hospital: Wilmington, N.C.
Espy, Thomas B.		Baptist	31st Alabama
Evans, Charles F.	1841–1917	Methodist	Louisiana Crescent Rifles

CONFEDERATE CHAPLAINS *continued*

Name	Life Dates	Denomination	Association
Evans, George W.		Methodist	36th Arkansas
Evans, Robert F.	1839–1908	Methodist	4th Georgia
Everett, L. D.			Georgia State Troops
Ewing, Daniel Blaine	1821–1886	Presbyterian	Post: Gordonsville, Va.
Fairley, David S.	1831–1912	Presbyterian	27th North Carolina
Faison, Julian Poydras	–1890	Missionary Baptist	38th North Carolina
Fancher, R. F.		Baptist	13th Texas Cavalry
Farley, Francis A.		Methodist	21st Virginia Cavalry
Farrish, J. R.	1835–1913	Baptist	13th Mississippi
Farrow, W. F.		Presbyterian	1st South Carolina Regulars
Fears, Augustus Browder	1810–	Disciples of Christ	30th Georgia
Featherstone, George W.			30th Tennessee
Fife, J. A.	1828–1907	Methodist	Martin's 1st Mississippi
Fikes, Azariah M.		Methodist	23rd Alabama
Findlay, James			53rd Alabama
Finley, James S.			32nd Tennessee
Finney, Franklin			43rd Mississippi
Fisher, Charles M.			22nd Virginia
Fisher, James L.	1813–1882	Methodist	47th North Carolina
Fisher, William	1818–1898	Baptist	22nd Virginia
Fitzgerald, Frederick		Episcopalian	2nd North Carolina
Fitzgerald, O. D.		Baptist	32nd Mississippi
Fitzpatrick, John B.		Methodist	37th Virginia
Fleming, William Honour	1821–1877	Methodist	1st South Carolina
Flinn, William	1818–1894	Presbyterian	16th Georgia; Phillips's Georgia Legion
Flora, Joseph			63rd Tennessee
Flowers, Thomas W.	1828–1907	Methodist	7th Mississippi
Fly, D. W.			24th Texas Cavalry
Fones, Henry Harrison		Baptist	55th Virginia
Fontaine, Patrick Henry	1841–1915	Baptist	53rd Virginia

CONFEDERATE CHAPLAINS *continued*

Name	Life Dates	Denomination	Association
Ford, John T.			3rd Georgia Battalion
Ford, Miles Harper	1822–1872	Methodist	Ballentine's Mississippi Cavalry
Foster, William Lovelace		Baptist	35th Mississippi
Foust, W. J.			41st Tennessee
Fox, John N.		Baptist	Hospital: Culpeper, Va.
Frayzier, Beriak			3rd Tennessee Mounted
Frazer, Donald			2nd Florida
Frazier, Robert L.		Cumberland Presbyterian	4th Alabama
Freeman, James F. W.	1805–1876	Presbyterian	Hospital: Raleigh & Salisbury, N.C.
Frierson, Madison Wilson	–1864	Presbyterian	22nd Mississippi
Fry, Cyrus Franklin		Baptist	Hospital: Staunton, Va.
Fry, John G.			7th Georgia
Fulwood, Charles A.	1829–1905	Methodist	48th Georgia
Gache, Louis–Hippolyte	1817–1907	Roman Catholic	10th Louisiana
Gadsden, Christopher Philip	–1871	Episcopalian	Palmetto Guard South Carolina Artillery
Gaillard, Savage Smith	1818–1879	Presbyterian	Hampton's South Carolina Legion
Gardner, William Fowler	1840–1907	Episcopalian	24th Virginia
Garland, James Powell	1835–1906	Methodist	49th Virginia
Garrison, Edwin A.		Methodist	48th Mississippi
Garrison, H. Y.		Methodist	McNeill's Arkansas Regiment
Garrison, James A.			20th Georgia
Gatewood, Robert		Episcopalian	Stark's Virginia Artillery Battalion
Gaulman, W. B.			6th Mississippi
Gaultney, William R.			1st North Carolina
Geer, Edwin		Episcopalian	Hospital: Wilmington, N.C.
Giles, Enoch H.	1836–1908	Methodist	6th Florida
Gillaspie, Charles F.			8th Mississippi

CONFEDERATE CHAPLAINS *continued*

Name	Life Dates	Denomination	Association
Gillis, Neil	1830–1907	Methodist	57th Alabama
Gilmer, George Hudson, Sr.	1836–1891	Presbyterian	Price's Virginia Light Artillery
Gilmer, Thomas Walker	1834–1869	Presbyterian	II Corps Artillery, Army of Northern Virginia
Gilmore, James Harvey	1838–1900	Presbyterian	21st Virginia
Girardeau, John Lafayette	1825–1898	Presbyterian	23rd South Carolina
Gitt, Woodward R.		Baptist	59th Virginia
Glass, Hiram M.	1828–1918	Methodist	20th Texas
Godbey, E. Crockett	1818–1901	Methodist	63rd Tennessee
Godrey, James A.	1819–1890	Methodist	14th Louisiana
Godfrey, James Erwin, Sr.	1809–1889	Methodist	54th Georgia
Goforth, Napoleon Bonaparte	1828–	Baptist	31st Tennessee
Goldberg, Charles			18th Texas
Goodnight, Thomas M.			6th Kentucky
Gordon, Charles M.			36th Mississippi
Gould, Archibald			1st Florida Cavalry
Goulding, Francis Robert	1810–1881	Presbyterian	Hospital: Macon, Ga.
Grace, Joshua Johnson		Methodist	17th Alabama
Graham, William Wallace	1839–1921	Methodist	28th Alabama
Granbery, John Cowper	1829–1907	Methodist	11th Virginia
Grandin, Joshua Marsdin	1814–1896	Methodist	33rd Virginia
Graves, Azariah R.	–1871	Presbyterian	3rd Mississippi
Gray, George Thomas		Episcopalian	63rd Virginia
Gray, William A.	–1863		2nd Mississippi
Gray, William Crane	1835–1919	Episcopalian	4th Tennessee
Green, Edward Melvin	1838–1927	Presbyterian	2nd Arkansas
Green, J. Jasper	1837–1899	Baptist	38th Mississippi
Green, Samuel M.			16th South Carolina
Green, T. D.			4th South Carolina
Greene, John M.		Methodist	32nd Georgia
Gregory, John T. M.		Methodist	26th Alabama

CONFEDERATE CHAPLAINS *continued*

Name	Life Dates	Denomination	Association
Gregory, James L.			8th Kentucky
Griffin, George W.		Baptist	5th North Carolina
Griffin, John William	–1864	Episcopalian	19th Virginia
Grimsley, Aldridge Madison			Hospital: Shenandoah Valley, Va.
Grisham, John			9th Tennessee
Guthrie, Benjamin F.	1837–1862	Methodist	33rd North Carolina
Gwaltney, William Robert		Baptist	1st North Carolina
Gwin, Thomas D.		Baptist	Hagood's 1st South Carolina
Hackett, John Alexander		Baptist	18th Mississippi
Hafford, W. D. E.			13th Tennessee
Haines, F. M.			35th Mississippi
Haley, Littleberry James	1832–1917	Baptist	Ewell's Artillery, Army of Northern Virginia
Hall, B. F.		Disciples of Christ	McCullock's Texas Rangers
Hall, James B.		Cumberland Presbyterian	48th Alabama
Hall, William A.		Presbyterian	Louisiana's Washington Artillery
Hall, William Thomas	1835–1911	Presbyterian	30th Mississippi
Hall, Willis	1808–1888		26th Georgia
Halladay, Soloman F.			1st Florida Battalion
Hamilton, Alexander L.		Methodist	16th Alabama; S. Wood's Staff
Hamilton, Ephraim E.		Methodist	5th Tennessee
Hamilton, Wylie Taylor	1838–1902	Methodist	4th Georgia Cavalry
Hammond, Wesley C.		Methodist	3rd Virginia
Hanks, W. E.			32nd Mississippi
Hanner, John Wesley	1840–1907	Methodist	2nd Kentucky Cavalry
Hard, W. J.			Post: Augusta, Ga.
Hardie, Robert, Jr.		Methodist	2nd Louisiana
Harding, Ephraim Henry	1832–1923	Presbyterian	45th Virginia
Hardwick, John B.		Baptist	Hospital: Petersburg, Va.
Hargrove, Robert Kennon	1829–1905	Methodist	51st Alabama Cavalry

CONFEDERATE CHAPLAINS *continued*

Name	Life Dates	Denomination	Association
Harp, Robert James		Methodist	52nd Georgia
Harper, P. O.			Gordon's Georgia Brigade
Harrington, Whitfield		Methodist	Post: Vicksburg, Miss.
Harris, B. F.			Georgia State Troops
Harris, Benoni	1827–1892	Methodist	Price's Missouri Army
Harris, Buckner	1837–1908	Methodist	6th Texas
Harris, George C.		Episcopalian	26th Tennessee
Harris, George William		Baptist	8th Virginia
Harris, J. J.	–1903		5th Tennessee Cavalry
Harris, James O.			4th Tennessee
Harris, James R.	1836–1922	Methodist	7th Tennessee
Harris, Jesse J.	1827–1904	Methodist	26th Tennessee
Harris, John Kellogg	1832–1910	Presbyterian	23rd Virginia Battalion
Harris, John M.			7th North Carolina Cavalry Battalion
Harris, William		Baptist	15th Tennessee Cavalry
Harrison, Edmund R.	1832–1910	Methodist	35th Arkansas
Harrold, James Albert		Episcopalian	1st Virginia; Surgeon
Harrow, John W.			11th Virginia; Assistant Surgeon
Harvey, James R.	1837–1907	Methodist	2nd Arkansas
Haskell, William	–1863	Methodist	154th Tennessee
Haslett, William			21st Georgia
Haslup, Lemuel Wilson	1832–1909	Methodist	Hospital: Charlottesville, Va.
Hatcher, Harvey		Baptist	I Corps Artillery, Army of Northern Virginia
Hatcher, Hilary Eugene	1832–1892	Baptist	61st Virginia
Haughton, Thomas Benbury	–1894	Episcopalian	50th North Carolina
Hauser, William C., Sr.			48th Georgia
Hawkins, Perry			2nd South Carolina
Hawks, W. N.		Episcopalian	Post: Columbus, Georgia
Hawthorne, James Boardman	1837–1910	Baptist	24th Alabama

CONFEDERATE CHAPLAINS *continued*

Name	Life Dates	Denomination	Association
Haygood, Atticus Greene	1839–1896	Methodist	15th Georgia
Haygood, Francis Marion		Baptist	35th Alabama
Haynes, George Washington			16th North Carolina
Haynes, James	1838–1900	Presbyterian	60th Virginia
Hearn, S. C.		Baptist	5th Tennessee
Hearn, William Croghan	1829–1908	Methodist	41st Mississippi
Helms, William T.		Episcopalian	1st Tennessee
Hemmingway, W. A.	–1867	Methodist	21st South Carolina
Henderson, F. H. M.	1810–1899	Methodist	56th Georgia
Henderson, Greenville T.	1803–1888	Methodist	2nd Tennessee
Hendrix, William H.		Cumberland Presbyterian	8th Tennessee Cavalry
Hendry, John M.			3rd Florida
Henkel, David S.		Lutheran	28th North Carolina
Hershey, Andrew Moses	1809–1888	Presbyterian	Chimborazo Hospital: Richmond, Va.
Hickerson, Festus		Lutheran	5th Florida
Hicks, George W.		Baptist	Hospital: Richmond, Va.
Hicks, William	1811–1882	Methodist	16th North Carolina
Hidden, Elisha Burnham			30th Georgia
Hiden, James Conway	1837–1918	Baptist	Wise's Legion; Hospital: Charlottesville, Va.
Highley, Burton S.			51st Virginia
Hight, Medicus H.	1834–1862	Methodist	North Carolina State Troops
Hill, Felix Robertson	1844–1917	Methodist	Forrest's Tennessee Cavalry
Hill, Halbert Green	1831–1924	Presbyterian	13th North Carolina
Hill, Henry T.	1838–1922	Methodist	16th Tennessee
Hill, Samuel Jacob	1835–1884	Methodist	42nd North Carolina
Hilliard, Francis W.		Episcopalian	Hospital: University of Virginia
Hines, James J.	1827–1901	Methodist	Hoke's North Carolina Brigade
Hinton, J. W.			3rd Georgia Cavalry

CONFEDERATE CHAPLAINS *continued*

Name	Life Dates	Denomination	Association
Hodgson, Telfair		Episcopalian	1st Alabama Cavalry
Hogan, Henry D.	1830–		24th Tennessee
Hoge, Moses Drury	1819–1899	Presbyterian	Camp Lee, Va.
Hoge, William James	1825–1864	Presbyterian	Post: Petersburg, Va.
Hogue, Ezekiel			11th Arkansas
Holifield, M. J.			12th Kentucky Cavalry
Holland, Robert Afton	1844–1909	Methodist	Buford's Kentucky Cavalry
Holman, Russell			41st Alabama
Holmes, Adam Tunno		Baptist	Camp: Decatur, Ga.
Holt, James H.			Camp: Fayetteville, N.C.
Holt, John S.			34th Alabama
Hooper, Thomas Williamson	1832–1915	Presbyterian	Hospital: Liberty, Va.
Hoover, William			33rd Mississippi
Hopkins, Abner Crump	1835–1911	Presbyterian	2nd Virginia
Hopson, Winthrop Hartley	1823–1889	Disciples of Christ	Morgan's Kentucky Cavalry
Houser, William			48th Georgia
Houston, James W.			8th Missouri
Houston, William Wilson	1839–1891	Presbyterian	McIntosh's Virginia Artillery
Howard, Joseph L.		Lutheran	2nd Missouri; F. M. Crockrell's Staff
Howard, William		Baptist	36th Alabama
Howard, William George	1813–1865		7th Louisiana
Howell, James K.		Baptist	1st North Carolina
Howerton, Samuel W.		Baptist	15th North Carolina
Howle, S. H.			13th Alabama
Hoyle, Samuel Vinton	1836–1892	Methodist	12th Virginia
Hoyt, Henry Francis	1833–1912	Presbyterian	2nd Georgia Cavalry
Hubert, Darius	1823–1893	Roman Catholic	1st Louisiana
Huckins, James			Hospital: Charleston, S.C.
Huddleston, J. N.		Methodist	40th Mississippi
Hudson, Edward	–1875		6th Texas Cavalry

CONFEDERATE CHAPLAINS *continued*

Name	Life Dates	Denomination	Association
Hudson, John N.		Methodist	17th Georgia
Hughes, Francis Goodman	1838–1908	Methodist	65th Georgia
Hughes, William Holmes	1828–1916	Methodist	19th Texas
Hume, Thomas, Sr.		Baptist	Post: Petersburg, Va.
Hume, Thomas, Jr.	1836–1912	Baptist	3rd Virginia
Hunter, Robert Smith	1834–1909	Methodist	1st Kentucky Cavalry
Hunter, Theodore		Presbyterian	25th Georgia
Hutton, Cornelius Marion	1835–1923	Presbyterian	36th Alabama
Hyde, George W.	1838–1917	Baptist	Hospital: Huguenot Spring, Va.
Hyde, John Poisal	1836–1914	Methodist	10th Virginia
Hyman, John James	1833–1906	Baptist	49th Georgia
Ivy, Fitz Henry			57th Georgia
Ivy, James A.		Methodist	16th Louisiana
James, Albert Allison	1824–1910	Presbyterian	18th South Carolina
James, John T.			8th South Carolina
Jamison, P. G.		Methodist	11th Tennessee
Jarboe, Joseph		Roman Catholic	2nd Tennessee
Jarrell, Anderson Joseph	1840–1896	Methodist	19th Georgia
Jenkins, Paul Gervais	–1911	Episcopalian	Hospital: Columbia, S.C.
Jennings, Jacob Mead	1804–1872	Methodist	3rd Alabama
Jennings, Thomas C.	1823–1871	Methodist	11th Virginia
Jessup, B. F.			Hospital: Wilmington, N.C.
Jeter, Jeremiah Bell	1802–1880	Baptist	Post: Richmond, Va.
Jewell, Horace	1832–1917	Methodist	33rd Arkansas
Johnson, B. G.	1823–1903	Methodist	Arkansas State Troops
Johnson, B. J.			8th Alabama
Johnson, George W.			1st Missouri
Johnson, H. T.			45th Mississippi
Johnson, Harvey F.	1831–1886	Methodist	3rd Mississippi Battalion
Johnson, John Lipscomb	1835–1915	Baptist	17th Virginia
Johnson, John T.	1825–1906	Methodist	8th Virginia Cavalry

CONFEDERATE CHAPLAINS *continued*

Name	Life Dates	Denomination	Association
Johnson, John W.		Methodist	37th Tennessee
Johnson, Littleton H.		Methodist	Trans–Mississippi Department
Johnson, Richard		Episcopalian	1st South Carolina Cavalry
Johnson, Samuel			15th Texas Cavalry
Johnson, W. B.			South Carolina's Hampton Legion
Johnson, William Crockett	1825–1902	Methodist	Mississippi Cavalry, S.D. Lee's Staff
Johnston, William G.		Methodist	11th Alabama
Johnston, B. I.			8th Florida
Johnston, Frontis Howe	1834–1901	Presbyterian	48th North Carolina
Johnston, Pickney A.	1839–1901	Methodist	38th Mississippi
Jones, Andrew W.	1834–1890	Methodist	55th Georgia
Jones, Griffin S.			106th North Carolina Militia
Jones, Harry H.			55th Virginia
Jones, John	1815–1893	Presbyterian	Rome, Ga.
Jones, John Buttrick	1824–1876	Baptist	3rd Arkansas Cherokee Mounted Volunteers
Jones, John William	1836–1909	Baptist	13th Virginia
Jones, John William		Baptist	25th Virginia
Jones, Lucius Henry	–1863	Episcopalian	4th Texas Cavalry
Jones, Ransom Julaney	1837–1902		2nd Mississippi State Troops
Jones, William Borden		Baptist	61st North Carolina
Jones, William Edward	1831–1900	Methodist	22nd Georgia
Jones, William G. H.			24th Virginia
Jordan, Joseph H.			17th Louisiana
Jordan, Thomas H.	1830?– 1863	Methodist	2nd Georgia Battalion
Jordan, William		Roman Catholic	18th North Carolina
Joyce, William J.	–1919	Methodist	5th Texas Cavalry
Joyner, James E.	–1868	Methodist	57th Virginia
Kavanaugh, Benjamin T.	1805–1888	Methodist	1st Missouri Cavalry

CONFEDERATE CHAPLAINS *continued*

Name	Life Dates	Denomination	Association
Kavanaugh, Hubbard Hinde	1836–1892	Methodist	6th Kentucky
Keep, W. W.		Baptist	6th Mississippi Battalion
Kennedy, Francis Milton	1834–1880	Methodist	28th North Carolina
Kennedy, William M.		Methodist	Hospital: Richmond, Va.
Kerr, David			1st North Carolina
Kerr, Leander		Congregational	Camp Winder, Va.
Kerr, William Montgomery	1820–1895	Methodist	45th Virginia
Kimball, Francis A.		Methodist	16th Alabama
Kindrick, W. P.			19th Tennessee Cavalry
King, John E.		Baptist	14th Tennessee
King, W. H.			1st South Carolina Cavalry
Kirkland, Alexander	1839–1910	Presbyterian	5th North Carolina Cavalry
Kistler, Paul Franklin	1827–1901	Methodist	24th South Carolina
Kittrell, Lemuel		Methodist	12th Missouri
Knapp, Theodore Judson			11th North Carolina
Koger, Thomas Jefferson	1807–1862	Methodist	41st Mississippi
Kramer, George C. M. R.	1835?– 1875	Methodist	39th Georgia
Lacy, Beverly Tucker	1819–1900	Presbyterian	T. J. Jackson's Corps, Army of Northern Virginia
Lacy, Drury	1802–1884	Presbyterian	Hospital: Raleigh, N.C.
Lacy, William E.		Presbyterian	48th Alabama
Lacy, William Sterling	1842–1899	Presbyterian	47th North Carolina
Lafferty, John James	1837–1909	Methodist	62nd Virginia
Laird, John S.			1st Missouri
Lambeth, Samuel Sommerfield	1838–	Methodist	10th Virginia
Landrum, J. G.			13th South Carolina
Landstreet, John	1818–1891	Methodist	1st Virginia Cavalry
Lane, J. S.		Methodist	13th Alabama
Langhorn, Maurice	1816–1886		6th Virginia
Lanier, William O.	1835–1894	Methodist	20th Tennessee

CONFEDERATE CHAPLAINS *continued*

Name	Life Dates	Denomination	Association
Latta, F. M.			16th Arkansas
Lattimore, J. L.		Baptist	46th Mississippi
Lauck, Jacob M.	1833–1912	Methodist	26th Virginia Cavalry Battalion
Law, Thomas Hart	1838–1923	Presbyterian	Fort Caswell, N.C.
Leachman, Jerry M.	1827–1881	Baptist	20th Virginia Cavalry
Lee, Burwell	1809–1877	Methodist	27th Arkansas
Lee, Charles S. M.			5th Virginia
Lee, Edmund	1809–1892	Presbyterian	Hospital: Savannah, Ga.
Lee, William M.			9th Arkansas
Leith, William Henry	1840–1902	Methodist	Hospital: Columbus, Miss.
Leps, James Henry	1823–1889	Presbyterian	31st Virginia
Leray, Francis Xavier		Roman Catholic	Hospital: Mississippi
Lester, G. B.			8th Tennessee
Lester, Robert B.	1823–1893	Methodist	3rd Georgia
Lewellen, James			74th North Carolina Militia
Lewis, Henry T.		Methodist	Hospital: Clinton, La.
Lewis, Reuben	1809–1886	Presbyterian	Hospital: Emory & Henry College, Va.
Ley, J. C.	–1909	Methodist	2nd Florida Cavalry
Leyburn, George William	1809–1875	Presbyterian	34th Virginia
Link, John Bodkin	1825–1894	Baptist	2nd Missouri Cavalry
Linthicum, Charles Frederick	1838–1864	Methodist	8th Virginia
Little, James		Presbyterian	9th Florida
Loate, A. H.			Hospital: Virginia
Lockhart, Patrick J.	1831–	Methodist	22nd Virginia Cavalry
Lomax, Alexander A.	1830–1906	Baptist	15th Mississippi
Long, Benjamin F.		Methodist	4th & 12th North Carolina
Long, J. S.		Methodist	North Carolina Troops
Long, John Cralle		Baptist	Hospital: Danville, Va.
Lord, William Wilberforce		Episcopalian	1st Mississippi Light Artillery
Lowe, John C.	1834–1910	Methodist	28th Mississippi

CONFEDERATE CHAPLAINS *continued*

Name	Life Dates	Denomination	Association
Lowe, Thomas G.		Baptist	5th North Caroina
Lowry, James		Presbyterian	48th Georgia
Mack, Joseph Bingham	1832–1912	Presbyterian	50th Tennessee
Mackey, James	1838–1893	Methodist	5th Arkansas
Madigan, Patrick Henry		Roman Catholic	15th Missouri Cavalry
Madison, B. F.			3rd Arkansas
Madison, H.			Hospital: Shenandoah Valley, Va.
Madison, Louis B.	1835–1906	Methodist	58th Virginia
Magell, John			52nd Virginia
Mahon, Robert Henry			20th Tennessee Cavalry
Mahon, William Jackson	1816–1905	Methodist	13th Tennessee
Malloy, William C.		Methodist	44th Mississippi
Mangum, Adolphus Williamson	1834–1890	Methodist	6th North Carolina
Manion, A. B.		Methodist	18th Texas Cavalry
Mann, James Emory	1832–1890	Methodist	59th North Carolina
Manning, Archibald D.		Methodist	6th Mississippi
Manucy, Dominic		Roman Catholic	Hospital: Alabama
Marable, Benjamin Franklin II	1831–1892	Presbyterian	North Carolina Militia; William Mann's Staff
Markham, Thomas Railey	1828–1894	Presbyterian	1st Mississippi Light Artillery
Marsh, Robert Henry	1837–1924	Missionary Baptist	26th North Carolina
Marshall, Asa Monroe		Baptist	12th Georgia
Marshall, Matthias Murray		Episcopalian	7th North Carolina
Martin, John J.			18th Tennessee
Martin, Joseph Edward	1840–1900	Methodist	1st Virginia
Mashburn, John Harvey, Sr.	1803–1876	Methodist	38th Georgia
Massey, Jacob	1821–		62nd North Carolina
Massey, William E.		Baptist	8th Alabama
Mathis, Hiram M.			51st Georgia
Mathis, John S.	1830–1905	Methodist	9th Texas
Matthews, Andrew C.	1837–1905	Methodist	1st Tennessee

CONFEDERATE CHAPLAINS *continued*

Name	Life Dates	Denomination	Association
Maury, Magruder	1830–	Episcopalian	12th Virginia Cavalry
Maury, T. D.			Hospital: Virginia
McAfee, William Hamilton		Methodist	22nd Georgia
McAuley, George			51st Georgia
McBryde, Alexander	1816–1862	Methodist	5th Mississippi
McBryde, William P.		Cumberland Presbyterian	5th Mississippi
McCabe, John Collins		Episcopalian	Post: Richmond, Va.
McCall, Moses			Georgia State Troops
McCall, T. D.			23rd Alabama
McCallaine, A. R.			15th South Carolina
McCallum, H. B.		Episcopalian	15th South Carolina
McCarey, Josiah			9th Missouri Battalion
McCarthy, Florence M.	1838–	Baptist	7th Virginia; 9th Louisiana
McCauley, George			50th Georgia
McClelland, John			3rd Virginia Cavalry
McClure, Charles M.			Georgia Cherokee Legion
McCollough, John Dewitt	–1902	Episcopalian	South Carolina Holcombe Legion
McCormick, W. J.			7th Florida
McCown, John White	1833–1910	Baptist	Zollicoffer's Tennessee Brigade
McCoy, Henry Pendleton Rose	1830–1914	Presbyterian	Hospital: Virginia
McCoy, Robert	–1879	Presbyterian	6th Tennessee
McCraw, J. M.			9th Texas
McCulloh, W. D.			23rd Mississippi
McCutchen, Greenville S.	1818–1915		Swan's Virginia Cavalry Battalion
McCutchen, James B.	1829–1870	Methodist	7th Kentucky Mounted
McCutchen, John F.		Cumberland Presbyterian	24th Tennessee
McCutcheon, J. A.		Methodist	34th Alabama
McDaniel, Simeon C.			19th Georgia
McDiarmid, Whitfield S.		Baptist	38th North Carolina

CONFEDERATE CHAPLAINS *continued*

Name	Life Dates	Denomination	Association
McDonald, Benjamin W.		Presbyterian	50th Alabama
McDonald, Caliborne	1826–1913	Methodist	21st Mississippi
McDowell, James	1832–1913	Presbyterian	6th South Carolina Sharpshooters
McElzea, E. C.			23rd Mississippi
McFerrin, John Berry		Methodist	2nd Tennessee
McGee, William	1821–1891	Methodist	Hospital: Lynchburg, Va.
McGehee, Lucius		Methodist	49th Alabama
McGill, John	1840–1925	Episcopalian	52nd Virginia
McGruder, A. I.			2nd South Carolina
McGuire, John Peyton		Episcopalian	Hospital: Richmond, Va.
McHan, Harvey H.	1827–1895	Methodist	36th Georgia
McIlwaine, Richard	1834–1913	Presbyterian	44th Virginia
McInnis, Richmond	1817–1881	Presbyterian	Hospital: Newton, Miss.
McIver, J. W.	1835–1868	Methodist	12th Mississippi
McJunkin, Samuel B.		Baptist	15th Alabama
McKennon, H. J.		Methodist	15th Alabama
McKennon, Luther	1840–1916	Presbyterian	36th North Carolina; 2nd North Carolina Artillery
McKenzie, J. W. P.	1806–1881	Methodist	8th Texas
McKim, Randolph Harrison	1842–1920	Episcopalian	2nd Virginia Cavalry
McKnight, Daniel A.	1830–1880	Methodist	5th Missouri
McLain, Robert		Presbyterian	37th Mississippi
McMahan, J. J.		Presbyterian	51st Virginia
McMannen, John A.			45th North Carolina Militia
McMurran, John Williams	1830–1867	Presbyterian	49th Virginia
McMurry, G. W.			45th Tennessee
McNair, E. M.	1814–1886	Presbyterian	1st Alabama
McNair, Evander	1833–1918	Presbyterian	24th North Carolina
McNeer, William Randolph		Methodist	4th Virginia
McNeilly, James Hugh	1838–1922	Presbyterian	49th Tennessee

CONFEDERATE CHAPLAINS *continued*

Name	Life Dates	Denomination	Association
McRae, Cameron John	1812–1872	Episcopalian	15th North Carolina
McRae, John H. D.	1831–1911	Methodist	24th Georgia
McSparran, James Erasmus	1833–1921	Methodist	11th Virginia
McVay, Amos H.		Methodist	28th Georgia
McVeigh, A. D.			Post: Farmville, Va.
McVeigh, Townsend James		Baptist	2nd Virginia
McVoy, Alexander Diego	1832–1905	Methodist	38th Alabama
Meek, Jefferson			42nd Mississippi
Mendenhall, Cyrus Erastus			49th North Carolina
Mercer, Francis A.	1829–1902	Methodist	27th Virginia
Meredith, Jacquelin Marshall	1833–1920	Episcopalian	47th Virginia
Meredith, William C.		Episcopalian	4th Virginia Cavalry
Meynardie, Elias James	1826–1890	Methodist	2nd South Carolina
Mickle, Robert Alexander	1831–1905	Presbyterian	14th Georgia
Miles, C. A.			Hospital: Lynchburg, Va.
Miller, Benjamin M.		Episcopalian	Post: Mobile, Ala.
Miller, Charles Addison	1819–1893	Presbyterian	4th Virginia
Miller, Charles W.	1837–1885	Methodist	6th Kentucky Cavalry
Miller, John A.	1832–1912	Methodist	9th Mississippi
Miller, John M.			3rd Tennessee
Miller, John Wesley		Methodist	Hospital: Summerville, S.C.
Miller, Lewis Caperton	1840–1889	Methodist	26th Georgia
Miller, William Gaines		Methodist	46th Virginia
Milliken, Leonard H.		Baptist	13th Tennessee
Mills, John W.	1819–1874	Methodist	5th Florida
Millsaps, John J.	1835–1862	Methodist	20th Mississippi
Minchall, Richard			5th Missouri Cavalry
Minchell, J. M.			Shelby's Missouri Cavalry
Mister, Wilbur Fisk			15th Mississippi
Mitchell, Jacob Duche	1806–1877	Presbyterian	Hospital: Lynchburg, Va.
Mitchell, James	1813–		8th Missouri

CONFEDERATE CHAPLAINS *continued*

Name	Life Dates	Denomination	Association
Mitchell, Joseph W.			18th Arkansas
Moncure, Walter Raleigh Daniel	1837–1900	Baptist	30th Virginia
Monger, H. B.		Episcopalian	Border's Texas Cavalry
Monk, Francis M.		Episcopalian	56th Alabama Cavalry
Monroe, Hugh			55th North Carolina Militia
Montgomery, L. M.		Presbyterian	22nd Mississippi
Mood, Francis Ashbury	1830–1884	Methodist	Post: Charleston, S.C.
Moore, A. B.			17th Tennessee
Moore, Alexander W.		Methodist	Holcombe's South Carolina Legion 14th Georgia
Moore, Henry Dannelly	1838–1902	Methodist	12th Alabama
Moore, Hewlett S.		Baptist	7th Arkansas
Moore, Junius Pulliam	1815–1878		21st North Carolina State Troops
Moore, James A.			R.S. Garnett's Virginia Command
Moore, Richard R.			50th North Carolina Militia
Moore, Styring Scarboro			26th North Carolina
Moore, Theopilus Wilson	1832–1907	Methodist	23rd North Carolina State Troops
Moore, William H.	1838–1916	Methodist	Scales's North Carolina Brigade
Moorehead, R. M.			1st Kentucky Cavalry
Moran, Robert S.		Methodist	50th North Carolina
Moretz, Christian		Lutheran	48th North Carolina
Morrison, G. R.		Presbyterian	19th Mississippi
Morrison, Hugh McEwen	1828–1893	Presbyterian	19th Mississippi
Morse, Albert Augustus	1819–1894	Presbyterian	17th South Carolina
Mortimer, G. J.		Methodist	1st Mississippi Cavalry
Morton, John Houston	1833–1892	Baptist	3rd Tennessee Cavalry
Morton, Paul Carrington	1837–1902	Presbyterian	23rd Virginia
Moses, Peter Allen	1828–1919	Methodist	8th Arkansas
Motheral, N. W.			9th Tennessee Cavalry
Mouton, John Baptist		Roman Catholic	Hospital: Mobile, Ala.

CONFEDERATE CHAPLAINS *continued*

Name	Life Dates	Denomination	Association
Mowbray, William			58th Virginia Militia
Mullally, Francis Patrick	1830–1904	Presbyterian	1st South Carolina
Mullen, J. H.			39th Tennessee
Mullin, Samuel H.			31st Virginia
Murphee, John			49th Alabama
Murphy, Joseph W.		Episcopalian	32nd & 43rd North Carolina
Myers, James M.			42nd Georgia
Nabors, James H.			44th Alabama
Neal, Thomas B.		Presbyterian	24th North Carolina
Neel, A. A P.	1841–1909	Methodist	II Corps Hospital: Army of Northern Virginia
Neely, P. P.			1st Mississippi State Troops
Neese, James L.			28th Texas Cavalry
Nelson, James	1841–1921	Baptist	II Corps Artillery, Army of Northern Virginia
Nelson, Robert	1818–1886	Episcopalian	21st Virginia
Nelson, William Meade		Episcopalian	Army of Northern Virginia, Trimble's Staff
New, Robert Anderson			11th Louisiana
Nicholson, A. B.	1826–1900	Methodist	4th Mississippi Cavalry
Nicholson, Joseph J.		Episcopalian	Post: Talladega, Ala.
Nicholson, Peter C.		Baptist	49th North Carolina
Niven, Thornton McNess, Jr.	1836–1908	Presbyterian	II Corps Artillery, Army of Northern Virginia
Norris, William B.			Smith's Legion, Georgia Rangers
Norton, George Hartley, Jr.	1824–1893	Episcopalian	17th Virginia
Norton, Paul		Episcopalian	23rd Virginia
Norton, R. W.		Baptist	19th Tennessee
Norton, Wilbur Fisk	1840–1906	Methodist	39th Alabama
O'Connell, Laurence P.	1826–1891	Roman Catholic	Hospital: Virginia

CONFEDERATE CHAPLAINS *continued*

Name	Life Dates	Denomination	Association
O'Keefe, Michael	1828–1906	Roman Catholic	Blanchard's South Carolina Reserves
O'Reilly, Thomas	1831–1872	Roman Catholic	Hospital: Atlanta, Ga.
Ogburn, Daniel A.		Methodist	South Carolina State Troops
Oldham, Montcalm			39th Virginia
Oliver, Charles James	1831–1914	Methodist	Troop Artillery Battalion, Georgia
Oslin, William W.	1831–1891	Methodist	43rd Georgia
Otkin, Charles H.			45th Mississippi
Overton, George Buck	1839–1917	Methodist	2nd Kentucky
Owen, William B.	–1865	Methodist	17th Mississippi
Page, James J.		Episcopalian	II Corps Artillery, Army of Northern Virginia
Page, Jesse Hayes	1831–1904	Methodist	17th North Carolina
Page, Tilmon	1839–1878	Methodist	51st Tennessee
Painter, Robert	–		10th Missouri
Palmer, Edward Porter	1826–1905	Presbyterian	14th Georgia
Paris, John	1809–1883	Methodist	54th North Carolina
Parks, William Asbury	1834–1910	Methodist	Waul's Texas Legion; 52nd Georgia
Parks, J. C.			Missouri State Guard
Parks, R. F.			43rd Georgia
Parsons, William Gaston			20th Texas Cavalry
Patterson, George E.	–1891?	Episcopalian	3rd North Carolina
Patterson, William McKendree	1838–1889	Methodist	6th Missouri
Pattillo, F. J.			28th Texas Cavalry
Pattillo, George Henry	1837–1888	Methodist	27th Georgia
Pattillo, William P.			3rd Texas Cavalry
Payne, William S. L.		Methodist	8th Tennessee
Pealer, Joseph			3rd Tennessee Mounted
Pearson, William Franklin	1831–1894	Presbyterian	2nd South Carolina

CONFEDERATE CHAPLAINS *continued*

Name	Life Dates	Denomination	Association
Pearson, William Wesley	1837–1872	Methodist	31st Mississippi
Peeler, James			28th Georgia
Pegram, Thomas H.	1829–1906	Methodist	68th North Carolina Militia
Pellicer, Anthony D.		Roman Catholic	Hospital: Alabama
Penick, William Sydnor	1836–1907	Baptist	53rd Virginia
Pennington, Isaac, Jr.		Baptist	23rd Arkansas
Pennington, Isaac, Sr.		Baptist	9th Missouri
Pepper, Clarendon Martin	1830–1895	Methodist	Camp:Wilmington, N.C.
Perkins, Edmund Taylor	1829–1911	Episcopalian	55th Virginia
Perry, Benjamin Franklin	1836–1868	Methodist	37th Alabama
Perry, J. W.	–1879	Methodist	35th Alabama
Perry, William G.		Methodist	44th Alabama
Person, L. S.			55th Georgia
Peterson, Peter Archer	1828–1893	Methodist	12th Virginia
Petrie, George Laurens	1840–1931	Presbyterian	22nd Alabama
Pettigrew, John L.		Baptist	31st Georgia
Petway, Ferdinand S.		Methodist	44th Tennessee
Phelps, Gerard W.		Episcopalian	17th North Carolina
Philips, B.			Hospital: Richmond, Va.
Philips, Josiah			Hawes's Arkansas Brigade
Phillipi, Alexander	1833–1915	Lutheran	29th Virginia
Phillips, Nathan G.	–1862	Presbyterian	43rd Alabama
Phillips, Preston	1829–1892	Methodist	32nd Texas Cavalry
Phillips, Richard Henry	1813–1890	Episcopalian	52nd Virginia
Pickett, Joseph Desha	1822–1900	Disciples of Christ	2nd Kentucky
Pierce, R. W.			5th Texas Mounted Rifles
Pierce, Thomas F.	1825–1904	Methodist	Georgia State Troops
Pilley, Stephen A.	1837–1909	Methodist	53rd Alabama, Partisan Rangers
Pilley, William B.	1835–1917	Methodist	54th Alabama
Pinkerton, Samuel J.		Episcopalian	Hospital: Atantla, Ga.
Pirtle, John Milton		Methodist	14th Tennessee

CONFEDERATE CHAPLAINS *continued*

Name	Life Dates	Denomination	Association
Pitts, Fountain Elliott	1808–1874	Methodist	11th Tennessee
Pitzer, Alexander White	1834–1827	Presbyterian	Army of Tennessee
Pledger, Wesley Parks	1833–1879	Methodist	12th Georgia
Plyler, Calvin	1830–	Methodist	48th North Carolina
Poindexter, J. W.		Cumberland Presbyterian	35th Tennessee
Pointer, John V.	1839–1880	Methodist	9th Texas
Pont, Francis		Roman Catholic	Hospital: Mississippi
Pope, Cadsman			Arkansas Hempstead Rifles
Porter, Anthony Toomer	1829–1902	Episcopalian	25th South Carolina; Hampton South Carolina Legion
Porter, David H.	1830–1873	Presbyterian	5th Georgia Cavalry
Porter, George John	1834–1891	Presbyterian	6th North Carolina Cavalry (65th North Carolina)
Porter, Joseph D.	1821–1879	Presbyterian	5th Alabama
Porter, James A.			Holcombe's South Carolina Legion
Porter, Robert Gilderoy	1839–1908	Methodist	10th Mississippi
Porter, Rufus Kilpatrick	1827–1869	Presbyterian	Cobb's Legion; 2nd Georgia
Potter, A. L.			3rd Mississippi
Potter, Andrew Jackson	1830–1895	Methodist	26th Texas Cavalry
Poulson, Thomas Layman			1st Maryland
Poulton, John F.			38th Virginia
Power, William Carr	1831–1916	Methodist	14th North Carolina
Powledge, Francis Gideon	1831–1912	Methodist	12th Georgia
Poynter, Robert Harrison	–1902	Methodist	10th Missouri
Prachensky, Joseph	1822–1890	Roman Catholic	3rd Alabama
Pratt, George W.		Methodist	4th Florida
Pratt, Henry Berrington	1832–1912	Presbyterian	5th North Carolina Cavalry

CONFEDERATE CHAPLAINS *continued*

Name	Life Dates	Denomination	Association
Preston, Thomas Lewis	1835–1895	Presbyterian	II Corps, Army of Northern Virginia
Price, Blackford, Jr.			48th Alabama
Price, Charles William	1834–1885	Presbyterian	8th Kentucky Cavalry
Price, Richard Nye	1830–1923	Methodist	26th North Carolina
Price, William			39th Mississippi
Price, William Thomas	1830–1921	Presbyterian	11th Virginia Cavalry
Pritchard, Thomas Henderson	1836–1914	Baptist	Gordon's Georgia Brigade
Proctor, Joseph A.	1830–1910	Methodist	2nd North Carolina Cavalry
Pryor, Theodorick Bland	1805–1890	Presbyterian	Camp: Camp Lee, Va.
Pugh, John William	1829–1912	Presbyterian	41st Virginia
Quaite, W. G. L.			1st Arkansas Cavalry
Quarles, William			48th Tennessee
Quarterman, Nathaniel Pratt	1839–1915	Presbyterian	20th Georgia Cavalry Battalion
Quigg, Henry	1827–1907	Presbyterian	42nd Georgia
Quinby, James Hamilton		Episcopalian	Post: Charleston, S.C.
Quintard, Charles Todd	1824–1898	Episcopalian	1st Tennessee
Raby, John W.	1838–	Methodist	58th North Carolina
Ragsdale, S.			7th Kentucky Mounted
Raines, A. G.		Baptist	14th Alabama
Randle, J. R.	1839–1915	Methodist	5th Tennessee
Randolph, Alfred Magill	1836–1918	Episcopalian	Hospital: Danville, Va.
Randolph, John			19th Tennessee Cavalry
Randolph, John			31st Tennessee
Ransom, Lemuel C.		Cumberland Presbyterian	20th Alabama
Ransom, R. R.		Methodist	62nd Tennessee
Ratcliffe, William P.		Methodist	9th Arkansas
Ray, David J.			57th North Carolina Militia
Ray, Fountain P.	1830–1905	Methodist	19th Texas Cavalry
Ray, George Henry	1832–1911	Methodist	4th Virginia Cavalry

CONFEDERATE CHAPLAINS *continued*

Name	Life Dates	Denomination	Association
Reed, Edward	–1862	Episcopalian	Hospital: South Carolina
Reed, R. H.			5th Louisiana
Reeves, Isaac Newton	–1910	Methodist	16th Mississippi
Reeves, Timothy		Baptist	3rd Missouri Cavalry
Reeves, William		Baptist	15th Missouri Cavalry
Renfroe, George W.	1823–1890	Methodist	62nd Tennessee
Renfroe, John Jefferson D.	1830–1888	Baptist	10th Alabama
Renfroe, John B.			13th Texas Cavalry
Renneck, Robert			12th Missouri Cavalry
Repiton, Alphonse Paul, Sr.		Methodist	Hospital: Wilmington, N.C.
Reynolds, John A., Jr.	1827–1921	Methodist	24th Georgia
Reynolds, Perry G.		Methodist	23rd Arkansas
Rice, John H.	1828–1864	Methodist	38th Arkansas Mounted Rifles
Richards, John Gardiner	1828–1915	Presbyterian	10th South Carolina
Richardson, John P.	–1862	Methodist	4th Mississippi
Richardson, W. B.		Methodist	32nd North Carolina
Richie, James H.		Methodist	18th Tennessee
Riddle, J. J.		Baptist	30th Texas Cavalry
Riddle, William L.		Baptist	11th Kentucky Cavalry
Ridley, J. S.			11th North Carolina
Riggin, John H.	1834–1913	Methodist	15th Arkansas
Ritchey, David P.		Presbyterian	35th Tennessee
Roach, James M. B.		Cumberland Presbyterian	10th Alabama
Robbins, Jeffrey H.	1829–1869	Methodist	12th North Carolina Cavalry
Robbins, W. M.		Methodist	7th Arkansas
Robert, Patrick Gibson	1827–1904	Episcopalian	34th Virginia; 2nd Louisiana
Roberts, R. R.		Methodist	1st Arkansas
Robins, William Fiske	1835?– 1895	Methodist	56th Virginia
Robinson, Adam A.	1815–1892	Methodist	11th Georgia Artillery Battalion
Robinson, H. H.			3rd Mississippi

CONFEDERATE CHAPLAINS *continued*

Name	Life Dates	Denomination	Association
Robinson, Nathaniel G.			30th Virginia Battalion
Robinson, William Fisher	1840–1905	Methodist	15th Georgia
Roby, Wesley Moorman	1832–1889	Methodist	78th North Carolina Militia
Rodefer, Charles P.		Episcopalian	Post: Bristol, Tenn.
Rodgers, Samuel	1825–1894	Methodist	22nd Virginia
Rodman, Erskine Mason		Episcopalian	Pegram's Virginia Artillery
Rogers, George W.		Baptist	3rd Missouri
Rogers, J. A.		Baptist	Hospital: Mobile, Ala.
Rogers, J. W.		Episcopalian	Camp: Cahawba, Ala.
Rogers, Sydney L.			15th Alabama
Rose, Sheldon H.	–1861	Methodist	16th Mississippi
Rosser, Moses Franklin		Methodist	41st Georgia
Rosser, William Ledyard	1836–1899	Presbyterian	8th Tennessee Cavalry
Royall, William Bailey	1823–1893	Missionary Baptist	35th North Carolina
Rush, Leonard	1808–1897	Methodist	3rd Georgia Cavalry
Rush, William Boyd		Methodist	1st Tennessee Cavalry
Rush, Zebidee	1821–1907	Methodist	62nd North Carolina Militia
Russell, James M.			46th Alabama
Russell, Samuel L.			19th Alabama
Rutledge, Thomas Jonathan	1835–1882	Methodist	3rd Alabama
Ryan, Abram Joseph	1839–1886	Roman Catholic	8th Tennessee
Ryan, Patrick		Roman Catholic	Post: Charleston, S.C.
Rybon, Peter Matthew	1829–1901	Methodist	7th Georgia Cavalry
Ryland, Robert	1805–1899	Baptist	Post: Richmond, Va.
Ryland, William Semple	1836–	Baptist	13th Virginia
Samford, William			28th Texas Cavalry
Sandals, John			Post: Fort Smith, Ark.
Sanford, William Frank	–1890?	Methodist	52nd North Carolina
Savage, H. G.			22nd Mississippi
Schwarar, John Miller		Episcopalian	4th Tennessee
Scott, John Andrew, Sr.	1820–1895	Presbyterian	1st Virginia Reserves

CONFEDERATE CHAPLAINS *continued*

Name	Life Dates	Denomination	Association
Scott, Thomas W.			Chimborazo Hospital: Richmond, Va.
Scrivener, B. M.			19th Texas
Scruggs, J. A.			22nd Texas
Scurlock, Joshua Fletcher	1834–1902	Methodist	Louisiana Crescent Rifles
Searcy, J. B.		Baptist	26th Arkansas
Sears, Oscar A.	1830–1867	Roman Catholic	Hospital: Lynchburg, Va.
See, Charles Sydney Matthews	1826 1903	Presbyterian	5th Virginia
Selman, Benjamin Lafayette	1831–1910	Methodist	23rd Alabama
Shane, Richard		Presbyterian	2nd North Carolina Cavalry
Sharp, E. G.	1834–		22nd Texas
Sharp, Joseph D.	1810–1887	Presbyterian	18th Texas
Shaver, David		Baptist	Hospital: Richmond, Va.
Shaw, Colin	1812–1905	Presbyterian	51st North Carolina
Sheeran, James B.	1819–1881	Roman Catholic	14th Louisiana
Sheppard, Samuel	1830–?		17th Virginia Cavalry
Shurlock, J.			2nd Kentucky Cavalry
Sikes, S. S.			Post: Montgomery, Ala.
Simer, A. P.			5th Tennessee
Simmons, William Ashbury	1823–1890	Methodist	11th Georgia
Sinclair, James	1814–1883	Presbyterian	5th North Carolina
Sison, C. P.			14th Alabama
Skinner, Thomas E.			38th North Carolina Militia
Slaughter, George		Episcopalian	58th Virginia
Slaughter, Philip	1808–1890	Episcopalian	19th Virginia
Slaven, Francis M.	1839–?		36th Virginia
Sloan, Henry Thompson			Orr's 1st South Carolina Rifles
Sloat, A. H.			Hospital: Liberty, Va.
Smedes, Bennett	–1901?	Episcopalian	5th North Carolina
Smith, Andrew Pickens	1832–1895	Presbyterian	2nd South Carolina

CONFEDERATE CHAPLAINS *continued*

Name	Life Dates	Denomination	Association
Smith, Aristides Spyker	1803–1892	Episcopalian	11th North Carolina
Smith, Austin W.	1836–1875	Methodist	25th Tennessee; George Dibrell's Staff
Smith, Busbey B.		Methodist	Hospital: Montgomery County, Va.
Smith, Charles M.		Episcopalian	22nd Virginia
Smith, G. T.		Episcopalian	Post: Staunton, Va.
Smith, George Gillman	1836–1913	Methodist	Phillips's Georgia Legion
Smith, George W.			9th Missouri Battalion Sharpshooters
Smith, Henry Martyn	1828–1894	Presbyterian	Post: Jackson, La.
Smith, Samuel H.	1835?–	Methodist	60th Georgia
Smith, Thompson L.		Episcopalian	22nd Virginia
Smith, William Alexander		Methodist	Garnett's Command, Va.
Smulders, Egidius	1815–1900	Roman Catholic	8th Louisiana
Smythe, Robert L.		Presbyterian	1st Georgia
Sneed, Henry			1st Georgia Battalion Sharpshooters
Snodgrass			Hardeman's Texas Cavalry
Snodgrass, David Swauzee	1826–1909	Baptist	Post: Demopolis, Ala.
Snow, J. J.		Methodist	3rd South Carolina State Troops
Southerland, Silus Bruce	1817–	Methodist	29th Tennessee
Sowe, J. C.			28th Mississippi
Spainhower, James H.	–1861		1st North Carolina
Spangler, Isaac	–1874	Methodist	6th Louisiana Cavalry
Sparks, James O. A.	1842–1869	Methodist	4th Georgia
Spiller, Benjamin Cleviers	1819–1883	Methodist	13th Virginia Cavalry
Sprunt, James Menzies	1818–1884	Presbyterian	20th North Carolina
Stafford, Andrew Jackson	1834–1910	Methodist	8th South Carolina
Stanley, Augustin O.		Methodist	37th Georgia; 41st Georgia
Stanley, Frank		Methodist	Hospital: Danville, Va.

CONFEDERATE CHAPLAINS *continued*

Name	Life Dates	Denomination	Association
Stanley, Thomas C.		Methodist	46th Georgia
Stansberry, J. M.		Baptist	Hospital: Dalton, Ga.
Starr, William Gabriel	1840–1916	Methodist	47th Alabama
Stell, Reuben	1802–1876		64th Virginia
Stephens, Alexander B.		Methodist	1st South Carolina
Stephens, Berry M.	1826–1898	Methodist	25th Tennessee
Stevens, Allen B.		Methodist	11th South Carolina
Stewart, Kensey Johns		Episcopalian	6th North Carolina
Stickney, George W.		Episcopalian	14th Louisiana
Stockton, William R. D.	1834–1897	Methodist	1st Texas Cavalry
Stoddard, William R.	1835–1865	Presbyterian	Lauderdale Springs, Miss.
Stoddert, William S.	1824–1885	Presbyterian	18th Virginina
Stokes, David C.		Methodist	7th Georgia
Stokes, Franklin			118th North Carolina Militia
Stokes, James M.	1832–1875	Methodist	3rd Georgia
Stone, Henry Clay		Methodist	Post: Selma, Ala.
Stone, James Bell	1814–1897	Baptist	5th Mississippi
Stone, James Boyd	1831–1913	Methodist	43rd Mississippi
Stough, Albert L.	1827–	Methodist	37th North Carolina
Street, J. K.			14th Texas Cavalry
Strick, Samuel S.		Episcopalian	59th Tennessee
Strickland, John	1826?–1862	Methodist	40th Georgia
Strickler, William M.			5th Louisiana
Stringfield, James King	1839–1870	Methodist	1st Tennessee
Stroud, A. L. W.		Methodist	13th Alabama
Stuart, Charles B.			8th Louisiana Cavalry
Stuart, Samuel Davies	1815–1895	Presbyterian	54th Virginia
Sturgeon, James Calvin	1829–1914	Presbyterian	Howard's Grove Hospital: Richmond, Va.
Sullins, David	1827–1918	Methodist	19th Tennessee
Sullivan, William T. J.	1829–1911	Methodist	37th Mississippi

CONFEDERATE CHAPLAINS *continued*

Name	Life Dates	Denomination	Association
Surratt, Samuel B.	1832–1881	Methodist	19th Louisiana
Sutton, James Henderson			31st Georgia
Sutton, P. S.			7th North Carolina Cavalry Battalion
Swan, Praxiteles			5th Texas
Swinney, Samuel T.		Methodist	1st Louisiana Cavalry
Sykes, S. S.			Post: Knoxville, Tenn.
Tage, Tillman			51st Tennessee
Talbott, Nathanael M.	1805–1872	Methodist	16th Missouri
Talley, George Riley	1818–1873	Methodist	6th Alabama
Talley, John Wesley	1800–1886	Methodist	Hospital: Richmond, Va
Talley, Stephen Christian	1831–	Methodist	2nd Tennessee Cavalry
Talley, William H.			39th North Carolina
Taylor, Benjamin M.		Cumberland Presbyterian	23rd Tennessee
Taylor, George Boardman	1832–1907	Baptist	25th Virginia
Taylor, James Barnett, Jr.	1837–1911	Baptist	10th Virginia Cavalry
Taylor, James Barnett, Sr.	1804–1871	Baptist	Post: Richmond, Va.
Taylor, Jasper Newton		Baptist	14th Mississippi
Taylor, John H.		Baptist	35th Georgia
Taylor, Robert Fleming	1822–1896	Presbyterian	Hospital: Jackson, Miss.
Taylor, Robert J.	1816–1873	Presbyterian	9th Virginia
Taylor, William P.		Baptist General	49th North Carolina Militia
Tebbs, Foushee C.		Methodist	4th Virginia
Teeling, John		Roman Catholic	1st Virginia
Tennant, John C.		Episcopalian	32nd North Carolina
Terrill, James W.		Baptist	15th Texas Cavalry
Terry, Elisha			12th Texas Cavalry
Thigpen, Alexander M.	1832–1889	Methodist	6th Georgia
Thomas, Albizi Gano	1833–1903	Disciples of Christ	7th Georgia
Thomas, Charles W.		Episcopalian	Georgia State Troops; Hospital

CONFEDERATE CHAPLAINS *continued*

Name	Life Dates	Denomination	Association
Thomas, James D.		Lutheran	19th Virginia Artillery
Thomas, Woodliff	1828–1888	Baptist	18th Texas Cavalry
Thompson, Eugene W.	1833–1877	Methodist	43rd North Carolina
Thompson, J. H.		Methodist	Hospital: Richmond, Va.
Thompson, John Ransom	1832–1916	Methodist	Clayton's Division, Army of Tennessee
Thompson, Richard Watson	1834–1912	Methodist	27th Texas Cavalry
Thompson, Z.			25th Louisiana
Thomson, J. C.			32nd Arkansas
Tichenor, Isaac Taylor	1825–1902	Baptist	17th Alabama
Tidball, William Buchanan	1822–1896	Presbyterian	Haskell's Virginia Artillery
Tilley, L. A.		Methodist	53rd Alabama
Tillinghast, John Huske	1835–	Episcopalian	44th North Carolina
Timberlake, John W.		Methodist	2nd Florida
Timmons, John M.		Baptist	Watkin's East Tennessee Regiment
Timmons, Robert Abijah	1837–1904	Methodist	Hilliard's Alabama Legion
Tinkerton, L. I.			Hospital: Atlanta, Ga.
Tinsley, Peter Archer	1833–1908	Episcopalian	28th Virginia
Tompkins, John H.			7th Florida
Toy, Crawford Howell	1836–1919	Baptist	53rd Georgia
Treadwell, Henry Bass	1830–1902	Methodist	10th Georgia Infantry Battalion
Treadwell, John Emory	1837–1923	Methodist	Post: Selma, Ala.
Trevillian, G. C.		Baptist	Hospital: Liberty, Va.
Tribble, Allen	1820–1881	Methodist	34th Tennessee
Trimble, Robert Wilson			1st Arkansas
Truslow, John F.	1815–1887	Methodist	6th Arkansas
Tucker, David		Cumberland Presbyterian	8th Tennessee
Tupper, Henry Allen	1828–1902	Baptist	9th Georgia
Turgis, Francois Isadore		Roman Catholic	30th Louisiana

CONFEDERATE CHAPLAINS *continued*

Name	Life Dates	Denomination	Association
Turner, P.			3rd Louisiana Cavalry
Tutt, J. M.			9th Missouri
Tyler, James B.			10th Virginia Cavalry
Tyson, Thomas S.		Methodist	20th Arkansas
Underwood, John Levi		Baptist	30th Alabama
Ungerer, J. J.		Lutheran	3rd Kentucky Mounted
Vanderhurst, William M.	−1862		6th Texas Cavalry
Vann, William A.	1840–1864	Baptist	13th North Carolina
Vass, Lachlan Cumming	1831–1896	Presbyterian	27th Virginia
Vaughan, Maurice Hamilton		Episcopalian	3rd North Carolina State Troops
Verdery, William M.			59th Georgia
Vertegans, Edward			16th Virginia Cavalry
Vick, Iredell R.		Baptist	1st Texas
Wabbon, E. P.			4th Kentucky
Waddel, John Newton	1812–1895	Presbyterian	Army of Mississippi
Wade, Thomas Smith	1838–1911	Methodist	19th Virginia Cavalry
Waggoner, James Richard	1830–	Methodist	56th Virginia
Walker, James A.		Baptist	Hospital: LaGrange, Ga.
Walker, John F.			Hoffman's Tennessee Battalion
Walker, John Garrott	1836–1918	Methodist	24th Mississippi
Walker, Joseph	1804–1895	Baptist	Howard's Grove Hospital: Richmond, Va.
Walker, R. J.			48th Tennessee
Walkup, Joseph Walker	1826–1903	Presbyterian	9th Virginia
Wallace, Isaiah T.	1829–1891	Baptist	41st Virginia
Wallace, James Albert	1810–1880	Presbyterian	Hospital: Ft. Gaines, Ga.
Walters, William E.		Baptist	2nd South Carolina Rifles
Walters, William			4th South Carolina
Walton, Edward Payson		Baptist	5th Virginia
Walton, Robert Hall	1833–1876	Presbyterian	Phillips's Georgia Legion
Ward, John Wyatt	1827–1905	Baptist	3rd Virginia

CONFEDERATE CHAPLAINS *continued*

Name	Life Dates	Denomination	Association
Wardlaw, Francis H.	1820–1895	Methodist	Post: Opelika, Ala.
Ware, Thomas Alexander	1810–1897	Methodist	8th Virginia
Watson, Alfred Augustine	1818–1905	Episcopalian	2nd North Carolina
Watson, John Franklin	1839–1870	Presbyterian	16th North Carolina
Waugh, Henry P.	1824?–1898	Methodist	64th North Carolina
Weatherly, J. H.			46th Alabama
Weaver, J. H.			28th Tennessee
Weaver, James H.			13th Georgia
Webb, Richard Stanford	–1901	Methodist	44th North Carolina
Webb, William R.		Baptist	44th North Carolina Militia
Weller, M. Leander	–1862	Episcopalian	9th Mississippi
Wellons, Willie			41st North Carolina Militia
Wells, Abram N.	1830–1895	Methodist	26th North Carolina
Wells, Marshall Harrison	1836–1916	Methodist	Hospital: Washington, Ark.
Wells, Martin V.	1833–1861	Methodist	9th Mississippi
West, Elbert A.	1836–1872	Methodist	25th Alabama
West, Hezekiah	1831–	Methodist	Thomas's North Carolina Legion
West, Joel T.			21st Georgia
West, Thomas Sterling	1835–1896	Methodist	13th Mississippi
West, Thomas			13th Arkansas
Westbrook, John Ivey			43rd Arkansas
Wetmore, W. R.			Missouri State Troops
Wexler, Edwin C.	–1865	Methodist	29th North Carolina
Whaley, R. M.			6th Missouri Cavalry
Wharey, James Morton	1839–1909	Presbyterian	Poague's Virginia Artillery Battalion
Wharton, Lyman Brown	1831–1907	Episcopalian	59th Virginia
Wheat, A. J.		Methodist	Hospital: Jackson, La.
Wheat, J. T.			Hospital: Salisbury, N.C.
Wheelan, Peter		Roman Catholic	Post: Fort Pulaski, Ga.
Wheeler, J. E.			31st Louisiana

CONFEDERATE CHAPLAINS *continued*

Name	Life Dates	Denomination	Association
Wheelwright, William Henry	1824–1879	Methodist	9th Virginia Cavalry
White, Charles	–1891	Presbyterian	Arsenal: Savannah, Ga.
White, Fred		Methodist	16th Louisiana; 18th Texas
White, H. D.			1st Georgia
White, Henry Martyn	1836–1910	Presbyterian	1st Virginia Artillery
White, Joseph E.			19th Georgia
White, Thomas Ward	1838–1900	Presbyterian	Richmond Howitzers
Whitehead, Richard H.	1836–1912	Baptist	20th Mississippi
Whittsett, William Heth	1841–1911	Baptist	4th Tennessee Cavalry
Whitten, Moses L.	1832–1893	Methodist	9th Alabama
Wiatt, William Edward	1826–1919	Baptist	26th Virginia
Wier, Thomas Coke	1827–1920	Methodist	37th Mississippi
Wiggins, David W.	1812–1862	Methodist	30th Mississippi
Wiggins, Joseph A.	1832–1920	Methodist	2nd Tennessee Cavalry
Wiggins, Robert Lemuel	1841–1915	Methodist	4th Florida
Wiley, Ephraim Emerson	1814–	Methodist	Hospital: Emory, Va.
Williams, George T.		Episcopalian	1st South Carolina; 13th North Carolina
Williams, Hazard S.		Methodist	45th Virginia
Williams, J. W.			Hospital: Richmond, Va.
Williams, John A.		Methodist	7th Arkansas
Williams, John G.			3rd South Carolina Cavalry
Williams, Marcus G.	1831–1894	Methodist	3rd Tennessee
Williams, Thomas N.		Cumberland Presbyterian	42nd Virginia
Williams, William Harrison	1840–1893	Baptist	Winder Hospital: Richmond
Williamson, J. E.		Methodist	Stuart Hospital: Richmond
Willis, Edward Jefferson	1820–1902	Baptist	15th Virginia
Willoughby, J. H.			18th Alabama
Wilmer, George Thornton		Episcopalian	6th Virginia Cavalry
Wilson, Charlton Henry	1828–1864	Presbyterian	7th South Carolina

CONFEDERATE CHAPLAINS *continued*

Name	Life Dates	Denomination	Association
Wilson, E. A.		Methodist	67th North Carolina
Wilson, Edward Portlock	1822–1895	Methodist	56th North Carolina
Wilson, George W.			29th North Carolina
Wilson, J. W.			35th Alabama
Wilson, Joseph			Hospital: Knoxville, Tenn.
Wilson, Luther Halsey	1837–1914	Presbyterian	14th Tennessee
Wilson, Robert A.	–1894	Methodist	36th Alabama
Wilson, William Chalmers	1836–1903	Methodist	42nd North Carolina
Wilson, William P.		Methodist	16th Arkansas
Wilson, William Venable	1819–1908	Presbyterian	Hospital: Lynchburg, Va.
Winchester, George L.	–1863	Presbyterian	6th Tennessee
Winfield, Augustus Robert		Methodist	12th Arkansas
Winkler, Edwin Theodore	1823–1883	Baptist	25th South Carolina
Winter, William			15th Mississippi
Wise, Henry Alexander, Jr.	1835–1869	Episcopalian	Wise's Virginia Brigade
Witherspoon, Andrew Jackson	1824–1891	Presbyterian	21st Alabama
Witherspoon, Thomas Dwight	1836–1898	Presbyterian	2nd & 48th Mississippi
Wolf, John			10th Arkansas
Wood, Franklin Harris	1836–1913	Methodist	22nd North Carolina
Wood, Myron Doty		Presbyterian	11th South Carolina
Wood, William Andrew	1831–1900	Presbyterian	4th North Carolina
Woodfin, Augustus Beverly		Baptist	61st Georgia
Woodlief, Thomas			16th Texas Cavalry
Worrell, A. S.		Baptist	34th Georgia
Wright, James Lillbourne	1822–1903	Methodist	Hospital: Louisiana and Mississippi
Wright, Joseph B.			5th Missouri Cavalry
Yarborough, George Wesley	1838–1922	Methodist	35th Georgia
Yates, Edwin Asbury		Methodist	1st North Carolina
Young, James			22nd Tennessee
Young, Newton B.	1830–1907	Methodist	Hospital: Mississippi

CONFEDERATE CHAPLAINS *continued*

Name	Life Dates	Denomination	Association
Young, William M.		Baptist	Post: Petersburg, Va.
Zelner, Marion			12th Tennessee Cavalry
Zimmerman, George Henry	1838–1899	Methodist	12th Virginia Cavalry
Zively, John N.	1824–1905	Presbyterian	5th Texas Cavalry